Lecture Notes
in Business Information Processing   447

More information about this series at https://link.springer.com/bookseries/7911

Ana Paula Cabral Seixas Costa ·
Jason Papathanasiou · Uchitha Jayawickrama ·
Daouda Kamissoko (Eds.)

Decision Support Systems XII

Decision Support Addressing Modern Industry,
Business, and Societal Needs

8th International Conference on Decision
Support System Technology, ICDSST 2022
Thessaloniki, Greece, May 23–25, 2022
Proceedings

Editors
Ana Paula Cabral Seixas Costa (iD)
Federal University of Pernambuco
Recife, Brazil

Uchitha Jayawickrama (iD)
Loughborough University
Loughborough, UK

Jason Papathanasiou (iD)
University of Macedonia
Thessaloniki, Greece

Daouda Kamissoko
Ecole des Mines d'Albi
Albi, France

ISSN 1865-1348   ISSN 1865-1356 (electronic)
Lecture Notes in Business Information Processing
ISBN 978-3-031-06529-3   ISBN 978-3-031-06530-9 (eBook)
https://doi.org/10.1007/978-3-031-06530-9

This Springer imprint is published by the registered company Springer Nature Switzerland AG
The registered company address is: Gewerbestrasse 11, 6330 Cham, Switzerland

Preface

This twelfth edition of Decision Support Systems published in the LNBIP series presents a selection of reviewed and revised full papers from the Eighth International Conference on Decision Support System Technology (ICDSST 2022), held in Thessaloniki, Greece, during May 23–25, 2022. The conference's main theme was "Decision Support Addressing Modern Industry, Business and Societal Needs" and the principal aim was to investigate how the new business models in the digital age accentuate the demand for customized and intelligent decision support capable of meeting the needs of modern industry, business, and society.

The Euro Working Group on Decision Support Systems (EWG-DSS) planned the ICDSST series, starting with ICDSST 2015 in Belgrade, to consolidate the tradition of annual events organized by the EWG-DSS in offering a platform for European and international DSS communities, comprising the academic and industrial sectors, to present state-of-the-art DSS research and developments, to discuss current challenges that surround decision making processes, to exchange ideas about realistic and innovative solutions, and to co-develop potential business opportunities.

Building on this tradition, ICDSST 2022 included the following scientific topic areas:

- Decision Support Systems: Advances and Future Trends
- Multi-Attribute and Multi-Criteria Decision Making
- Knowledge Management, Acquisition, Extraction, Visualization, and Decision Making
- Multi-Actor Decision Making: Group and Negotiated Decision Making
- Collaborative Decision Making and Decision Tools
- Discursive and Collaborative Decision Support Systems
- Mobile and Cloud Decision Support Systems
- GIS and Spatial Decision Support Systems
- Data Science, Data Mining, Text Mining, and Sentimental Analysis
- Big Data Analytics
- Imaging Science (Image Processing, Computer Vision, and Pattern Recognition)
- Human-Computer Interaction
- Internet of Things
- Social Network Analysis for Decision Making
- Simulation Models and Systems, Regional Planning, Logistics, and SCM
- Business Intelligence, Enterprise Systems, and Quantum Economy
- Machine Learning, Natural Language Processing, Artificial Intelligence
- Virtual and Augmented Reality
- New Methods and Technologies for Global Crisis Management
- Analytics for Mitigating the Impact of Pandemics
- Intelligent DSS for Crisis Prevention
- Innovative Decision Making During Global Crises
- New DSS Approaches for Post-Crisis Recovery of Economy

- Decision Making in Modern Education
- Decision Support Systems for Sports
- General DSS Case Studies (Education, E-Government, Energy, Entrepreneurship, Environment, Healthcare, Industrial Diversification and Sustainability, Innovation, Logistics, Natural Resources, etc.)

These topics reflect some of the essential areas of study within Decision Support Systems, as well as the research interests of the group members. This rich variety of themes, advertised not only to the (more than three hundred) members of the group, but to a broader audience as well, allowed us to gather contributions regarding the implementation of decision support processes, methods, and technologies in a large variety of domains. Hence, this EWG-DSS Springer LNBIP volume collates contributions of full papers, selected through a single-blind paper reviewing process. In particular, at least two members of the Program Committee reviewed each submission in the first part of a rigorous two-stage process. The second stage involved the volume editors judging whether the revised versions did indeed address the issues that the reviewers had raised. Papers that didn't address properly all the issues were either accepted to the conference but not included in this volume or were not accepted at all. Finally, we selected 15 out of 46 submissions, which corresponds to a 32% acceptance rate, to be included in this twelfth edition of Decision Support Systems.

We proudly present the selected contributions, organized in three sections:

1. *Decision Support Addressing Modern Industry:* This section explores the application of contemporary technologies to decision support in modern industry. First, "Blockchain Technology Potential to Transform Global Value Chains" by Zoran Wittine, Antea Barisic, and Sanja Franc deals with the governance of global value chains, using blockchain technology as a new way of organizing global production. Then, Mathieu Lega, Corentin Burnay, and Stéphane Faulkner present "Predicting the Rating of an App Beyond its Functionalities: Introducing the App Publication Strategy", exploring whether a publication strategy has an impact on the success of a mobile app, in order to support companies decisions regarding their publication strategy, using machine learning techniques. Next, "Improving Machine Self-Diagnosis with an Instance-Based Selector for Real-Time Anomaly Detection Algorithms", by Philip Stahmann, Jon Oodes, and Bodo Rieger, prototypically implements a real-time anomaly detection algorithm selector to support decision making regarding machine self-diagnosis. Following this, "Blockchain and Artificial Intelligence in Real Estate" by Christos Ziakis offers a systematic review of the literature related to the usage of the blockchain technology and machine learning in the real estate industry. Finally, Nikolaos Nousias, George Tsakalidis, Sophia Petridou, and Kostas Vergidis present "Modelling the Development and Deployment of Decentralized Applications in Ethereum Blockchain: A BPMN-based approach", proposing a BPMN approach to design blockchain-based applications.
2. *Decision Support Addressing Business and Societal Needs:* This section applies decision support approaches, methods, and systems addressing societal and business needs. First, "Strengthening EU Resilience: Labor Market Integration as a Criterion for Refugee Relocation" by Anastasia Blouchoutzi, Georgios Tsaples, Dimitra

Manou, and Christos Nikas supports the decision of relocation, based on migrant labor market integration prospects, favoring social inclusion. Then, "Towards an Inclusive Europe: Ranking European Countries Based on Social Sustainability Indicators" by Jelena Stankovic, Marija Dzunic, and Ivana Marjanović assesses the state of social sustainability throughout Europe, based on the inclusion of various indicators reflecting the social dimension of sustainable growth. Next, Jonas Kirchhoff, Christoph Weskamp, and Gregor Engels present "Decision Support Ecosystems: Definition and Platform Architecture", an architecture of a shared platform for a decision support ecosystem and an application for regional energy distribution network planning. Following this, "A systematic research methodology for business model decision making in commercialising innovative healthcare diagnostic technologies", by Aira Patrice Ong, Shaofeng Liu, Genhua Pan, and Xinzhong Li, proposes a new methodology to develop business models for healthcare incorporating multidimensional implications of various stakeholder perspectives in decision making. Finally, Chenhui Ye, Pascale Zaraté, and Daouda Kmissoko present "A DSS based on a control tower for supply chain risks management", a decision support system for supply chain risk management in a multi-source data and risk environment.

3. *Multiple Criteria Approaches:* This section presents multicriteria models and methods applied in different contexts of societal, business, and modern industry decisions. First, "Using the FITradeoff Method for solving a truck acquisition problem at a midsize carrier", by Mariana Wanderley Cyreno, Lucia Reis Peixoto Roselli, and Adiel Teixeira de Almeida, explores the FITradeoff method that integrates holistic evaluation with elicitation by decomposition to solve a truck acquisition multicriteria decision problem. Next, "Maturity assessment in the context of industry 4.0 - an application using FITradeoff method in a textile industry" by Duan Ferreira and Ana Gusmão proposes and applies a maturity assessment procedure, in the context of industry 4.0, based on the FITradeoff multicriteria method. Then, Glykeria Myrovali and Maria Morfoulaki present "Sustainable Mobility Engagement and Co-planning: a Multicriteria Analysis-based Transferability Guide", which exploits multicriteria analysis for evaluating the transferability potential of good practice in citizens' sensibilization and engagement in sustainable mobility. The next paper, "A DSS for the multi-criteria vehicle routing problem with pickup and delivery and 3d constraints" by Themistoklis Stamadianos, Magdalene Marinaki, Nikolaos Matsatsinis, and Yannis Marinakis, proposes a DSS that combines optimization and a multicriteria model for solving a particular case of a vehicle routing problem. The last paper in this section, "A multicriteria tool to support decision-making in the early stages of energy efficiency investments" by Aikaterini Papapostolou, Filippos Dimitrios Mexis, Charikleia Karakosta, and John Psarras, presents a decision tool based on the ELECTRE TRI multicriteria method to evaluate energy efficiency investments.

We would like to thank the many people who contributed to the success of ICDSST 2022 and this LNBIP book. First of all, we would like to thank Springer for providing us with the opportunity to guest edit this edition of Decision Support Systems, and we wish to express our sincere gratitude to Ralf Gerstner and Christine Reiss, who dedicated their time to guide and advise us during the volume editing process. Secondly, we need to thank all the authors for submitting their state-of-the-art work for consideration to this volume, managing to overcome all the obstacles that arguably affected scholars around the globe. From our point of view, this is yet another confirmation that the DSS community is vivid, active, and has a great potential for contributions to society. It really gives us courage and stimulates us to continue the series of International Conferences on Decision Support System Technology. Finally, we express our deep gratitude to the reviewers — members of the Program Committee who volunteered to assist in the improvement and the selection of the papers under (to be honest) a tight schedule. We believe that this EWG-DSS Springer LNBIP volume has made a rigorous selection of high-quality papers addressing the conference theme. We hope that readers will enjoy the publication!

April 2022   Ana Paula Cabral Seixas Costa
                                                      Jason Papathanasiou
                                                   Uchitha Jayawickrama
                                                     Daouda Kamissoko

Organization

Conference Chairs

Jason Papathanasiou   University of Macedonia, Greece
Ana Paula Cabral Seixas Costa   Federal University of Pernambuco, Brazil

Steering Committee – EWG-DSS Coordination Board

Shaofeng Liu	University of Plymouth, UK
Boris Delibašić	University of Belgrade, Serbia
Jason Papathanasiou	University of Macedonia, Greece
Isabelle Linden	University of Namur, Belgium
Pavlos Delias	International Hellenic University, Greece
Ana Paula C. S. Costa	Federal University of Pernambuco, Brazil

Program Committee

Adiel Teixeira de Almeida	Federal University of Pernambuco, Brazil
Alberto Turón	University of Zaragoza, Spain
Alexander Smirnov	Russian Academy of Sciences, Russia
Alexis Tsoukias	Université ParisDauphine, France
Ana Paula C. S. Costa	Federal University of Pernambuco, Brazil
Ben C. K. Ngan	Worcester Polytechnic Institute, USA
Boris Delibašić	University of Belgrade, Serbia
Carlos Henggeler Antunes	University of Coimbra, Portugal
Christian Colot	University of Namur, Belgium
Daouda Kamissoko (Co-chair)	Ecole des Mines d'Albi, France
Dragana Bečejski-Vujaklija	Serbian Society for Informatics, Serbia
Emilio Larrodé	University of Zaragoza, Spain
Fátima Dargam	SimTech Simulation Technology/ILTC, Austria
Fernando Tricas	University of Zaragoza, Spain
Francisco Antunes	Beira Interior University, Portugal
Gloria Philipps-Wren	Loyola University Maryland, USA
Hing Kai Chan	University of Nottingham, Ningbo, China
Isabelle Linden	University of Namur, Belgium
Jason Papathanasiou	University of Macedonia, Greece
Jean-Marie Jacquet	University of Namur, Belgium
João Lourenço	Universidade de Lisboa, Portugal

Jorge Freire de Sousa	University of Porto, Portugal
José Maria Moreno-Jiménez	Zaragoza University, Spain
Kathrin Kirchner	Technical University of Denmark, Denmark
María Teresa Escobar	University of Zaragoza, Spain
Marc Kilgour	Wilfrid Laurier University, Canada
Marko Bohanec	Jozef Stefan Institute, Slovenia
Nikolaos Matsatsinis	Technical University of Crete, Greece
Panagiota Digkoglou	University of Macedonia, Greece
Pascale Zaraté	IRIT/Toulouse University, France
Pavlos Delias	Kavala Institute of Technology, Greece
Rita Ribeiro	UNINOVA, Portugal
Rudolf Vetschera	University of Vienna, Austria
Sandro Radovanovic	University of Belgrade, Serbia
Sean Eom	Southeast Missouri State University, USA
Shaofeng Liu	University of Plymouth, UK
Stefanos Tsiaras	Aristotle University of Thessaloniki, Greece
Stelios Tsafarakis	Technical University of Crete, Greece
Uchitha Jayawickrama (Co-chair)	Loughborough University, UK
Wim Vanhoof	University of Namur, Belgium

Local Organizing Team

Georgios Tsaples	University of Macedonia, Greece
Jason Papathanasiou	University of Macedonia, Greece
Pavlos Delias	International Hellenic University, Greece

Sponsors

European Working Group on Decision Support Systems
(https://ewgdss.wordpress.com)

Association of European Operational Research Societies
(www.euro-online.org)

Institutional Sponsors

Research Committee of the University of Macedonia,
Department of Business Administration,
Thessaloniki, Greece
(http://www.uom.gr/index.php?newlang=eng)

International Hellenic University, Greece
(https://www.ihu.gr/en/enhome)

Federal University of Pernambuco, Brazil
(https://www.ufpe.br/inicio)

Graduate School of Management, Faculty of Business,
University of Plymouth, UK
(http://www.plymouth.ac.uk/)

Faculty of Organisational Sciences, University of Belgrade, Serbia
(http://www.fon.bg.ac.rs/eng/)

**UNIVERSITÉ
DE NAMUR**

University of Namur, Belgium
(http://www.unamur.be/)

Contents

Multiple Criteria Approaches

Decision Support Addressing Modern Industry

Blockchain Technology Potential to Transform Global Value Chains

Zoran Wittine[✉], Sanja Franc, and Antea Barišić

Faculty of Economics and Business, University of Zagreb, Zagreb, Croatia
`zwittine@efzg.hr`

Abstract. Technological changes in transport and communications have shown to be one of the most important determinants of geographic fragmentation of production process which led to shaping of global value chains (GVCs). Governance of these complex production systems is becoming increasingly challenging, especially due to the lack of information about the processes and actors in the chain, which leads to sustainability issues and higher costs of assuring resilience and robustness. Blockchain technology (BT) provides opportunities to address these challenges. This paper provides a systematic overview of BT potential to transform GVCs. It points out transparency as one of the most important features of BT, which provides traceability and efficiency gains potential in a range of areas, as it enables real-time information-based decision making of leading firms and other members of GVCs. It also points out that BT can provide decision-support to consumers through information that was not previously available to them, thus facilitating their choices. Furthermore, it can facilitate government's international trade regulation enforcement. These changes have the potential to contribute to upgrading opportunities and bring another global production reorganization. Decision-support is needed to foster and facilitate BT adoption process.

Keywords: Global value chains · Decision support · Information-based decision making · Governance · Blockchain

1 Introduction

Global industrial organization has transformed during the several recent decades along with technological improvements, political and ideological changes and multilateral and regional economic cooperation incentives [1, 2]. GVCs can be defined as a range of activities (design, research and development, producing components, logistics, assembly, marketing, sales, customer support etc.) conducted by a set of firms across different countries worldwide to bring a product from its inception to final consumption [3, 4]. These new production networks are often very complex, geographically dispersed and intertwined, e.g. Apple iPhone production consists of a GVC of 785 suppliers from 31 countries from all over the world [5]. GVCs have been widely analyzed across different fields from international trade and development, political economy [6–8] to governance [9–11]. They are closely linked and intertwined to the supply chains (SC) and global strategy (GS) literature which focuses on their management and logistics [12–14]. So, a

© Springer Nature Switzerland AG 2022
A. P. Cabral Seixas Costa et al. (Eds.): ICDSST 2022, LNBIP 447, pp. 3–15, 2022.
https://doi.org/10.1007/978-3-031-06530-9_1

broad stream of research includes different research perspectives to GVCs, from macro to micro-level.

Technological progress is considered to be one of the most important factors impacting the evolution of GVCs [11]. New technologies brought through the 4IR are providing incentives for GVCs reconfiguration [15], further pushed by the COVID-19 pandemic which revealed some of its fragilities and posed a focus on their resilience and robustness through diversification [16, 17]. Thus, there is a tendency of extending already very complex GVCs. Some of the current "hot" topics in this field include micro-foundations of GVC governance, GVC mapping, learning, impact of lead firm ownership and strategy, dynamics of GVC arrangements, value creation and distribution, digitization, financialization, the impact of GVCs on their macro-environment, and chain-level performance management [18]. This paper strives to address several of them.

Blockchain technology (BT) and its potential implementation has been vastly explored in recent years [19-22]. BT has recently entered debates in the field of GVCs [23-26]. Existing research mostly include perspectives of GVC governance, SC management and logistics. They point out a range of potential usages of BT in GVCs. Several BT characteristics can be used to address some of the most important challenges that GVCs are facing. So, some of the previously mentioned important topics in the field of GVCs can be significantly affected through the BT implementation.

The main objective of this paper is to provide a systematic overview of BT potential to transform GVCs, especially its governance systems and decision making. This study aims to contribute to the current literature through providing an overview of perspectives of different stakeholders (GVC participants, consumers and governments). It strives to point out GVCs challenges, opportunities to address them through BT, and threats to BT implementation and usage. Research is divided into five parts. Section 2 includes an overview of current industrial organization through GVCs. Main characteristics of BT and its implementation is analyzed in the Sect. 3. Section 4 provides a systematic overview transformational effects of BT implementation in GVCs. Conclusion synthesizes main findings and recommendations for further research.

2 Global Value Chains as the New Global Industrial Organization Form

GVC economy is structurally different to its predecessors as the trade it includes is mostly in intermediate and not in finished goods, leading to a higher level of interconnectedness between countries at all levels of development [27]. Due to changes in the global industrial organization "made in" concept is largely considered to be outdated, as most of the products contain value added from several different countries, thus making the label "made in the world" a more appropriate one [28]. The decrease of different international trade costs has enabled the development of these geographically fragmented networks of production. This primarily refers to the decrease of international trade barriers, transport costs and communication costs which enabled firms to outsource and offshore some of their non-core activities. Besides the ideological changes and facilitation of process by multilateral institutions and regional economic integrations, a significant role is due to technological improvements including containerization and airplane shipment which increased the speed and decreased the costs of trade, while using internet and mobile phone networks decreased communication costs and some of the information asymmetries [2].

In GVC analysis, "top-down" (governance - focused on lead firms and global industries organization) and "bottom-up" (upgrading - focused on strategies countries implement to improve their positions in the global economy) perspectives encompass the vast amount of literature, and power dynamics are at the center of value optimization including transactions complexity, knowledge codifiability and suppliers capabilities [10]. GVCs involve complex forms of governance as they consist of a range of firms making various decisions and handling specific operations and activities. GVC governance reveals how firms join GVC, how fast they can gain product capabilities, how are GVC profits distributed, who decides on the key GVC initiatives and who provides technical support [29]. GVC lead firms have important role in efficiency increasing using joint strategy, enabling a multilateral feedback, ensuring rules, inclusion of non-business intermediaries with a goal of improving coordination along the chain, fostering innovation and development of new capabilities while attaining the key role [9]. Governance structure can vary from market-based governance to vertical integration, depending on the level of coordination among firms in the GVC [10]. The form of governance explains the power of firms to affect the distribution of profits and risks within an industry [31]. The power in GVCs comes from the control of various key resources (e.g. for Apple it is design and distribution) [9], and risks are the main reason for process specification, usually deriving from the gap between the market requirements in developed and developing countries [29]. GVC governance can explain upgrading success and development of different countries [31].

Through the process of GVC development the forms of governance have been changing. At the beginning there were buyer-led and producer-led GVCs [3]. Although these forms of governance have been important until today, governance has become much more complex following the changes in GVCs. While at the beginning the focus of GVC governance was on the process of global activities dispersion [3], later it was on the coordination of dispersed production linkages [10]. It is important to point out that governance model changes along the development of certain industry and/or firms. GVC governance is not static and the rise of the countries from the "Global South" importance is expected, given their increasing share in the global income [4]. Some approaches also emphasize the importance of international organizations and government agencies through posing standards and other stakeholders such as licensed certifiers, experts and non-profit organizations [10, 29].

SC does not have to include the "global" component, as it can be organized within one country. There are different definitions of SCs and one of the most encompassing one defines it as "a set of three or more entities (organizations or individuals) directly involved in the upstream and downstream flows of products, services, finances, and/or information from a source to a customer" [32]. GVC concept is closely linked to SCs as production networks have become global. Thus, contemporary SCs have become more disaggregated and geographically fragmented. But, even when SCs are global, they provide a different perspective as they focus on management and logistics. The SC management literature refers to the firm-level and investigates the flow along the distribution channel from suppliers to ultimate users, searching for the ways to improve it in a wide range of areas (e.g. planning and control, leadership, different cultures that participating entities encompass) [33]. Although much of the market trends have changed (e.g. demand for unique products and customers journeys) together with technological advancements, interorganizational collaboration remained at core of SC management, which has become even more important in the digital economy [34]. A more dynamic view of changes among the actors in the chain that involves the effects of different disruptions on global SCs can be beneficial to GVCs understanding.

Another closely linked field is GS which focuses on how multinational companies organize and manage cross-border activities more efficiently (firm-perspective), while the focus of GVC literature is on the industry level and GVC activities [14]. While key issues for GS are competitive advantage, firm's performance and value appropriation, for GVCs key issues are societal impact, bargaining power and GVC governance. Important contextual factors for GS are culture, institutions, and costumer preferences, while in GVCs these are power relations, technology dynamics and industry standards. GS offers a firm to network perspective and GVC network to firm perspective [14, 27]. So, it is clear that GS and SC literature are management oriented, while GVC literature provides a more holistic and descriptive view emphasizing linkages and not only individual GVC actors [14]. Together GVC perspective and these international business perspectives provide a systemic view of activities and relationships constituting GVCs [27]. Integrating these different literature streams and investigating the same phenomenon from different perspectives, can be mutually beneficial due to their shared underlying concepts and mechanisms which lead to important themes [14]: management of cross-border activities, network-optimization, upgrading and strategic coevolution. Thus, the analysis of BT potential effects on GVCs will also include micro-level effects.

3 Blockchain Technology Implementation in Global Value Chains

Blockchain is a specific digital technology solution characterized by its decentralized structure, with the characteristics of shared recordkeeping, immutability, decentralization, distributed trust, consensus, security, resiliency, transparency, audibility, permissibility, disintermediation, programmability and verifiability [23, 35, 36]. Its two important aspects are the distributed ledger and system of trust. Distributed ledger technology implies that transaction data is automatically shared with other participants of the network, rather than being held in a single host commuter or a central server [36]. It implies a novel and fast evolving approach to recording and sharing data across multiple data stores (ledgers) [36]. Blockchain includes a range of transactional records (blocks) connected in a digital chain. Cryptography and algorithmic methods are used to record and synchronize network data and not to allow blocks to be retrospectively altered by any network member [36]. Trust is provided as the stored information can't be changed or deleted after the entry without going through a rigorous validation using network consensus algorithms, thus enabling mutually mistrusting entities to exchange financial value without intermediaries [37]. We can differentiate between permissionless (open and decentralized - so anyone can join the network as a reader or a writer) and permissioned (proposed to limit a set of readers and writers who have the permission of a central entity to participate) blockchains [37].

BT is still in its early stages and it is expected to mature in a range of areas along with the research body growth. Worldwide spending on BT solutions has been increasing steeply in the last few years and it is expected to further increase significantly. While blockchain has so far been used mostly in financial industry, other industries also have a high potential to implement it [36, 38]. There is potential of BT use in healthcare (information management), in finance (financial services) and in SC management for a range of different uses [35]. IBM stresses that billions could be saved through providing more accurate and trustworthy bills of landing attached to containers. An early case of BT use in SCs includes their initiative of maritime container management through BT with Maersk [39]. Unilever, Walmart and Nestle have recently decided to collaborate to trace food contamination in SCs using BT, to improve their corporate social responsibility (CSR). Also, a blockchain service provider sought to integrate BT in sea food SC to increase transparency and validity of sustainable practices [20]. Microsoft, IBM, Visa and MasterCard started developing distributed ledger technology products and services which could eventually provide the same level of trust and confidence as the traditional IT systems today [36]. They propose its potential use in managing SCs, authenticating products (e.g. arts, pharmaceuticals, luxury products) and managing intellectual property registration, trade finance, managing invoices, loyalty programs etc.

BT can have an important role in GVCs through improving traceability of goods along the production process. Several research point out benefits of BT usage in SCs: increasing transparency, trust and security while decreasing costs, leading to efficiency gains [39, 20]. Besides recording all asset SC flows, tracking orders, receipts, invoices, payments and other documents and digital assets (e.g. warranties, certifications, bar codes, copyright) in a unified blockchain, it can also contribute to sharing information about the production process, delivery and maintenance between suppliers and sellers [19]. This can enable managing food safety, tracking protected species trade or identifying counterfeit medicines. BT offers real-time information to all stakeholders in the production process, enabling better control over the whole SC activities and product characteristics. It can improve interoperability between various GVCs [40].

Production and maintenance of these trusted information is not free but having in mind the high administrative costs of todays' transactions and being it very error prone and open to frauds, benefits can be clearly seen [39]. BT can be used to store transaction files and execute tasks based on agreed conditions, and not only hold transaction information [24]. Through digitizing physical assets and creating digital track records that enable tracing the asset from production to end use, it can provide greater GVC transparency. BT could be an incentive to global trade as "smart contracts" based on this type of technology could eliminate some uncertainness regarding classic financial instruments (e.g. letter of credit). Smart contracts usually refer to software programs which store rules and actions between parties [20]. They are a protocol or a program within the blockchain that executes the transaction, once all the conditions have been met [25]. So, BT can de-commoditize products as it can provide granulated and detailed information regarding to previously unknown characteristics [39].

Blockchain can be used with simple QR codes which can be scanned by phones, but human involvement can't provide fundamental security except to transaction cost efficiency gains [39]. But, if more sophisticated technologies e.g. sensors are used (smart contracts based on IOT where sensors record information e.g. temperature, GPS etc.) human error would be decreased due to technology-centered data input. Using IOT in GVCs can provide visibility of each item, its position and attributes, at any time, providing high transparency [26]. This can also increase profitability as it can decrease the need of surplus goods, enable faster reactions to changing demand and availability of suppliers, possibilities of shipping optimization etc. BT used with IoT improves GVC scalability, security and traceability, while it allows for convergence of logistics systems and increasing GVC efficiency in terms of expenses, consistency, distribution and versatility, so it can provide a comparative advantage for those implementing it. Thus, blockchains can help firms to execute activities across organizational boundaries even if they cannot agree on a trusted third party as IoT together with BT enables a secure and trustworthy product information transfer in GVCs and helps to shorten the feedback cycle which facilitates a faster decision making through improving efficiency of transmitting information related to the whole process [26, 41].

There are a range of challenges in blockchain implementation. From those intra-organizational and inter-organizational to policy-oriented ones [20]. As this is a bleeding-edge technology [36], a full-fledged implementation option is hard to find and investment in new hardware and software are expected to be high [20]. A challenge might be employees' digital skills, as all GVC participants need to learn how to use it [24]. In case of its asymmetrical application its benefits may vanish, so support would be needed to include SMEs, especially those in less developed countries. Also, several blockchain platforms have emerged and have been used in diverse applications. Recently decision models for blockchain platform selection problem have emerged, reducing the time and costs of decision-making process among software firms that want to implement it [42]. Interoperability of different solutions might be another challenge.

Transparency brings reputation implications and the fact that more information might be available to auditors, public and other GVC participants, could increase scrutiny of the whole process, as some of the inputs might include unattractive practices [8]. Privacy and security are another concern if the transactions are open and visible to all network members, although they can be encrypted, and the user identity hidden [36, 40]. Some blockchain technologies can't guarantee that certain private information would not be misused. An issue of BT could be credibility as if more than a half of the computers working as nodes "tell a lie", than a lie becomes the truth. Contract law can help solve this problem by creating obligations on those involved in the community consensus process to maintain the authenticity and accuracy of the records. So, although decentralization is one of the most important advantages of BT, it can be a disadvantage in case of a problem or information breach if there is no entity obligated to solve the problem [40]. Other potential legal and regulation challenges include forming industry standards, providing legal clarity over ownership and jurisdiction, forming a system of resolving transaction disputes, and combating the terrorism financing regulations [36]. Benefits might be hampered by legislative complexities and lack of joint standards across world markets [26]. Laws and other regulation represent an important part of GVC functioning and all firms in the GVC need to abide the existing legislative framework. As goods are distributed to customers in domestic or export markets, more consumer-oriented law applies, as well as those conditions of contracts between businesses and consumers.

Representations around the sustainability of products are typically made in contract law, and breaches of these can result in damages paid to those suffering losses due to these misrepresentations [25]. From regulatory point of view, governments have to create a new or modify the existing legislative framework while carefully considering that regulation protects consumers and doesn't hamper with digital innovation. If regulations and rules are too strict innovation creation is discouraged, and complex and unstable regulatory environment can limit activities of SMEs. However, despite some of the mentioned concerns, BT brings various benefits which have a potential of transformational effects to global production system.

4 Potential Transformational Effects of Blockchain Technology on Global Value Chains

BT can provide disruption for design, organization, operations, and management in GVCs [20]. Furthermore, 4IR provides a set of opportunities for improvement of global SC management through implementation of BT. These include IoT, sensors and big data, which together with smart trucks, containers and pallets enable monitoring and making better decisions [19]. So far, technological improvements, did not only affect prices, but completely changed trade patterns and constructed a new production system. BT might challenge governance and relationships of existing GVCs, with an opportunity to alter the size and configuration of GVCs, and help lead firms to reduce transaction costs, at the same time benefiting SMEs worldwide. Disruptions are expected to bring pressures for strategy change of leading firms and GVCs geographical reorganization [14]. 4IR has already been transforming the role of lead firms and the GVC activities dispersion and has brought new lead firms in Industry 4.0. GVC relationships and work organization have changed through platform economy using big data, cloud technology and powerful algorithms, providing a new way of governing a GVC through controlling the platform and thus, appropriating superior value.

Large firms usually have better access to information and other resources and have better overview of the whole path of goods. Small firms often contribute to just a few steps in the production process and do not have complete information on goods. Digital platforms and BT contribute to the elimination of information asymmetry, enabling participation of firms from countries with weak institutional and legislative framework [25]. So, digitization, BT and IoT have the potential to strengthen GVCs and provide various benefits [26]. Intermediaries decrease the profitability of producers, while increasing the prices to consumers due to their services (e.g. product offerings determination) and transaction facilitation (e.g. logistics, transaction settlement, trust). They can be defined as all those GVC participants which have the function of matching buyers and sellers. Disintermediation refers to the evolution of shorter GVCs in the digital economy [35]. BT is expected to mitigate opportunism from making dependent other members of the GVC [20]. Complexity of GVCs could be reduced as the role of intermediaries in building the trust would not be needed any more, leading to decreasing transaction costs. This does not mean that intermediaries are expected to vanish, but their traditional role that has been changing is expected to be redefined to be more facilitating [14].

Today most of the firms in GVCs don't have the full knowledge on how, when and where all components of products are made, manufactured and used, given the complexity of the production networks including retailers, logistics companies, distribution companies and suppliers [43]. This kind of visibility is rarely existing over a second and further tier suppliers, except in a very few companies which provide GVC visualization using end-to-end manner source map [43]. BT can provide production process transparency and trace the value flow from raw materials to final consumption. Thus, BT can address existing information lack in which can bring several changes to GVC patterns and dynamics, such as facilitate new forms of governance, shift power to GVCs ends through decreasing information asymmetry, de-commoditize goods and disaggregate price signals, and lower reliance on quality proxies [39]. Both producers and consumers have a lack of information on the production process and this asymmetric information can be addressed through BT. Primary producers higher bargaining power can emerge through reducing their information asymmetries enabling them to restructure SCs and dynamically switch between them [39].

Turning data and information into knowledge can help in decision-making, so digital technologies facilitate lead firms' quest to codify transactions and convert knowledge-intensive activities into standardized, routine and low-knowledge ones [44]. The key advantage of digitalization is in facilitating product upgrading and introduction of new business models [45]. In the digital era, real time decision-making is vital for competitiveness, and real time decision-support systems enable organizational and process flexibility thus enabling companies to respond to competitive pressures (e.g. through introducing new products more quickly, cheaply and of improved quality) [46]. BT can disrupt the global trade system with digital tools enabling the share of real-time information and reducing costs related to non-timely information, policing and enforcement in global economic transactions, administrative trade frictions, and minimizing major challenges in logistics (e.g. order delay, goods damaging, multiple data entry) [35]. Immutability and time-based network can increase the productivity of GVCs [35]. One of the options is using cryptocurrencies for financial transactions along GVCs as they allow real time money transfer with lower fees [47].

The use of IoT and BT-based information systems has a potential of a range of data- driven decision-support applications in different GVCs from manufacturing [22] to food quality assurance [21]. These technology advancements complemented with sophisticated decision-support systems enable designing, implementing and controlling strategies that are at the core of these integrated systems, using intelligent decision-making design utilizing artificial intelligence based on real-time big data [46, 48]. All data from the clearance form to bill of lading and insurance policy can be integrated in the block and available to suppliers, transporters, buyers, regulators and auditors, decreasing accounting and auditing costs [24]. Producers can be allowed to get information about goods and their final consumers after selling them, as well as on rents of the other participants of the GVC [39]. Table 1 systematizes current challenges, opportunities and potential impediments of BT implementation for GVC participants.

Table 1. Overview of blockchain technology potential transformation of GVCs

	GVC LEAD FIRMS	OTHER GVC PARTICIPANTS
Current challenges	Governance challenges related to lack of information on GVC processes and actors; transportation and logistics issues; high administrative costs of complex systems governance	Barriers to joining and upgrading in GVCs; lack of information of value appropriation along the chain; high cost of intermediaries and other administrative costs
Opportunities of implementing blockchain technology	Traceability and in-depth GVC overview; ensuring sustainability; efficiency rise; real-time decision making; agile management; facilitating product upgrading; security (decentralization); enabling real-time transactions with lower fees (cryptocurrencies); product de-commoditization	Traceability and better overview of value creation; decreasing information asymmetries and barriers to entry GVCs; de-commoditization of products; easier communication; decreasing intermediaries' costs; higher bargaining power (due to decrease of information asymmetry)
Impediments to blockchain implementation	Additional financial resources for financing basic infrastructure; Employees digital skills; Regulatory oversight; Unwanted transparency (reputation implications); uncertain return on investment	Additional financial resources for financing basic infrastructure; digital skills, interoperability of different solutions; changing intermediaries roles; Regulatory oversight; Unwanted transparency (to other stakeholders)

Source: Authors according to literature research.

Sustainability of SCs consists of three pillars: social, environmental and business [20]. Lead firms have been pressured to take over the responsibility for bad CSR practices, what has been challenging to those that do not have the comprehensive information and thus are not able to completely guarantee the compliance with environmental, human and labor rights in their GVC [21]. As consumers do not have the complete information they tend to rely on proxies [39]. Issues such as unethical labor, environmental issues and counterfeit products increase the demand for transparent GVCs [43]. GVC sustainability is increasingly becoming important to consumers as the public awareness of production under bad working and environmental standards has risen [35]. Social justice and sustainability of GVCs are coming in the focus [14]. To differentiate products, determine their subjective value and make the purchase, consumers seek information regarding products' legitimacy, quality and provenance especially in food purchases [39]. BT can increase knowledge of production process social and environmental characteristics and enable identifying ethical sources [20]. Only the authorized GVC participants can record the data so counterfeit products can be easily detected [39].

Providing the detailed information on the social sustainability along the SC can even improve the decision-making of firms. It improves and facilitates the evaluation process of suppliers and can be a source of competitive advantage [49]. Pioneering firms will realize this competitive advantage of transparency which provides increased buyers' trust leading them to increased purchases and bringing additional revenues and profits [20].

Research has shown that consumers strive for more information to make information-based decisions, thus making it more recommendable to invest in transparency instead of certifications [50]. Tracing the carbon footprint of each SC becomes easier with BT and it can enable consumers to choose the products with lower carbon footprint [20]. Besides GVC partners and consumers of their products, another important stakeholders are governments and regulators which to check the compliance of products to different regulations (e.g. biosecurity, sanctions, minimum ethical and labor standards) need product information, especially regarded to food safety [39]. Use of BT in customs office can reduce trade costs, increase transparency, safeguard against fraud and reduce the time of customs clearance [24]. Table 2 systematizes current challenges and opportunities of BT implementation for consumers and government.

Table 2. Overview of challenges and blockchain technology potential disruptions in GVCs for consumers and governments

	CONSUMERS	GOVERNMENTS
Current challenges	Limited data production process CSR data; "made in" label might be misleading due to high value of inputs from various countries; need to rely on proxies for quality	Facilitating industries and companies to enter and upgrade in GVCs; long time and complex customs clearance procedures; faulty and counterfeit products
Opportunities of implementing blockchain technology	De-commoditized goods with provided information for making information-based purchase decisions; providing possibility to make more sustainable choices and lower reliance on quality proxies; clear product specificities information for more easily detecting counterfeit and bad quality products	More detailed information on GVCs enabling easier insight of industrial organization and spotting the upgrading opportunities; increased transparency leading to safeguard against frauds; increased transparency reducing customs clearance time

Source: Authors according to literature research.

Thus, BT can support collection of data, storage and managing thus supporting significant information along the chain and addressing complex issues in GVCs to pursue sustainable development [35]. It can provide an option to assure transparency and decrease a range of costs along the GVC leading to potentials for increased profitability and sustainability. So, it is important that all GVC stakeholders see BT as an opportunity, but stay aware of its implementation impediments [20].

5   Conclusion

This paper provides a systematic overview of BT potential to transform GVCs. The emphasis was given on potential effects of blockchain implementation on decision-making of lead firms, other chain participants, consumers and governments. The literature analysis led to systematization of key opportunities of blockchain implementation for key GVC stakeholders. The main opportunity for GVC lead firms is transparency which BT enables leading to traceability, in-depth overview of all actors in the chain and facilitating real-time decision making. Transparency is also beneficial for other GVC participants, consumers and governments, as it decreases information asymmetries. It leads to goods de-commoditization and allows sustainability practices differentiation, thus facilitating decision-making for consumers and providing competitive advantages for certain companies. It reduces customs clearance time and safeguards against frauds, while allowing governments a better understanding of the upgrading process and enabling them to form policies promoting it. The role of traditional intermediaries is expected to decrease and transform, given the trust that decentralized system provides. Shifting to more agile management can lead to significant efficiency gains and facilitate faster and more successful product upgrading. Lead firms will have to bring complex decision on the implementation of this technology. More research on the BT implementation in different GVCs is needed to provide decision-support to lead firms in technology adoption and case studies of BT implementation in GVCs would be useful for building empirical knowledge in this field.

References

1. Baldwin, R., Okubo, T.: GVC journeys: industrialisation and deindustrialisation in the age of the second unbundling. J. Jpn. Int. Econ. **25**, 53–67 (2019)
2. Amador, J., Cabral, S.: Global value chains: surveying drivers and measures. In: European Central Bank Working Paper, Working Paper, vol. 1739, pp. 1–45 (2014)
3. Gereffi, G.: The organization of buyer- driven global commodity chains: how U.S. retailers shape overseas production networks. In: Gereffi, G., Korzeniewicz, M. (eds.) Commodity Chains and Global Capitalism, pp. 95–122. Praeger, London (1994)
4. Horner, R., Nadvi, K.: Global value chains and the rise of the global south: unpacking twenty-first century polycentric trade. Global Netw. **18**(2), 207–237 (2018)
5. Clarke, T., Boersma, M.: The governance of global value chains: unresolved human rights, environmental and ethical dilemmas in the apple supply chain. J. Bus. Ethics **143**(1), 111–131 (2015). https://doi.org/10.1007/s10551-015-2781-3
6. Dünhaupt, P., Herr, H.: Global value chains–a ladder for development? Int. Rev. Appl. Econ. **35**(3–4), 456–474 (2021)
7. Ravenhill, J.: Global value chains and development. Rev. Int. Polit. Econ. **21**(1), 264–274 (2014)
8. Wood, A.: Value chains an economist's perspective. IDS Bull. **32**(3), 41–45 (2001)
9. Kano, L.: Global value chain governance: a relational perspective. J. Int. Bus. Stud. **49**(6), 684–705 (2018)
10. Gereffi, G., Humphrey, J., Sturgeon, T.: The governance of global value chains. Rev. Int. Polit. Econ. **12**(1), 78–104 (2005)
11. Gereffi, G.: Beyond the producer-driven/buyer-driven dichotomy the evolution of global value chains in the internet era. IDS Bull. **32**(3), 30–40 (2001)
12. Koberg, E., Longoni, A.: A systematic review of sustainable supply chain management in global supply chains. J. Clean. Prod. **207**, 1084–1098 (2019)
13. Notteboom, T., Rodrigue, J.P.: Containerisation, box logistics and global supply chains: the integration of ports and liner shipping networks. Marit. Econ. Logistics **10**(1), 152–174 (2008)
14. Pananond, P., Gereffi, G., Pedersen, T.: An integrative typology of global strategy and global value chains: the management and organization of cross-border activities. Glob. Strateg. J. **10**(3), 421–443 (2020)

15. Rehnberg, M., Ponte, S.: From smiling to smirking? 3D printing, upgrading and the restructuring of global value chains. Global Netw. **18**(1), 57–80 (2018)
16. Javorcik, B.: Reshaping of global supply chains will take place, but it will not happen fast. J. Chin. Econ. Bus. Stud. **18**(4), 321–325 (2020)
17. Barišić, A.: Covid-19 pandemic and global value chains: is the reconfiguration on the way? In: Tipurić, D., Cindrić, L. (eds.) 9th International OFEL Conference Book of Proceedings, pp. 196–206. CIRU, Zagreb (2021)
18. Kano, L., Tsang, E.W., Yeung, H.W.C.: Global value chains: a review of the multi-disciplinary literature. J. Int. Bus. Stud. **51**(4), 577–622 (2020)
19. Tijan, E., Aksentijević, S., Ivanić, K., Jardas, M.: Blockchain technology implementation in logistics. Sustainability **11**(4), 1185 (2019)
20. Saberi, S., Kouhizadeh, M., Sarkis, J., Shen, L.: Blockchain technology and its relationships to sustainable supply chain management. Int. J. Prod. Res. **57**(7), 2117–2135 (2019)
21. Tsang, Y.P., Choy, K.L., Wu, C.H., Ho, G.T.S., Lam, H.Y.: Blockchain-driven IoT for food traceability with an integrated consensus mechanism. In: IEEE Special Section on Data Mining for Internet of Things, vol. 7 (2019)
22. Pal, K.: Information sharing for manufacturing supply chain management based on blockchain technology. In: Cross-Industry Use of Blockchain Technology and Opportunities for the Future, pp. 1–17. IGI Global (2020)
23. Treiblmaier, H.: The impact of the blockchain on the supply chain: a theory-based research framework and a call for action. Supply Chain Manag. Int. J. (2018)
24. Botton, N.: Blockchain and trade: not a fix for Brexit but could revolutionise global value chains (if governments let it), ECIPE Policy Brief No. 1/2018 (2018)
25. Nikolakis, W., John, L., Krishnan, H.: How blockchain can shape sustainable global value chains: an evidence, verifiability, and enforceability (EVE) framework. Sustainability **10**(11) (2018)
26. Egwuonwu, A., Mordi, C., Egwuonwu, A., Uadiale, O.: The influence of blockchains and internet of things on global value chain. Strateg. Chang. **31**(1), 45–55 (2022)
27. McWilliam, S.E., Kim, J.K., Mudambi, R., Nielsen, B.B.: Global value chain governance: intersections with international business. J. World Bus. **55**(4) (2020)
28. Ferdows, K.: Made in the world: the global spread of production. Prod. Oper. Manag. **6**(2), 102–109 (1997)
29. Humphrey, J., Schmitz, H.: Governance in global value chains. IDS Bull. **32**(3), 19–29 (2001)
30. Gereffi, G., Lee, J.: Why the world suddenly cares about global supply chains. J. Supply Chain Manag. **48**(3), 24–32 (2012)
31. Ponte, S., Sturgeon, T.: Explaining governance in global value chains: a modular theory-building effort. Rev. Int. Polit. Econ. **21**(1), 195–223 (2014)
32. Mentzer, J.T., et al.: Defining supply chain management. J. Bus. Logist. **22**(2), 1–25 (2001)
33. Cooper, M.C., Lambert, D.M., Pagh, J.D.: Supply chain management: more than a new name for logistics. Int. J. Logistics Manag. **8**(1), 1–14 (1997)
34. Min, S., Zacharia, Z.G., Smith, C.D.: Defining supply chain management: in the past, present, and future. J. Bus. Logist. **40**(1), 44–55 (2019)
35. Tseng, C.T., Shang, S.S.: Exploring the sustainability of the intermediary role in blockchain. Sustainability **13**(4) (2021)
36. Natarajan, H., Krause, S., Gradstein, H.: Distributed ledger technology and blockchain. FinTech Note No. 1. World Bank, Washington, DC (2017)
37. Wüst, K., Gervais, A.: Do you need a blockchain? In: 2018 Crypto Valley Conference on Blockchain Technology (CVCBT), pp. 45–54. IEEE (2018)
38. Statista: Blockchain Statista dossier (2021). https://www.statista.com/study/39859/blockchain-statista-dossier/. Accessed 5 Nov 2021

39. Allen, D., Berg, A., Markey-Towler, B.: Blockchain and supply chains: V-form organisations, value redistributions, de-commoditisation and quality proxies. J. Br. Blockchain Assoc. **2**(1), 57–65 (2019)

40. Clohessy, T., Clohessy, S.: What's in the box? Combating counterfeit medications in pharmaceutical supply chains with blockchain vigilant information systems. In: Treiblmaier, H., Clohessy, T. (eds.) Blockchain and Distributed Ledger Technology Use Cases. PI, pp. 51–68. Springer, Cham (2020). https://doi.org/10.1007/978-3-030-44337-5_3

41. Mendling, J.: Towards blockchain support for business processes. In: Shishkov, B. (ed.) BMSD 2018. LNBIP, vol. 319, pp. 243–248. Springer, Cham (2018). https://doi.org/10.1007/978-3-319-94214-8_15

42. Farshidi, S., Jansen, S., España, S., Verkleij, J.: Decision support for blockchain platform selection: three industry case studies. IEEE Trans. Eng. Manage. **67**(4), 1109–1128 (2020)

43. Abeyratne, S.A., Monfared, R.P.: Blockchain ready manufacturing supply chain using distributed ledger. Int. J. Res. Eng. Technol. **5**(9), 1–10 (2016)

44. Cano-Kollmann, M., Cantwell, J., Hannigan, T.J., Mudambi, R., Song, J.: Knowledge connectivity: an agenda for innovation research in international business. J. Int. Bus. Stud. **47**(3), 255–262 (2016)

45. Szalavetz, A.: Digitalisation, automation and upgrading in global value chains – factory economy actors versus lead companies. Post-Communist Econ. **31**(5), 646–670 (2019)

46. Al-Mudimigh, A.S., Zairi, M., Ahmed, A.M.M.: Extending the concept of supply chain: the effective management of value chains. Int. J. Prod. Econ. **87**(3), 309–320 (2004)

47. Pournader, M., Shi, Y., Seuring, S., Koh, S.L.: Blockchain applications in supply chains, transport and logistics: a systematic review of the literature. Int. J. Prod. Res. **58**(7), 2063–2081 (2020)

48. Ekawati, R., Arkeman, Y., Suprihatin, S., Sunarti, T.C.: Design of intelligent decision support system for sugar cane supply chains based on blockchain technology. In: 2nd International Conference on Industrial Electrical and Electronics, pp. 153–157 (2020)

49. Bai, C., Kusi-Sarpong, S., Badri Ahmadi, H., Sarkis, J.: Social sustainable supplier evaluation and selection: a group decision-support approach. Int. J. Prod. Res. **57**(22), 7046–7067 (2019)

50. Toussaint, M., Cabanelas, P., González-Alvarado, T.E.: What about the consumer choice? The influence of social sustainability on consumer's purchasing behavior in the Food Value Chain. Eur. Res. Manag. Bus. Econ. **27**(1) (2021)

Predicting the Rating of an App Beyond Its Functionalities: Introducing the App Publication Strategy

Mathieu Lega[✉][iD], Corentin Burnay[iD], and Stéphane Faulkner

Namur Digital Institute (NADI/PReCISE), University of Namur, Namur, Belgium
mathieu.lega@unamur.be

Abstract. Mobile applications (or apps) are present on every portable device and have become the center of tremendous attention from developers and software vendors. Some apps meet significant success with high profitability, but most of them tend to remain anonymous, with weak returns on investment. The risk incurred when launching a new app is therefore significant. In this article, we introduce the concept of Publication Strategy, resulting from the numerous decisions made by an app designer on all the variables which are publicly visible on the stores (screenshots, description, title, etc.). This paper studies the extent to which the success of an app may be predicted using such Publication Strategy. To do this, we use metadata about more than 40,000 apps from both the Google Play Store and the Apple App Store and adopt a machine learning research strategy by training and testing a number of classification models. We observe that in about 50% of the cases, it is possible to predict the rating of an app based solely on its Publication Strategy. The results are very similar between the 2 stores. These results bring us to the definition of a number of research avenues to further explore the notion of App Publication Strategy which can be used to support apps designers in their decisions.

Keywords: Mobile applications · Apps · Publication strategy · Empirical study · Machine learning · Google play store · Apple App Store · Decision support

1 Introduction

Nowadays, more than two thirds of the global population owns a smartphone [12]. On average, a smartphone is used 3 h a day and contains 100 applications [12]. In 2018, more than $100 billions were spent by users on mobile applications (also called mobile apps or apps) via in-app purchases, paid downloads and subscription fees [7] and 194 billions of mobile apps were downloaded [20]. Some predictions state that the global mobile apps revenue could get near to $1000 billions by 2023 [20].

© Springer Nature Switzerland AG 2022
A. P. Cabral Seixas Costa et al. (Eds.): ICDSST 2022, LNBIP 447, pp. 16–28, 2022.
https://doi.org/10.1007/978-3-031-06530-9_2

It is clear from these numbers that the generated revenue is growing faster each year and that this evolution is expected to continue in the next years. This in turn emphasizes the fact that mobile applications now represent a huge market and therefore a significant source of opportunities for businesses.

However, designing and selling an app is not trivial; some apps are downloaded/purchased much more frequently than others, and pushing an app on the market may therefore not always represent a good move for a company as it requires a lot of resources. In other words, developing a new app does not always come with financial success and companies should be cautious about it.

We also know that the rating of a mobile application has an impact on the ranking of the app in search results for the App Store [2]. Knowing that more or less 50% of the customers use these stores to discover apps, rating has a direct impact on the discovery of an app [3,5]. Moreover, 80% of the customers check the rating of an app before downloading it [5]. If an app has a rating of 2 stars out of 5, only 15% of the customers state that they will consider downloading it [3,5]. This percentage increases to 96% if the rating is 4 stars [3,5]. We can thus say that the rating also has an impact on the conversion rate to download and thus the success of an app.

All these reasons brought us to look at the extent to which the rating (used as proxy for the success), and more precisely the number of complete stars, of a mobile application can be predicted using only what we call the "Publication Strategy" of the companies developing and commercializing the app (latter called "the companies"). This Publication Strategy includes the variables controlled by the companies and displayed when a customer arrives on the page of the app on an app store. Our objective in doing so is to discover if the concept of Publication Strategy has an impact on the success of an app. If the Publication Strategy truly plays a role in the success of an app, better understanding this concept would allow companies to take better decisions regarding their Publication Strategy (which is easier to change than the functionalities of the app) and thus to minimize the number of low rated (and thus riskier) apps launched on the market for a given quality/functionality level. We also try to discover the most important variables/features (the 2 words will be used interchangeably in this work) of a Publication Strategy. Our research questions can be stated as follows:

- To which extent is it possible to predict the rating of a mobile application using only its Publication Strategy?
- Which are the most important variables in the Publication Strategy of a mobile application?

For this purpose, we first create two databases containing metadata about applications, one for the Google Play Store and one for the Apple App Store. Then, feature engineering is used in order to extract the most important variables from the raw data. Finally, machine learning is applied to train prediction models. We use the following classification algorithms: decision tree, random forest, k-nearest neighbors, support vector machine and neural networks. The results of these algorithms are compared and discussed.

The remainder of this paper is structured as follows. In Sect. 2, we present some related works in the field of mobile applications. In Sect. 3, we explain with more details our methodology for the creation of the databases, the use of feature engineering and the training of the models. In Sect. 4, we present our results. In Sect. 5, we discuss our results, the limitations of our work and some research avenues. Finally, we conclude our work in Sect. 6.

2   Related Works

This section presents some related works about apps success factors and the prediction of the rating of mobile apps. We also detail our positioning compared to the presented articles.

2.1   Models of App Success Factors

The reasons behind the success of a mobile application has been studied in several ways in the literature. Lee and Raghu [11] decided to look at how the success in an app market is impacted by both app-related and seller-related characteristics. For this purpose, they tracked the presence of apps in the top 300 grossing charts of the Apple App Store and analyzed the factors allowing an app to stay in these charts or not [11]. For this purpose, they used a generalized hierarchical modeling approach, a hazard model and a count regression model [11]. They concluded that, at a seller-level, it is very important to diversify across categories to achieve sales performance [11]. At an app-level, the following factors may impact positively the way an app performs in terms of sales: being free, higher initial popularity, the fact of investing in less popular categories, continuously updating the features of the app and an higher number of user feedbacks [11].

Picoto, Duarte and Pinto [16] also used the tops grossing for their study. The aim of their study was to find the factors that could have an impact on the ranking and the success of an app [16]. For this purpose, they took 500 top grossing apps from the Apple App Store from which they extract the top 50 and bottom 50 for analysis [16]. Once they had identified potential antecedents for an app's ranking, they used a multivariate logistic regression and a Fuzzy Set Qualitative Comparative Analysis (fsQCA) to identify the factors that could determine the success of an app [16]. They found that the following factors make it more likely for an app to be in the top 50: category popularity, number of languages supported, package size, and app release date [16]. A surprising result is that the higher the user rating, the lower the probability for this app to be in the top 50 [16]. Finally, they found that the attributes, functionalities, and longevity of an app have a bigger impact on the success of an app than the user rating [16].

Yang [21] tried to predict the use of mobile apps, the attitudes of customers towards these apps and the intent to use with the Theory of Planned Behavior, the Technology Acceptance Model, and the Uses and Gratification Theory. The author tested the proposed model with a web survey answered by American college students [21]. The results state that the following factors may be used to predict the attitude of consumers related to apps: perceived enjoyment, usefulness, subjective norm, and ease of use [21]. If the aim is to predict the use of applications, the significant factors are: perceived usefulness, mobile internet use, mobile apps intent, personal income, and gender [21].

Lu, Liu and Wei [13] decided to focus only on two factors: enjoyment and mobility. In their study, they tried to understand the link between the perception of these factors and the intention to continue using an app [13]. They used a second-stage continuance model and data of 584 smartphone users collected with a survey [13]. As a result, they discovered that "the salience of disconfirmation and beliefs in enjoyment and mobility serve as the primary driver of the changes in satisfaction and attitude toward continuance intentions" (Lu, Liu & Wei, 2016, p.1). Another result is that more than 60% of the variance related to the attitude after usage can be attributed to: perceived enjoyment, mobility and satisfaction [13].

2.2 Prediction of Ratings

The prediction of the user rating of an application is a well-known problematic. Monett and Stolte [15] have tackled this problem in their work. They used a corpus of 1,760 annotated reviews about 130 mobile apps available on the Google Play Store [15]. Their goal was to predict the rating based on the polarity of subjective phrases found in the reviews [15]. For this purpose, several computational models have been used and evaluated [15]. They concluded that rating could be well predicted even using only phrase-level sentiment polarity [15].

Meng, Zheng, Tao and Liu [14] implemented a weight base matrix factorization (WMF) capturing user-specific interests in order to predict an app rating for a specific user. The used dataset containing logs of user's downloaded and uninstalled apps involved 5057 users and 4496 apps [14]. Their model got convincing results, performing better than some other prediction models [14].

A third approach can be found in [4]. In order to predict the rating of applications, Daimi and Hazzazi decided to use the following algorithms: Linear Regression, Neural Networks, Support Vector Machines, Random Forest, M5 Rules, REP Tree and Random Tree [4]. They used an Apple Store dataset composed of 7197 apps and the following attributes: user rating count for all version, user rating count for current version, average user rating for all version (the attribute to predict), average user rating for current version, number of supporting devices, number of screen shots showed for display and number of supported languages [4]. They found that Random Forest produced the best results when predicting the rating of an application from the Apple Store dataset [4].

Finally, Sarro, Harman, Jia and Zhang [18] focused on predictions achieved by Case Based Reasoning (CBR) taking only the technical features of the apps into account. They used a dataset dating from 2011 containing 9588 apps and 1256 extracted features from the BlackBerry App World store and 1949 apps and 620 extracted features from the Samsung Android App store [18]. As a result, they discovered that, in 89% of the cases, the rating of an app could be perfectly predicted [18]. They also discovered that only 11–12 applications were sufficient to achieve the best prediction when using a case-based prediction system [18]. They thus concluded that it is possible to accurately predict the rating of an app taking only its features into account [18].

2.3   Positioning of This Work

Our work differentiates from all the studies about apps success factors presented above because we do not use feedbacks from users to test a model, neither focus on top charts. Instead, we try to maximize our precision when predicting the rating (that acts as proxy for the success) given by the customers of an app. More precisely, we try to predict the number of stars an app will receive using classification algorithms. We thus use the well-known star rating used by several stores.

What distinguishes this work from the other works about the prediction of the rating of an app is the fact that we only use the Publication Strategy as predictor. Indeed, we investigate the impact of the Publication Strategy on the success, observed by the number of stars an app receives on the stores. We thus only focus on variables that may be leveraged by the companies and that are displayed on the stores because this is by definition what we consider to be the Publication Strategy.

Moreover we differentiate apps from the Apple App Store and apps coming from the Android Play Store. For this purpose, we gathered metadata about more than 80 000 applications for the former and 90 000 applications for the latter. Our final output is thus trained models of machine learning able to predict a rating (the number of stars) for an application.

3   Methodology

3.1   Creation of the Databases

To answer our research questions, the first step is to collect data about mobile applications including the rating of each app and a maximum of variables controlled by the companies and displayed on the store. For this purpose, we use the API of 42matters (https://42matters.com/app-market-data). We chose this one for several reasons. First of all, it allows us to retrieve metadata from both Android (from the Google Play Store) and IOS (from the Apple App Store) apps. Then, all the fields available on the stores are included and more precisely the rating of each app and the variables about the Publication Strategy. There are also mechanisms to iterate over the applications using some criteria and filters allowing us to get a maximal amount of data. Finally, the results are returned under an easy to process format (this is explained later).

The risk while using data collected by another party is to get data of bad quality. However, 42matters extracts its data directly from the Apple App Store and the Google Play Store. Moreover, we checked the retrieved data of several apps (selected randomly) by comparing with the actual stores and found no error. We also checked for aberrant values in the different retrieved fields and found none. We thus infer that the obtained data is reliable.

In order to retrieve data from this API, a query must be built. There are different parameters that allow to specify the criteria that the returned apps must fulfill (these parameters may be found on the website of 42matters). As we are interested in the rating, we use this latter as selection criterion to retrieve apps. We thus divide the loading of the data in different steps, specifying a range of 0.5 for the rating at each time. We first collect apps with a rating lower or equal to 0.5 and then increment this step by step until we collect apps with a rating between 4.5 and 5. The API returns a maximum of 10,000 apps for a given set of criteria and the apps are returned and sorted in descending order of number of ratings which allows us to get the apps with the highest numbers of ratings (ans thus the most reliable ratings) for each range.

This allows us to build a database with several thousands of apps for each rating. This process is repeated for the Apple App Store and the Google Play Store. As the API returns Json files, we use MongoDB to store our data because it allows to work in a document-oriented way.

3.2 Feature Engineering

The second step, realised with Python, is to extract the different variables that will be later used in the prediction of the rating. The main criterion to choose these variables is that they must be controlled by the companies before launching the app on the market and displayed on the store. Indeed, the final goal is to study the importance of the Publication Strategy of an app on its rating.

We also analyze and adapt the raw data in order to detect potential problems (such as missing values or duplicated rows) and give it the right shape for the different algorithms. Indeed, some of them have requirements for the data in order to run successfully.

Moreover, we use dimensionality reduction techniques in order to check if it increases the performances of our models. Principal Component Analysis (PCA) and Random Forest are used for this purpose [1,19]. The former allows to create uncorrelated linear combinations of the existing features and the latter allows to extract the most important features of our dataset [1,19].

3.3 Training of the Models

Finally, classification algorithms are used because our goal is to predict the number of complete stars an app will receive and not the precise rating (this is thus a classification problem and not a regression one). This step is also performed using Python. We train the following models with the prepared data: (i) Decision Tree; (ii) Random Forest; (iii) K-Nearest Neighbors (KNN); (iv) Support Vector Machines (SVM); (v) Neural Networks and more specifically MultiLayer Perceptron (MLP).

Most of these models have been chosen using the flowchart presented in [8]. We just added the Decision Tree and the MLP that are not listed in the mentioned chart as the former is very simple and the latter is very flexible [6,9]. Also, we do not use the linear SVC (Support Vector Classifier) model as we already chose SVM. Indeed, the latter may be used with a linear kernel and, even if it represents another implementation, the results are often similar with the linear SVC [10].

The training process is the following for each model. We first divide our data into train data (80%) and test data (20%). The train data is used to tune the hyperparameters and the test data allows us to measure the accuracy of each model on data never seen before. In order to find the optimal hyperparameters for each model, we proceed in different steps. First, we analyze the evolution of the accuracy depending on the values of some hyperparameters. Then, a grid search is used to compare different configurations based on cross-validation. Once this tuning is finished, we test the final model with the test data.

Three kinds of accuracies are calculated for each model: a training accuracy, a validation accuracy and a testing accuracy. The first is the accuracy obtained when predicting the labels of the data used to train the model. The second is the accuracy obtained with the best configuration while tuning the hyperparameters. The third accuracy is obtained by predicting the labels of the test data. The training and the validation accuracies are biaised because they are used to enhance the model.

Python is also used for this step and more precisely the functions from the scikit-learn package. The performances of the different algorithms are discussed and compared. The performances of a random prediction are also computed in order to have a reference point.

4   Results

4.1   Feature Engineering

Selection of the Variables. For the Android apps, we obtained a database containing 96,178 rows and 53 fields. The entire list of fields may be found on the website of 42matters. Obviously, a big part of these variables did not interest us. As a reminder, we only wanted to keep the variables controlled by the companies and displayed on the store. Moreover, we had to transform some fields in order to make them usable. The kept fields are presented in Table 1. We did not take the list of countries where the app is available neither the languages supported by the app as features because we consider that these variables may be impacted by the success of the app after the commercialization.

The database of IOS apps counted 81,000 rows and 52 fields. It is important to note that some fields were available for Android but not for IOS and vice versa. This explains why different fields were used for IOS in comparison with Android. The used selection criteria was also that the variables must be controlled by the companies and displayed on the store. Table 2 presents the kept fields for IOS apps.

Table 1. Selected features for Android apps

Name	Description
Category	The category of the app
Promo video	Whether the app contains a promotional video
Price	The price of the app (in $)
Content rating	A rating of the content of the app
Number of screenshots	The number of screenshots displayed on the store
Size	The size of the app in bytes
In-app purchases	Whether in-app purchases are available in the app
Minimum in-app purchase	The minimum cost of in-app purchase
Maximum in-app purchase	The maximum cost of in-app purchase
Length of the description	The length of the description of the app
Length of the short description	The length of the short description of the app
Length of title	The length of the title of the app
Ads	Whether the app contains ads
Rating	The rating of the app

Table 2. Selected features for IOS apps

Name	Description
Length of the description	The length of the description of the app
Number of iPhone screenshots	The number of iPhone screenshots of the app
Number of iPad screenshots	The number of iPad screenshots of the app
iPhone	Whether the app is available on iPhone
iPad	Whether the app is available on iPad
VPP distribution	Whether the app supports VPP distribution
Content rating	A rating of the content of the app
Size	The size of the app in bytes
Game center	Whether the app supports Game Center
Primary category	The primary category of the app
Price	The price of the app
Length of the title	The length of the title of the app
Rating	The rating of the app

Analysis and Preparation of the Data. First of all, as we created our databases in different steps, there were some duplicated rows. Indeed, the rating of an app may change from one week to another. We thus deleted them.

Then, we managed the different categorical features (the category for example). We first checked the distribution of the values of each column to see if some of them were under-represented. When several values appeared less than 1000 times in a column, we aggregated them into a new category "other" in order to keep only the relevant values. As explained before, some algorithms are not able to handle categorical input. We therefore decided to use one-hot-encoding [17]. This method allows to transform a categorical column in several boolean columns (one for each category) [17].

The next step was the scaling of the numerical columns. This was another requirement for some of our models. We decided to use standardization ($z = (x - \mu)/\sigma$) to decrease the impact of the outliers in the features [17]. In order to avoid data leakage, we scaled the data using only the training sets.

We also had to modify the rating in order to have the classes that we wanted. We used the following rounding rules: rating class = 0 if rating < 0.5; rating class = 1 if rating $\geq$ 0.5 and < 1.5; rating class = 2 if rating $\geq$ 1.5 and < 2.5; rating class = 3 if rating $\geq$ 2.5 and < 3.5; rating class = 4 if rating $\geq$ 3.5 and < 4.5; rating class = 5 if rating $\geq$ 4.5.

Finally, as the number of rows with missing values in the resulting datasets was very low (less than 100), we just deleted them. We also kept only the applications with at least 50 ratings from the customers. Indeed, for several apps, the average rating was not calculated on enough individual ratings to be significant.

For the Android apps, our final dataset consisted of 64504 rows and 65 columns. An important consequence of the treatment described above is that there was no application with a rating of 0 star any more, reducing the number of classes to 5.

The final IOS dataset had 41856 rows and 31 columns. As for Android, there was no app with a rating of 0 star.

Reduction of Dimensionality. Two methods were used to decrease the number of features. First, we applied a Principal Component Analysis keeping 95% of the variance. This returned 24 principal components for the Android dataset and 15 principal components for the IOS dataset. Then, we used the built-in feature selection of the Random Forest to keep only the variables with a relative importance bigger than 0.01. Based on this process, 9 features remained for the Android dataset: the length of the description, the size, the length of the short description, the length of the title, the number of screenshots, the most expensive in-app purchase, the presence or absence of advertisements, the least expensive in-app purchase and the presence or absence of a promo video. Regarding the application of this second method to the IOS dataset, 10 features remained: the size, the length of the description, the length of the name, the number of screenshots, the number of screenshots on ipad, the fact that the app is a game or not, the fact that GameCenter is enabled or not, the fact that the app is free or not, the fact that the content of the app is rated "4+" or not and the fact that the category of the app is "other" or not.

4.2   Training of the Models

The results of the different models for Android apps is summarized in Table 3 and Table 4 summarizes the results of the different models for IOS apps. Each time, a reference point is given with a random prediction (1/number of classes). All these results have been achieved using the methodology presented in Subsect. 3.3. As a recall, the training accuracy is biaised because it is used during the optimisation of the parameters of the models. The validation accuracy is also biaised as it is used to tune the hyperparameters. The testing accuracy is thus the most significant approximation of the true accuracy of the model.

Table 3. Training of the models for Android apps

Model	Selected hyperparameters and final values	Training accuracy	Validation accuracy	Testing accuracy
Random	/	20%	20%	20%
Decision Tree	- Maximal depth = 10 - Maximal number of leaf nodes = 90	47.5%	46.4%	46.3%
Random Forest	- Maximal depth of the trees = 20 - Number of estimators = 75	78.9%	49.5%	50.1%
KNN	- Number of neighbors = 30	51.4%	46.9%	47.5% 44.3%[1] 46%[2]
SVM	- Regularization parameter (C) = 7	54.9%	45.2%[2]	48.8% 45.5%[1] 46.9%[2]
MLP	- Number of layers = 1 - Number of neurons = 20	50.3%	48.7%	49% 46.1%[1] 47.4%%[2]

1: using only the most important features.
2: using PCA.

Looking at the results for the Android dataset, we can see that the performances of all the models are rather close during the testing phase. It varies between 44.3% and 50.1% with Random Forest achieving the best score. This last result is more than twice the result of a pure random prediction. Another conclusion is that both feature selection methods fail to improve the results. Using the built-in feature importance evaluation of Random Forest, we can assess the relative importance of the different features. The most important features for Android are thus: the length of the description, the size, the length of the short description, the length of the title and the number of screenshots.

Table 4. Training of the models for IOS apps

Model	Selected hyperparameters and final values	Training accuracy	Validation accuracy	Testing accuracy
Random	/	20%	20%	20%
Decision Tree	- Maximal depth = 10 - Maximal number of leaf nodes = 200	49.1%	45.8%	46.4%
Random Forest	- Maximal depth of the trees = 15 - Number of estimators = 125	72%	48.1%	49.6%
KNN	- Number of neighbors = 30	49%	43.7%	45.2% 45.2%[1] 45.6%[2]
SVM	- Regularization parameter (C) = 2	48.7%	45.35%[2]	47.3% 47%[1] 47.5%[2]
MLP	- Number of layers = 1 - Number of neurons = 16	47.7%	47.2%	48% 47.3%[1] 47.7%[2]

1: using only the most important features.
2: using PCA.

Analyzing the results for the IOS dataset, Table 4 shows that all the models have close testing performances. It varies between 45.2% and 49.6% and the best score is achieved by Random Forest. We can see that the random prediction is completely outperformed. This time, PCA seems to enhance slightly the results for KNN and SVM. Using the built-in feature importance evaluation of Random Forest, the most important features for IOS are: the size, the length of the description, the length of the title and the number of iPhone screenshots.

5 Discussion

5.1 Comparison of the Performances

We can see that the models achieve rather close results when predicting the rating of applications from both the Apple App Store and the Google Play Store. The best score is achieved by the Random Forest model for both stores and is around 50%. This is more than twice the result of a random prediction (20%). This means that, in 50% of the cases, the number of stars that a mobile application will get may be predicted using only its Publication Strategy.

What these results suggest is that the concept of Publication Strategy defined earlier in this paper seems to be in practice a real and strong predictor of the rating of an app, and therefore of its potential success on a platform. Although we do no study a particular Publication Strategy in this paper, we find evidences that it actually matters, and that it could be leveraged by apps designers when making decisions about a new app.

Another conclusion is that the most important features are the same for both stores: the length of the description, the size, the length of the title and the number of screenshots.

5.2 Limitations and Future Works

First of all, the number of features extracted from the raw data could be increased to enhance the precision of the models. Indeed, the variables presented in this work are quite basic. In order to find more of them, a first idea would be to use text mining on the description and the title. These two fields seem to be very important in the prediction of the rating while taking only the length into account. More information could be extracted from these two fields.

Then, we only looked at the definition of the concept "Publication Strategy" and its importance in the prediction of the rating of an app. We did not study a particular Publication Strategy nor the different types of Publication Strategies. A future study could focus on the identification of patterns of Publication Strategies that apps designers could use to enhance the performance of their apps.

Another possibility would be to study a decision support system guiding the companies in the decisions about the Publication Strategy of their apps. This could reduce the uncertainty of their choices and reduce the number of low rated apps due to bad presentation.

Finally, it would also be interesting to analyze the impact of the Publication Strategy on the number of downloads for apps that have the same rating. It would allow to see if the presentation of an application makes a difference in terms of popularity for apps of the same quality.

6   Conclusion

We presented the concept of Publication Strategy of a mobile application and studied its importance by looking at the extent to which the rating of an app can be predicted solely based on its Publication Strategy. The following classification algorithms were used to predict the rating: decision tree, random forest, KNN, SVM, MLP. We used metadata about 64504 Android apps and 41856 IOS apps. The performances of the algorithms were compared and discussed. We discovered that, for both stores, 50% of the ratings could be predicted using only variables controlled by the companies before the commercialization and displayed on the store, i.e. the Publication Strategy. We thus concluded that this Publication Strategy actually matters for the success of an app and that more research is needed to support apps designers in their decisions regarding the Publication Strategy. Moreover, the most important variables for the predictions were the length of the description, the size, the length of the title and the number of screenshots. The limitations were discussed and some avenues for future research were presented.

References

1. Agarwal, R.: The 5 feature selection algorithms every data scientist should know (2019). https://towardsdatascience.com/the-5-feature-selection-algorithms-every-data-scientist-need-to-know-3a6b566efd2
2. Apple: Ratings, reviews, and responses (2020). https://developer.apple.com/app-store/ratings-and-reviews/
3. Colgan, M.: How important are mobile app ratings & reviews? (2019). https://tapadoo.com/mobile-app-ratings-reviews/
4. Daimi, K., Hazzazi, N.: Using apple store dataset to predict user rating of mobile applications. In: 2019 International Conference on Data Science, pp. 28–33 (2019)
5. Gordon, G.: User ratings & reviews: how they impact ASO - ultimate guide (2018). https://thetool.io/2018/user-ratings-reviews-aso-guide#How_does_User_Feedback_Impact_ASO
6. Gupta, P.: Decision trees in machine learning (2017). https://towardsdatascience.com/decision-trees-in-machine-learning-641b9c4e8052
7. Handley, L.: Nearly three quarters of the world will use just their smartphones to access the internet by 2025 (2019). https://www.cnbc.com/2019/01/24/smartphones-72percent-of-people-will-use-only-mobile-for-internet-by-2025.html
8. scikit learn: choosing the right estimator (2019). https://scikit-learn.org/stable/tutorial/machine_learning_map/index.html
9. scikit learn: neural network models (supervised) (2019). https://scikit-learn.org/stable/modules/neural_networks_supervised.html

10. scikit learn: support vector machines (2019). https://scikit-learn.org/stable/modules/svm.html
11. Lee, G., Raghu, T.S.: Determinants of mobile apps' success: evidence from the app store market. J. Manag. Inf. Syst. **31**(2), 133–170 (2014)
12. Legal'Easy: Les chiffres des utilisateurs d'applications (2019). https://www.my-business-plan.fr/chiffres-application
13. Lu, J., Liu, C., Wei, J.: How important are enjoyment and mobility for mobile applications? J. Comput. Inf. Syst. **57**(1), 1–12 (2017)
14. Meng, J., Zheng, Z., Tao, G., Liu, X.: User-specific rating prediction for mobile applications via weight-based matrix factorization. In: 2016 IEEE International Conference on Web Services (ICWS), pp. 728–731. IEEE (2016)
15. Monett, D., Stolte, H.: Predicting star ratings based on annotated reviews of mobile apps. In: 2016 Federated Conference on Computer Science and Information Systems (FedCSIS), pp. 421–428. IEEE (2016)
16. Picoto, W.N., Duarte, R., Pinto, I.: Uncovering top-ranking factors for mobile apps through a multimethod approach. J. Bus. Res. **101**, 668–674 (2019)
17. Rençberoğlu, E.: Fundamental techniques of feature engineering for machine learning (2019). https://towardsdatascience.com/feature-engineering-for-machine-learning-3a5e293a5114
18. Sarro, F., Harman, M., Jia, Y., Zhang, Y.: Customer rating reactions can be predicted purely using app features. In: 2018 IEEE 26th International Requirements Engineering Conference (RE), pp. 76–87. IEEE (2018)
19. Elite Data Science: Dimensionality reduction algorithms: strengths and weaknesses (2019). https://elitedatascience.com/dimensionality-reduction-algorithms#feature-selection
20. statista: mobile app usage - statistics & facts (2019). https://www.statista.com/topics/1002/mobile-app-usage/
21. Yang, H.: Bon appétit for apps: young American consumers' acceptance of mobile applications. J. Comput. Inf. Syst. **53**(3), 85–96 (2013)

Improving Machine Self-Diagnosis with an Instance-Based Selector for Real-Time Anomaly Detection Algorithms

Philip Stahmann[✉], Jon Oodes, and Bodo Rieger

University of Osnabrueck, Osnabrück, Germany
{pstahmann,joodes,brieger}@uni-osnabrueck.de

Abstract. The diffusion of smart sensor technology in production enables real-time monitoring of production conditions. Machine self-diagnosis shall serve the analysis of these conditions by differentiating expected data from anomalies. Several algorithms have been developed in practice and academia to detect anomalies in real-time and to support machine self-diagnosis, so that counteractions can be taken. However, due to the algorithms' different functionalities, they yield different results when applied to the same data. Our research aims to leverage complementary potentials among these algorithms. To this end, we use a design science research approach to design and prototypically implement a real-time anomaly detection algorithm selector to support decision making regarding machine self-diagnosis. The selector decides in real-time for each sensor-emitted data point, which algorithm yields the most reliable result in terms of anomaly detection. We evaluate functionality and feasibility with two real-world case studies. The evaluation shows that the algorithm selector may outperform single algorithms and that it is applicable in practice.

Keywords: Algorithm selection · Machine self-diagnosis · Real-time anomaly detection

1 Introduction

The digitalization radically impacts the core processes of industrial production companies [1]. One central factor for digitalization is the use of smart sensors, which increase transparency of entire production environments by emitting data in real-time [2]. Real-time data may also support production machine autonomy by enabling automated self-x competencies [3]. In this context, machines shall react autonomously to variable production conditions, self-diagnosis as one self-x competency refers to the real-time detection of anomalies in production data. The immediate detection of anomalies may be crucial to reduce production failures and machine downtime [2]. Due to the increasing flexibility of production and real-time requirements, conventional methods for anomaly detection, such as expert judgment, are inadequate for self-diagnosis [4]. Algorithms for real-time classification of data points into anomalies and expectable instances provide a promising approach to implement self-diagnosis. However, current real-time anomaly detection

A. P. Cabral Seixas Costa et al. (Eds.): ICDSST 2022, LNBIP 447, pp. 29–43, 2022.
https://doi.org/10.1007/978-3-031-06530-9_3

algorithms show qualitative deficiencies [5, 6]. Figure 1 shows an example of the application of five open source state-of-the-art algorithms for real-time anomaly detection in two data sets with temperature and CPU utilization measurements of a machine. The figure illustrates that different algorithms may lead to different results when they are applied to the same data for anomaly detection. These differences make it particularly difficult to decide whether an anomaly is present at a data point. In case decision makers decide against countermeasures if only some algorithms seemingly detect an anomaly at a certain data point, they risk missing causes for production failure. On the other hand, if decision makers decide to act on the indication of anomalies by few algorithms, they may react to false alarms, which may be costly, e.g. in case production has to be paused. Consequently, the different results show the need for a targeted selection of algorithms for anomaly detection.

Within this contribution, we aim to develop an instance-based selector for real-time anomaly detection algorithms. The selector does not address the challenge of anomaly elimination, but delivers a decision basis that may be necessary previous to the elimination step. Our selector shall indicate for each data point which algorithm is the best basis for deciding whether an anomaly is present. The algorithm selector shall leverage complementary potentials among real-time anomaly detection algorithms. Our research includes the identification, implementation and evaluation of design principles for real-time algorithm evaluation.

We formulate the research question: *How can an instance-based algorithm selector for real-time anomaly detection algorithms to support machine self-diagnosis capability be designed and implemented?*

Section two refers to related work on algorithm selection. In section three, we detail the selected design science research approach. Section four contains the design principles the developed algorithm selector presented in section five builds on. In section six we demonstrate and evaluate the algorithm selector using two case studies. Lastly, sections seven and eight contain limitations, future work and conclusions.

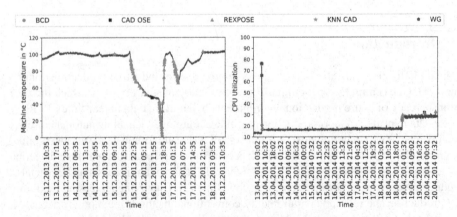

Fig. 1. Application of five real-time anomaly detection algorithms to two data sets.

2 Related Work on Algorithm Selection

The challenge of selecting the right algorithm from a number of alternatives to achieve the best possible analytic result is widespread in the information systems domain. [7] provides an overview of scientific publications on algorithm selection. All publications base on the observation that there is no universally best algorithm for a domain or a specific problem [8]. In general, two different algorithm selection approaches can be identified. On the one hand, there are methods for algorithm selection that require the consideration of entire data sets. For example, [9] pairwise compare the results of different machine learning algorithms after each has been fully applied to a dataset. On the other hand, there are per-instance approaches for algorithm selection. Here, the intention is always to leverage the complementarity of different algorithmic approaches, so that their combination provides better overall results than individual algorithms. An example is provided by [10] with the development of a per-instance selector, with the goal of combining complementary algorithms to solve an instance of the traveling salesman problem. In the context of our research, we restrict ourselves to the per-instance approach. For each data point added to a production sensor data stream, we want the selector to decide which algorithm provides the best possible result in terms of anomaly detection.

3 Application of Design Science Research Methodology

To structure design, prototypical implementation and evaluation of the algorithm selector, we follow the design science research methodology [11]. Our adaptation of the approach is depicted in Fig. 2. In this regard, the algorithm selector is considered an artefact that shall answer our research question. The different results of five state-of-the-art real-time anomaly detection algorithms were illustrated in Sect. 1 for problem identification and solution motivation. Subsequently, a structured literature research was conducted [12]. The results will be used to identify design principles (DPs). We used the databases *Google Scholar, IEEE Xplore, Scopus, Science Direct, Springer Link* and *Web of Science* to find scientific contributions. We combined the following three groups of search strings: *OR ("Real-time anomaly detection"; "Real-time outlier detection"; <None>) AND OR ("Algorithm selection"; "Algorithm prioritization"; "Algorithm ranking"; "Algorithm benchmarking"; <None>) AND OR ("Industrie 4.0"; "Industry 4.0"; "Intelligent manufacturing"; "Smart factory"; "Smart manufacturing"; "Industrial Internet Reference Architecture"; "Intelligent Manufacturing System Architecture"; <None>).* For the second group of search strings, we used terms equivalent or related to *algorithm selection* from the sources in [7]. Regarding the third group, we started with the term "Industry 4.0" and added equivalent terms that we found in literature.

34 publications were left after scanning titles and abstracts of the publications that resulted from the literature search. After reading these, 13 publications were discarded due to deviations in the topics, so that 21 publications remained for the derivation of DPs. The derivation process of the DPs is presented in Sect. 4. The DPs serve as guidelines for the prototypical implementation in the subsequent section. Before implementation, the required functionality was formalized as also shown in Sect. 5. The artefact was implemented in Python 3.8 by two researchers in an iterative process. In Sect. 6, the

prototypical implementation is demonstrated and evaluated. As the major risks are user-centric and technical at this stage of our research, we decided for a case study evaluation with qualitative and quantitative components (Venable et al., 2016).

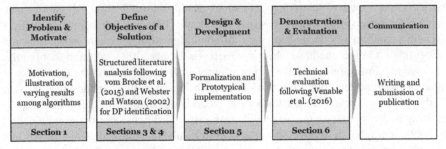

Fig. 2. Adapted research approach based on Peffers et al. (2007).

4   Problem Characteristics, Requirements and Design Principles

The second step of the methodology presented in the previous section focuses on the solution objectives. They determine how the artefact to be developed is supposed to solve identified problems that relate to the research question. To this end, all solution approaches have to originate in these problems [11]. We use the identified literature to formulate DPs as solution objectives for real-time algorithm selection to support machine self-diagnosis in production. Based on literature, we assume a supervised approach for our DPs and our implementation, where data sets with labeled anomalies are available. Based on these data sets, the algorithm selector to be developed can be trained and evaluated and later applied to unlabeled data.

First, the results from the structured literature analysis are classified into topics [13]. Figure 3 shows the three identified topics, namely measure, speed and quality of self-diagnosis. Within these three topics, we identified five problem characteristics (PCs), seven requirements (RQs), and finally three DPs.

Measure of self-diagnosis refers to the algorithmic results considered to decide for the best algorithm at a data point. The measure for self-diagnosis requires the establishment of comparability of results of anomaly detection algorithms. PC1 refers to the fact that different algorithms output different results when applied to the same data, as outlined in section one [14]. The problem characteristic leads to the requirement to develop a methodology to make the results of different real-time anomaly detection algorithms comparable (RQ1). PC1 also considers the finding that the openly available algorithms output a so-called anomaly score to indicate whether an anomaly is present [14, 15]. However, due to the algorithms' different functionalities, their anomaly scores are not directly comparable (PC2) (Wolpert and Macready 1997). RQ1 builds on these first two PCS and leads to DP1, which is the basis for the development of the artefact with respect to the first topic.

Speed of self-diagnosis refers to the time required by an algorithm to calculate and output an indication whether an anomaly is present. One central problem characteristic can be identified; anomaly detection procedures that do not indicate instantly whether an anomaly is present lead to delayed initiation of consequences to correct or mitigate production errors (PC3) [2]. A relevant requirement that must underlie the problem solution is therefore the consideration of low latency and real-time capability regarding sensor data receipt, algorithmic calculation and availability of information on anomalies (RQ2, RQ3). The algorithm selector shall be capable to select the best algorithm per instance in real-time, however the term real-time is not defined in literature. Consequently, we formulate DP2 with focus on anomaly detection as soon as possible to avoid delays.

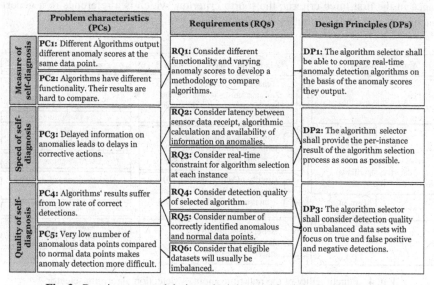

	Problem characteristics (PCs)	Requirements (RQs)	Design Principles (DPs)
Measure of self-diagnosis	PC1: Different Algorithms output different anomaly scores at the same data point.	RQ1: Consider different functionality and varying anomaly scores to develop a methodology to compare algorithms.	DP1: The algorithm selector shall be able to compare real-time anomaly detection algorithms on the basis of the anomaly scores they output.
	PC2: Algorithms have different functionality. Their results are hard to compare.		
Speed of self-diagnosis	PC3: Delayed information on anomalies leads to delays in corrective actions.	RQ2: Consider latency between sensor data receipt, algorithmic calculation and availability of information on anomalies.	DP2: The algorithm selector shall provide the per-instance result of the algorithm selection process as soon as possible.
		RQ3: Consider real-time constraint for algorithm selection at each instance	
Quality of self-diagnosis	PC4: Algorithms' results suffer from low rate of correct detections.	RQ4: Consider detection quality of selected algorithm.	DP3: The algorithm selector shall consider detection quality on unbalanced data sets with focus on true and false positive and negative detections.
	PC5: Very low number of anomalous data points compared to normal data points makes anomaly detection more difficult.	RQ5: Consider number of correctly identified anomalous and normal data points.	
		RQ6: Consider that eligible datasets will usually be imbalanced.	

Fig. 3. Requirements and design principles as objectives for the solution.

The third topic covers quality of self-diagnosis as anomaly detection algorithms often have low result quality (PC4) [6]. The quality has a direct impact on the reliability of production machines' self-diagnosis competency. Low reliability can lead to missed anomalies or false alarms and thus to low user acceptance and abandonment of self-diagnosis competency. One major reason for qualitative deficiencies is the nature of the data used during machine self-diagnosis [16]. Only very few anomalous and mainly normal data are present in real production data [17]. Unbalanced data makes the identification of the rarely occurring anomalies difficult (PC5) [6]. Derived from PC4, RQ4 states that the overall detection quality of the algorithms applied to a given data stream must be considered. Frequently used metrics to indicate the quality of algorithms, such as accuracy, do not work well for unbalanced data [18]. To meet the requirements of unbalanced data sets, we consider the sums of correctly and incorrectly identified anomalous and normal data points, when selecting the best algorithm for a data point (RQ5, RQ6) [5]. We derive DP3 from the three requirements on the topic of quality of self-diagnosis.

5 Formalization of the Algorithm Selector

Figure 4 illustrates the functionality of the prototypically implemented algorithm selector. The column on the left shows the application scenario. The algorithm selector chooses a real-time algorithm a from a pool of algorithms A. All $a \in A$ run on a constantly updated sensor data stream $D = (d_j, d_{j+1}, \ldots, d_m)$. The center column details the process for selecting the best algorithm. The selection process considers four criteria. The first three are anomaly score, timeliness and sum of correct detections (abbreviated as M, T and Q for convenience). If a best algorithm cannot be determined due to equivalent performance in the first three criteria, the fourth criterion, which is a reference to a generic benchmark, is decisive as outlined in the following.

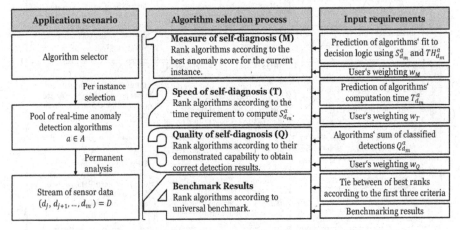

Fig. 4. Functionality of the real-time anomaly detection algorithm selector.

Regarding the first criterion, the anomaly score S is used. $S_{d_m}^a$ indicates for an algorithm a whether an anomaly is present at a certain data point d_m. Anomaly scores are bounded:

$$0 \leq S_{d_m}^a \leq 1 \tag{1}$$

As algorithmic results are not directly comparable, an algorithm-specific threshold TH_D^a is required for each $a \in A$ applied to dataset D. There is an indication for an anomaly if (2) applies:

$$TH_D^a \leq S_{d_m}^a \tag{2}$$

The decision logic is formulated for an algorithm $a \in A$ at datapoint d_m. In case that $d_m = anomalous$, it is checked whether there are algorithms for which (2) holds. If this is true, we calculate the difference between $S_{d_m}^a$ and TH_D^a for these algorithms. The algorithm with the best rank R_M^{best} is the one with the biggest difference between $S_{d_m}^a$ and TH_D^a. Consequently, we formulate:

$$R_M^{best}(a_{d_m}) = max(S_{d_m}^a - TH_D^a) \tag{3}$$

If there is no algorithmic result for which (2) holds although $d_m = anomalous$, we consider the algorithm with smallest difference between $S_{d_m}^a$ and TH_D^a as best algorithm as the anomaly score is closest to the threshold. To determine the best $a \in A$ at d_m, we formulate:

$$R_M^{best}(a_{d_m}) = min(TH_D^a - S_{d_m}^a) \tag{4}$$

In the case that $d_m = not\ anomalous$, we check if there are algorithms for which (2) does not hold. If this is the case, we calculate the difference between TH_D^a and $S_{d_m}^a$. The best algorithm has the $S_{d_m}^a$ that lies farthest below TH_D^a. Consequently, to determine the best $a \in A$ at d_m, we formulate:

$$R_M^{best}(a_{d_m}) = min(S_{d_m}^a - TH_D^a) \tag{5}$$

If $d_m = not\ anomalous$ and (2) holds for all algorithms, then the algorithm that outputs the biggest difference between $S_{d_m}^a$ and TH_D^a is considered most appropriate. In that case, to determine the best $a \in A$ at d_m, we formulate:

$$R_M^{best}(a_{d_m}) = max(TH_D^a - S_{d_m}^a) \tag{6}$$

In terms of the implementation of the real-time algorithm selector, a multiclass classification model shall use the presented decision logic. For each data point that is newly added to the data stream, this model should predict which of the algorithms will most closely match the decision logic.

Regarding the second criterion, the algorithm selector considers the time $T_{d_m}^a$, which each $a \in A$ requires to calculate $S_{d_m}^a$. To reduce potential time lags, we define that the faster an algorithm calculates $S_{d_m}^a$ the better its rank. In terms of the second criterion, the best rank of all $a \in A$ at d_m is determined as follows:

$$R_T^{best}(a_{d_m}) = min(T_{d_m}^a) \tag{7}$$

To add this criterion to the implementation of the real-time algorithm selector, a time-series forecasting model shall predict the calculation time required by each $a \in A$ for newly incoming data points.

The third criterion considers the number of correct and incorrect algorithmic results. For each algorithmic result, we define for each data point in D if it is a true or false positive or negative detection. We formulate these options as $tp_{d_m}^a, fp_{d_m}^a, tn_{d_m}^a$ and $fn_{d_m}^a$. If an algorithm correctly determines that there is an anomaly in d_m, then $tp_{d_m}^a = 1$, else 0. If an algorithm correctly determines that there is a normal data point in d_m, then $tn_{d_m}^a = 1$, else 0. Analogously, if an algorithm raises a false alarm by determining an anomaly at a normal data point d_m, then $fp_{d_m}^a = 1$, else 0. If an algorithm incorrectly determines a normal data point in d_m, although it is anomalous, then $fn_{d_m}^a = 1$, else 0.

In terms of the third criterion, for each algorithm, we sum up the correct results and subtract the incorrect results of the previous data points in D. Consequently, for each $a \in A$ at d_m we formulate:

$$Q_{d_m}^a = \sum_{j=1}^{m-1} tp_{d_j}^a + tn_{d_j}^a - fp_{d_j}^a - fn_{d_j}^a \tag{8}$$

The more often an algorithm was correct, the better it seems to be suited for real-time anomaly detection on D. Consequently, to determine the best $a \in A$ at d_m, we formulate:

$$R_Q^{best}(a_{d_m}) = max(Q_{d_m}^a) \tag{9}$$

As shown in Fig. 4, users can apply weights (w_M, w_T and w_Q) for the three criteria. The weights support individualization of algorithm selection according to user preference. The following constraints apply:

$$0 \leq w_M, w_T, w_Q \leq 1 \tag{10}$$

$$w_M + \overset{\bullet}{w_T} + w_Q = 1 \tag{11}$$

For each $a \in A$ at d_m, we multiply the weights with the rankings to determine the best algorithm. We formulate the overall evaluation of the algorithms according to the three criteria as a minimization problem. This means that the best rank in each criterion is assigned the value 1 as follows:

$$R^{best}(a_{d_m}) = min(w_M R_M(a_{d_m}) + w_T R_T(a_{d_m}) + w_Q R_Q(a_{d_m})) \tag{12}$$

In the case of a tie of best algorithms at d_m, a benchmark for real-time anomaly detection algorithms is used as fourth criterion. The most widely used benchmark in literature is the Numenta Anomaly Benchmark (NAB) developed by [5]. The benchmark is applied to instances of a data stream, resulting in a universal, but not instance-based ranking.

6 Demonstration and Evaluation

Our artefact has two main design risks, which are user-centric and technical [19]. Demonstration and evaluation therefore refer to the application of simulated real-world data and the assessment by experts. We present the artefact to two experts from different companies and apply it to two datasets. The experts were asked to describe the sensor data from a production process in an unstructured, qualitative interview.

Company 1: The first company produces metal gears as functional components for production machines. The interviewed expert is responsible for a production step of metal hardening. To harden and clean the gears, they are put into a water tank. To achieve targeted metal quality, water temperature must remain between 60 °C and 70 °C. A sensor emits data on water temperature about every second. Water temperature is regulated by immersion heaters. If water temperature reaches about 70 °C, immersion heaters are switched off automatically. The cooling process is supported by the addition of cold water. We created 100,000 data points using (13). The rate of anomalies is about 1%.

$$f(x) = 5 \, sin\left(x + \frac{sin\left(x + \frac{1}{2}sin(x)\right)}{1.7}\right) + 65 \tag{13}$$

Company 2: The second company is a car manufacturer. The interviewed expert occupies with the automated pressing of metal car parts. To avoid damage in the pressed parts, the machine must exert pressure between 3847.5 kN and 3852.5 kN. For each metal part, the machine has to return to its upper point. A sensor emits data on the exerted pressure about every second. In accordance with the interviewee, we modelled the pressure curve:

$$f(x) = 1925 \; sin\left(x + \frac{sin(2x)}{2}\right) + 1925 \tag{14}$$

We created 100,000 data points using the function from (14). The rate of anomalies is about 5%. Table 1 shows kinds and frequencies of production-specific anomalies for both processes. Both data sets have been published anonymously at: [20].

Table 1. Further information on anomalies.

	Cause description	Anomaly description	Freq.
Car	Errors in sensor functionality	Irregular spikes	2.5%
	Machine is maladjusted	Threshold violation	45%
	Machine is maladjusted	Unexpected slope	12.5%
	Metal parts do not lie adequately	Pressing machine stops	40%
Gear	Immersion heaters fail	Threshold violation	10%
	Immersion heaters fail	Unexpected slope	80%
	Sensor contaminated with dirt	Monotonous measurements	5–10%
	Sensor contaminated with dirt	Irregular jumps	0–5%

Both industry experts commented that they perceive a functioning algorithm selector as very useful. However, the process of data preparation to generate labels for anomalies was perceived as very tedious. For practical application, they recommended consideration of historical or simulated data that include anomalies. In addition, it was mentioned that the use of the artefact in practice would be more attractive with a user interface.

For the evaluation of the artefact's applicability, we use five openly available state-of-the-art real-time anomaly detection algorithms. All five algorithms serve for binary classification and have local learning capabilities, so that they are suitable for continuous data streams. The artefact works with supervised or unsupervised algorithms. We decided for unsupervised algorithms due to their potentially greater optimization potential. Also, labelling was perceived as very tedious and supervised alternatives may require more labels than necessary for the establishment of the criteria shown in the previous section. The selected algorithms output an anomaly score, which is a prerequisite for their selection to fit to the first criterion as outlined in the previous section. We apply these algorithms in parallel to both data sets and let the artefact decide for each data point, which algorithm is the best.

The algorithms are Bayesian Changepoint Detection (BCD) [21], Context Anomaly Detection Open Source Edition (CAD OSE) [14, 15], K Nearest Neighbors Conformal Anomaly Detection (KNN CAD) [22], relative entropy and expected similarity estimation (REXPOSE) [23] and Windowed Gaussian (WG) [14, 15].

We use the decision logic from the previous section for model-based prediction of the best algorithm according to the first criterion. For this purpose, the algorithms were applied to the data sets to obtain the anomaly scores. Each algorithm outputs one anomaly score per data point. For each algorithm, a dynamic threshold is calculated for each data set. For this purpose, a method called t-digest was applied to the data stream [24]. By using this method, it is possible to consider the percentiles of anomaly scores in real-time and to determine extremes. Setting the threshold below these extremes allows the delineation of normal and anomalous anomaly detection results. We emphasize the importance of critically reflected threshold setting due to its impact on the results and the entailed relevance in practice [16, 24]. We trained four types of models for multiclass classification to predict which algorithm most closely matches the decision logic for newly incoming data points. After implementation of the model types, their parameters were optimized using grid search. Also, during training, model validity with focus on parametrization was evaluated with a stratified k-fold cross-validation with $k = 10$. Stratified k-fold provides the ability to balance the classes in each fold, which is particularly useful in unbalanced problems such as anomaly detection [26]. The models used are Artificial Neural Network (ANN), Random Forest (RF), Support Vector Machine (SVM) and XGBoost Random Forest (XGB RF). The five algorithms are the five classes. Table 2 shows false positive rate (FPR), F-score and Matthew's correlation coefficient (MCC) for the four models, which are calculated according to (15)–(19). For the calculations, we used the one-vs-all confusion matrix of each model.

$$FPR = \frac{FP}{FP + TN} \tag{15}$$

$$Recall = \frac{TP}{TP + FN} \tag{16}$$

$$Precision = \frac{TP}{TP + FP} \tag{17}$$

$$F - score = \frac{Precision * Recall}{Precision + Recall} \tag{18}$$

$$MCC = \frac{TP * TN - FP * FN}{\sqrt{(TP + FP)(TP + FN)(TN + FP)(TN + FN)}} \tag{19}$$

Table 2. Metrics to evaluate multi-class classification models averaged over both data sets.

Model	FPR Mean	FPR St. Dev.	F-score Mean	F-score St. Dev.	MCC Mean	MCC St. Dev.
RF	0.11	0.02	0.83	0.03	0.64	0.07
ANN	0.14	0.09	0.77	0.04	0.71	0.11
XGB RF	0.09	0.02	0.89	0.04	0.71	0.05
SVM	0.13	0.1	0.81	0.07	0.69	0.04

Table 2 indicates the means of the metrics of both data sets over the ten folds. Since the XGB RF has the best metrics on average, but also for each single dataset, it is used as model to fulfill the first criterion.

When the algorithms were applied, the time taken to calculate the anomaly score per data point was also recorded for the second criterion. On this basis, we trained four models for predicting how long each algorithm would take to compute the anomaly score for a newly arriving data point. The models were validated using k-fold cross-validation with $k = 10$. The models are Generalised Autoregressive Conditional Heteroskedasticity (GARCH), Long Short-Term Memory (LSTM) and Neural NETwork AutoRegression (NNETAR). Further information on parametrization of all models is provided additionally [20]. The metrics Mean Absolute Error (MAE) and Root Mean Squared Error (RMSE) were used to evaluate the prediction of the time series. We calculated the metric as follows with $x_{d_j} = actual\ value$ and $y_{d_m} = predicted\ value$:

$$MAE = \frac{1}{m} \sum_{d_j}^{d_m} \left| y_{d_j} - x_{d_j} \right| \tag{20}$$

$$RMSE = \sqrt{\frac{1}{m} \sum_{d_j}^{d_m} \left(y_{d_j} - x_{d_j} \right)^2} \tag{21}$$

Table 3 shows the means of the metrics over both data sets. Since the LSTM shows the best metrics on average and for each single dataset, we use it to fulfill the second criterion.

Table 3. Metrics to evaluate time-series forecasting models averaged over both data sets.

Model	MAE Mean	MAE St. Dev.	RMSE Mean	RMSE St. Dev.
GARCH	0.68	0.07	0.84	0.19
LSTM	0.5	0.01	0.46	0.04
NNETAR	0.81	0.1	1.09	0.11

For fulfilling the third criterion, no training of a model is necessary as only true and false positives and negatives are counted for data with labels. As result from the expert interviews, we set the weights for the application of our artefact to $w_M = 0.2$, $w_T = 0.4$ and $w_Q = 0.4$ for the data from the car manufacturer and to $w_M = 0.2$, $w_T = 0.3$ and $w_Q = 0.5$ for the gear manufacturing data. Regarding the fourth criterion, we applied the NAB to obtain a ranking in case no decision can be made on the basis of the first three criteria [5].

Table 4 shows the final evaluation results including benchmark ranking. Again, we provide the average results from stratified k-fold validation with k = 10. We used an Intel(R) Core(TM) i7-8650U CPU @1.90 GHz and 16 GB RAM. Using this setup, we also measured calculation speed for algorithm selection, which was an average of 0.013 s per data point for car production data and 0.011 s per data point for gear production data.

Together with the BCD, the algorithm selector yields the lowest FPR mean with the lowest standard deviation for the car data set. Applied to the gear data set, it has the lowest FPR mean and a neglectable standard deviation. The selector raises less false alarms than the other algorithms when applied to both data sets. A low number of false alarms is especially important in digitized production [16]. Each false alarm may entail financial loss, when production has to be stopped to find the potential anomaly's cause.

Table 4. Evaluation of algorithms' and selector's performance.

	Metrics	FPR		F-Score		NAB
		Mean	St. Dev.	Mean	St. Dev.	
Car	**BCD**	0.07	0.01	0.89	0.09	4
	CAD OSE	0.12	0.04	0.85	0.09	2
	REXPOSE	0.47	0.11	0.51	0.12	3
	KNN CAD	0.26	0.17	0.72	0.14	6
	WG	0.07	0.03	0.9	0.08	5
	Selector	0.07	0.01	0.92	0.09	1
Gear	**BCD**	0.02	0	0.96	0.27	5
	CAD OSE	0.03	0	0.95	0.13	2
	REXPOSE	0.9	0.02	0.1	0.04	6
	KNN CAD	0.26	0.07	0.44	0.11	3
	WG	0.03	0	0.96	0.19	4
	Selector	0.01	0	0.97	0.1	1

For both data sets, the algorithm selector yields the highest F-score mean. This indicates that the selector has the highest accuracy for imbalanced binary classification into normal and anomalous data points for both data sets. In the car data set, the selector chose WG for 78.59% of data points. Applied to the entire car data set, WG yields the second best FPR mean and standard deviation and the best F-score mean among single algorithms. With 18.13%, CAD OSE is selected second most often, although it achieves worse FPR and F-score mean values than BCD, which is selected in 3.25% of the data points. REXPOSE is selected very rarely with 0.03% and KNN CAD is not selected at all. The omission of KNN CAD is due to its comparatively longer computation time. KNN CAD also has the lowest NAB rank for the car data set. There are 5,751 data points with ties in the car data set, where the fourth criterion becomes relevant. Applied to the gear data set, the selector also chooses WG and CAD OSE most often with 54.78% and 44.23%. BCD is chosen in 0.1%, REXPOSE and KNN CAD are not chosen at all. A major reason for the dominance of WG and CAD OSE is their good performance in the second and third criteria. There are 7,180 data points with ties in the gear data set. The number is considerably higher than in the car data set as the performances of WG and CAD OSE are markedly closer. Furthermore, the third factor shows a significant influence on the overall result.

7 Limitations and Outlook

Methodology and results of our research are not free from limitations as presented in the following. Despite adherence to guidelines provided by [12, 13], our literature research used to derive DPs has subjective components. The process to eliminate publications was subject to the researchers' judgment. The same applies to the categorization of relevant literature. Moreover, there is a potential limitation to the use of the demonstrated implementation of quality of self-diagnosis. Counters may mislead interpretation of results due to the imbalanced nature of anomaly detection. To mitigate this limitation, we use formula (8) only in combination with the other steps that are more robust to class imbalance. Also, for evaluation of the results we only use robust metrics (e.g. F1-Score, FPR and MCC). Future research may investigate more metrics that are robust to class imbalances, such as F2-score, which requires a weighting that may be done together with domain experts. As proposed by the experts, future research may also cover the development of an intuitive user interface.

Furthermore, the implemented decision model or selected steps may be integrated with tools for automated design of analytic pipelines, such as RapidMiner Auto Model, to analyze potentials of combining the steps flexibly for different data sets. Another field for future work is the combination with meta learning strategies, such as continuous feature extraction to obtain more information that may influence the instance-based choice of real-time anomaly detection algorithms.

8 Conclusion

The ongoing digitalization of production and the associated proliferation of sensor technology are leading to a sharp increase in data on machine states. Sensor data may be used to increase machine autonomy by means of the implementation of self-x competencies. Self-diagnosis is an important self-x core area as it is the basis for other autonomous functionalities such as self-repair. In terms of self-diagnosis, data from real-time data streams can be used to detect anomalies. Required algorithms must be able to decide in real-time whether a data point is anomalous. However, when applied to the same data, different algorithms lead to varying anomaly detection results. This inconsistency lowers the reliability of algorithm-based real-time anomaly detection. Consequently, there is a requirement for a real-time procedure to decide which algorithm performs best at which data point. This research makes three contributions to meet this requirement. Firstly, we contribute a structured derivation of design principles from literature for real-time algorithm selection in the field of production machine self-diagnosis. Secondly, we provide a formalization and prototypical implementation of a real-time anomaly detection algorithm selector. Design choices build on the design principles from the first step. Thirdly, we present a comprehensive evaluation that shows how the implemented artefact can outperform single algorithms by leveraging their complementarity. This evaluation includes the contribution of two labelled data sets from real-world case studies.

References

1. Buer, S.-V., Strandhagen, J.W., Semini, M., et al.: The digitalization of manufacturing: investigating the impact of production environment and company size. JMTM **32**(3), 621–645 (2021)
2. Schütze, A., Helwig, N., Schneider, T. Sensors 4.0 – smart sensors and measurement technology enable Industry 4.0. J. Sens. Sens. Syst. **7**(1), 359–371 (2018)
3. Cohen, Y., Singer, G.: A smart process controller framework for Industry 4.0 settings. J. Intell. Manuf. **32**(7), 1975–1995 (2021). https://doi.org/10.1007/s10845-021-01748-5
4. Hsieh, R.-J., Chou, J., Ho, C.-H.: Unsupervised online anomaly detection on multivariate sensing time series data for smart manufacturing 2019, pp. 90–97 (2019)
5. Lavin, A., Ahmad, S.: Evaluating real-time anomaly detection algorithms - the Numenta anomaly benchmark, pp. 38–44 (2015)
6. Apostol, I., Preda, M., Nila, C., et al.: IoT botnet anomaly detection using unsupervised deep learning. Electronics **10**(16), 1876 (2021)
7. Kotthoff, L.: Algorithm Selection Literature Summary. http://larskotthoff.github.io/assurvey/
8. Wolpert, D.H., Macready, W.G.: No free lunch theorems for optimization. IEEE Trans. Evol. Comput. **1**(1), 67–82 (1997)
9. Sun, Q., Pfahringer, B.: Pairwise meta-rules for better meta-learning-based algorithm ranking. Mach. Learn. **93**(1), 141–161 (2013). https://doi.org/10.1007/s10994-013-5387-y
10. Kerschke, P., Kotthoff, L., Bossek, J., et al.: Leveraging TSP solver complementarity through machine learning. Evol. Comput. **26**(4), 597–620 (2018)
11. Peffers, K., Tuunanen, T., Rothenberger, M.A., et al.: A design science research methodology for information systems research. J. Manag. Inf. Syst. **24**(3), 45–77 (2007)
12. Vom Brocke, J., Simons, A., Riemer, K., et al.: Standing on the shoulders of giants: challenges and recommendations of literature search in information systems research. CAIS **37** (2015)
13. Webster, J., Watson, R.T.: Analyzing the past to prepare for the future: writing a literature review. MIS Q. **26**(2), xiii–xxiii (2002)
14. Ahmad, S., Lavin, A., Purdy, S., et al.: Unsupervised real-time anomaly detection for streaming data. Neurocomputing **262**, 134–147 (2017)
15. Numenta Anomaly Benchmark. Numenta Anomaly Benchmark. https://github.com/numenta/NAB
16. Stahmann, P., Rieger, B.: Towards design principles for a real-time anomaly detection algorithm benchmark suited to Industrie 4.0 streaming data. In: 55th HICSS 2022 (2022)
17. Siegel, B.: Industrial anomaly detection: a comparison of unsupervised neural network architectures. IEEE Sens. Lett. **4**(8), 1–4 (2020)

18. Farquad, M., Bose, I.: Preprocessing unbalanced data using support vector machine. Decis. Support Syst. **53**(1), 226–233 (2012)
19. Venable, J., Pries-Heje, J., Baskerville, R.: FEDS: a framework for evaluation in design science research. Eur. J. Inf. Syst. **25**(1), 77–89 (2016)
20. "AnonymousPublisher1793" on GitHub. Data and additional information. https://github.com/anonymousPublisher1793/publication
21. Adams, E.P., MacKay, D.J.C.: Bayesian Online Changepoint Detection (2007)
22. Burnaev, E., Ishimtsev, V.: Conformalized density- and distance-based anomaly detection in time-series data (2016)
23. Schneider, M., Ertel, W., Ramos, F.: Expected similarity estimation for large-scale batch and streaming anomaly detection. Mach. Learn. **105**(3), 305–333 (2016). https://doi.org/10.1007/s10994-016-5567-7
24. Dunning, T.: The t-digest: efficient estimates of distributions. Softw. Impacts **7**, 100049 (2021)

Blockchain and Artificial Intelligence in Real Estate

Christos Ziakis[✉]

Department of Economic Sciences, International Hellenic University, 62124 Serres, Greece
ziakis@gmail.com

Abstract. Since their development, blockchain and artificial intelligence (AI) technologies have gained substantial momentum and immense adoption in different industries worldwide. The innovations of cryptocurrencies and machine learning algorithms have had significant implications for the growth and advancement of these technologies. The combination of the two presents incredible benefits to organizations in various sectors in terms of harnessing existing data for pattern recognition and insight identification. The technologies have impacted how industries do their businesses. This study includes a systematic review that explores how blockchain and AI, have changed the real estate industry, as well as the way the related businesses can take advantage of the technologies' capabilities to stay afloat within this new technological development. This research adopts the Prisma methodology to explore how the application of blockchain and AI has impacted the real estate sector. The main finding is that in real estate, the combination of blockchain and AI has great potential, especially in modeling data and valuation, storing information in digital formats and securing transactions.

Keywords: Blockchain · Artificial intelligence · Real estate

1 Introduction

Blockchain technologies provide secure ways for people to directly interact via decentralized and highly secure systems without the necessity of intermediaries. On top of their proficiencies, artificial intelligence can complement the technology and deal with most limitations associated with blockchain-based systems.

According to Treiblmaier, blockchain refers to distributed database typically shared between computer network nodes [1]. One of the critical advantages of blockchains is that they guarantee the security and fidelity of data records and generate trust minus the requirement for trusted third parties. Blockchain has introduced significant disruptions to the traditional business and operations processes since the transactions and applications that previously required trusted third parties for the centralized architectures for verification are now operating in a decentralized method with the help of blockchain [2]. Various inherent factors of the blockchain design and architecture provide the characteristics like robustness, transparency, security, and audibility. This is why blockchain is considered a distributed database with the organization of ordered blocks, and the committed blocks

A. P. Cabral Seixas Costa et al. (Eds.): ICDSST 2022, LNBIP 447, pp. 44–54, 2022.
https://doi.org/10.1007/978-3-031-06530-9_4

are immutable [3]. More and more organizations are investing in blockchain technology to minimize the design and architecture for the costs of transactions and decentralized, thus becoming transparent, inherently safer, and significantly faster [4]. The number of applications of blockchain technology today explains the importance of blockchain technology. As an example, it is readily being adopted for the application along with cryptocurrencies and is still growing as well. According to a Forbes article by Castillo & Schifrin, companies' and individuals' investment in blockchain technology is about $2.9 billion, representing an 89 percent increase from the previous two years [5].

The significant growth pace of the application of blockchain technology can also result in interoperability issues due to the heterogeneity of the different applications. Moreover, the horizon of the application is significantly increasing as the fields and technologies along with which blockchain technology is being implemented are increasing [6, 7].

The increased advancement in technology allows us to do tasks requiring higher levels of intelligence more conveniently. For instance, AI technologies can allow a machine to operate more efficiently and intelligently. According to Bachute & Subhedar, machine learning and deep learning that are critical parts of AI, particularly helping to accomplish its mission of making machines act and think like humans [8]. Machine learning focuses on a particular objective of giving a computer the ability to do a task minus the need for direct programming. In this, a computer system is typically fed structured data and 'learns' to be better at analyzing data and, with time, processing it. After being programmed, computers can indefinitely understand new data sort and act on it without requiring additional human involvement. In this case, structured data can be thought of as data inputs capable of being inputted in rows and columns. A category column in a spreadsheet named 'drinks, ' including row entries like 'water or 'milk, can be straightforward for a computer working with this form of 'structured' data. With time, the program may start identifying that 'water is a form of drink even after the user stops labeling the data. Such 'self-reliance' is key to machine learning. Machine learning can further be broken down into various forms based on the level of human intervention, for instance [9]:

1) Supervised and semi-supervised learning entails the most continuing human involvement. Computers are fed training data and models specially designed to teach how to respond to the data. The models can accurately handle any new dataset following the 'learned' pattern with time.
2) Semi-supervised learning involves computers being fed a combination of unlabeled and properly labeled data to search for patterns by itself.
3) Unsupervised learning – in this, the computers have the freedom of finding patterns and relations in data as they see fit, typically creating results that would have been invisible by human data analysts.
4) Reinforcement learning – this goes a step further ahead of unsupervised and supervised learning by identifying 'consequences' to the computers if they fail to accurately label or understand data.

While machine learning is mainly concerned with a machine's ability to do tasks without explicit programming, deep learning is primarily focused on their thinking and acting capabilities in the face of specific complex tasks.

Blockchain technologies provide secure ways for people to directly interact via decentralized and highly secure systems without the necessity of intermediaries. On top of their proficiencies, AI can complement the technology and deal with most limitations associated with blockchain-based systems. Combining the two (AI and blockchain technology) can be helpful in terms of providing high-performance and valuable results. A decade ago, several researchers focused on diversified applications of blockchain technology, which resulted in a linked structure, defining the various ways blockchain technology can be applied for problem-solving, avoiding double-spending issues, and maintaining the transaction orders [10, 11].

The main objective of this research is to explore the applications of blockchain and AI in the real estate sector. To achieve this objective, the study aims to find and discuss the existing literature on applying blockchain and AI technologies in the real estate sector. The works covered in this paper helps to explore and understand the concept of blockchain technology and determine how AI capabilities can be incorporated in blockchain technology-based systems and help facilitate the various processes in the real estate industry. The paper follows the PRISMA method of review to effectively explore materials related to the application of blockchain and AI in real estate and present evidence-based knowledge, which can be used for analysis, discussion, recommendation, and conclusion of the study. In addition, the paper also discusses some of the use cases and typical applications of the integrated approach of blockchain and AI.

2 Methodology

In order to provide a reproducible and transparent systematic literature review on the application of blockchain technology along with AI in Real Estate, the process suggested by Briner and Denyer [12] and the features presented in the PRISMA statement are adopted in this study [13]. This study's systematic literature review technique intends to locate literature relating to blockchain and artificial intelligence applications and choose and synthesize topics based on the research objective thoroughly and systematically. Also, the adopted review technique is based on a repetitive cycle of detecting the appropriate search keywords, assessing the relevant publications, and performing an analysis. An analysis protocol is also defined to outline the process from the protocol execution to gathering data and acquiring materials to be analyzed and studied.

The study adopts the appropriate data collection methodologies, including case studies and literature review, to get the firsthand perception of blockchain and AI technologies application in real estate.

The systematic literature review is carried out during January 2022, there are no time-frame restrictions, and the results are updated during February 2022. Various sources, including journals and online databases, such as Web of Science, ScienceDirect, Scopus, and the JSTOR database, were used to gather relevant information for the study.

The search term used to involve the following:

"Blockchain" AND "Artificial Intelligence" AND "Real Estate"

Moreover, additional search has been done with the usage of referenced work present in the relevant articles, with the help of the snowball effect [14, 15]. The research also includes the grey literature involving the unpublished research by the public or private institutions, and for that, the researcher evaluated the primary 100 hits on Google.

The database returned 272 publications as a result of the original search queries. Duplicates and articles with missing metadata (such as abstracts) were removed to improve the results. As a result, the number of publications dropped to 230. Using the four-eye principle, these were scrutinized and extensively inspected. These articles were then sorted by keywords, abstracts, titles, and content relevancy to blockchain and machine/deep learning marketing applications. The studies are evaluated based on inclusion and exclusion criteria as shown below (see Table 1). The studies are evaluated based on the screening of the title, screening of the abstract, and the screening of the full text as well.

Table 1. Exclusion and inclusion criteria

Selection criteria	Scientific database		Grey literature
Inclusion	Peer-reviewed research articles, book chapters, conference proceedings, review papers		English reports and studies
	Studies without time frame restrictions		No time frame restriction
Exclusion	During title screening	Non-English studies and articles	Generic articles and reports related to the blockchain-based technology
	During abstract screening	Generic articles related to blockchain	
	During full-text screening	Blockchain articles having a software-based orientation	
	During full-text screening	Articles involving technical characteristics and aspects of blockchain technology	

Only 58 publications made it beyond the first round of screening. Most articles describing blockchain and AI technologies' application in other industries such as finance, tourism, medical, agriculture, and others do not explicitly highlight their application implications in real estate, resulting in a significant drop in the number of articles. Only 24 studies were judged to align with the research aim after a comprehensive text reading and were thus retrieved for the final study. Each of these papers was considered relevant to the research and had texts highlighting the function and impact of blockchain and AI in real estate. The procedure of gathering data for the study is depicted in the diagram below (see Fig. 1).

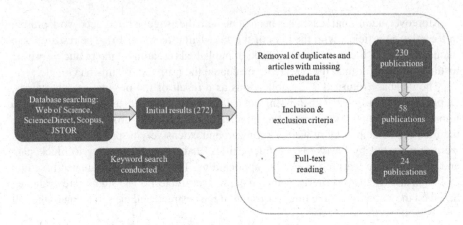

Fig. 1. Schematic representation of data collection.

The literature review method of data collection adopted in this case helps extract a body of information related to applying blockchain and artificial intelligence technologies in real estate from various sources. As a data collection tool, the literature review in this report includes activities like identifying, recording, understanding, meaning making and conveying information. The information collected here is done comprehensively.

3   Discussion

To begin with, blockchains store electronic information in digital formats. Block-chain is renowned for its fundamental role in a cryptocurrency system to maintain secure and decentralized transactions records. While they are closely related, Treiblmaier states that the data structure is a critical difference between blockchains and typical databases [1]. Blockchains gather information in a group, referred to as a block, which holds collections of information. A block includes a respective storage capacity. After it is complete, it is closed and connected to the previously entire blocks, creating chains of data referred to as the blockchains. All following new information after that newly added block is compiled into freshly made blocks that will consequently be added to the chain, as well, once complete [16]. Databases typically include data in the form of table structures. On the other hand, Blockchains, like its name implies, is structured into blocks threaded together. Inherently, those data structures make irreversible timelines of data when executed in decentralized manners. When blocks are filled, they are saved and become a part of that timeline. After adding them to the chains, all blocks are allocated particular time stamps. Leible et al. state that a blockchain is usually managed by peer-to-peer networks for use as publicly distributed ledgers, whereby nodes jointly follow protocols for communicating and validating a new block [17]. Today, there are private blockchains that can be used for business purposes. These blockchains have received mixed thoughts; for instance, Hampton referred to it as nothing more than 'snake oil' without appropriate security models [18]. On the other hand, others still argue that if a permissioned blockchain is carefully designed, it can be more decentralized and, thus, more secure practically than a permission-less one.

The models used in AI are modeled after the human brain and present very sophisticated approaches to machine learning to tackle various challenges. It includes inbuilt complex, multi-layered "deep neural networks" that facilitate data passing between nodes in vastly connected systems. Although it requires a lot of data for 'feeding and building' these systems, they can start generating results immediately with relatively minimal to no human intervention requirement after everything is in place [19]. The two primary forms of deep learning algorithms are convolutional neural networks and recurrent neural networks. The former are specially designed algorithms for working with imageries. The convolution part refers to the processes that apply weight-based filters within all elements of images to help computers understand and respond to elements in the individual picture.

Malhotra states that this can be rather useful when a user needs to scan various images for a particular feature or item, e.g., pictures of the sea floors for a sign of shipwrecks or an image of a multitude for a specific face of a person [19]. According to Sokolov, this discipline concerned mainly with analyzing and comprehending computer images and videos can be referred to as 'computer vision, and been a rapidly growing area over the past decade [20].

Blockchain and AI bring innovative capabilities to the sector of real estate. As a database, blockchains store electronic information in digital formats. Blockchain facilitates the recording and distribution of digital information, which can not be edited, destroyed, deleted, or altered in any way whatsoever [21]. This means that applying the technology can, for one, help in securing records of transactions in the real estate sector since they are unalterable, undeletable, and indestructible.

The blockchain platform introduces a form of tokenism in real estate [22]. The platform documents, stores, and verifies ownership tokens making it easier to buy, sell, and trade [23]. According to an article published in Rebellion Research, the commercial real estate industry has been operating under some form of secrecy when it comes to aspects such as rental rates, valuations, and prices of properties to keep a competitive edge [24]. Blockchain applications offer a way for real estate companies to effectively store and process the massive amounts of data existing in the industry. Currently, vast amounts of data are being kept in physical brokers' and builders' offices. Through blockchain and AI companies can migrate manual operations, from upcoming projects brochures to 'stacking' malls and other building plans, administration related paperwork, contracts, and other legal documents to digital formats, which can be quickly processed. From the customers' standpoint, the presence of conveniently accessible information showcasing preferable residential and commercial properties simplifies the clients' journey toward buying, sell or leasing decisions.

With increasing levels of digitization, however, clients are demanding transparency. To ease the distribution of property related information on the internet, real estate firms have adopted blockchain technology to replace transactions rooted in trust with those proved by mathematics [24].

With blockchain technology, users can carry out transactions without the need for a central authority. Blockchain is radically advancing the real estate sector by enabling the recording of all information in an immutable manner [25]. The technology eliminates third parties and brokers in real estate transactions making the entire process simple and transparent. According to a report, blockchain technology with its ability to create an immutable trail, increase trust, and data exchange, is preferred by industries such as real estate [26].

Moreover, blockchain in real estate is associated with cost reduction, increased transparency, and irrevocable documentation of processes [27]. But considering that the technology is still new and complex, there are challenges in terms of acceptance and implementation in companies. Blockchain allows optimization of retail and commercial property sales increases access to real estate funds and investment opportunities and streamlining of payments [28].

Liebkind observes that blockchain has opened up ways to change real estate transactions which are often conducted offline [29]. The author mentions that smart contracts in blockchain platforms have made it possible to tokenize assets like real estate. Companies worldwide are using smart contracts and ledgers offered by blockchain to carry out transparent and efficient real estate transactions [30, 31].

In real estate, prices mainly change every now and then after a property changes hands [32]. These changes usually result in high costs and huge volumes of transactions which can be hard to track and can even result in infrequent and inaccurate observations for some assets. In between a transaction, a real estate professional and investor needs to depend on valuations - the most possible prices to be acquired within the market, had the properties been put up for sale.

Although a valuation can be pretty straightforward, a lot more might be required when similar properties in the form of hedonic variables (also referred to as comparable) are transacted in the market near the valuation date [21]. When there are no consistent, similar transactions, the likely price of a property (whether commercial or residential) has to be calculated using a valuation process. While various processes can be used for the same, sophisticated econometric models such as the combination of blockchain and artificial intelligence would be able to provide even more accurate estimates of possible levels of discount rates and cashflows on top of providing the valuation. AI holds great promise for real estate valuation in providing high quality, timely, and accurate real estate data [33].

With the amounts of data existing related to real estate, implementing a balanced mix of modeling and data can be crucial for property valuation and other purposes. Although it requires a lot of data for 'feeding and building' these AI systems, they can start generating results immediately with relatively minimal to no human intervention requirement after everything is in place.

The capabilities provided by the technologies can also significantly influence the selling or buying decisions based on the perceived and analyzed present state of the real estate cycle and its expected future direction [34].

These advanced valuation techniques afforded by AI can analyze by simulating the player's thought processes to come up with decisions.

For instance, regression algorithms account for property characteristics like location, age, room count, size, and other aspects of home quality such as swimming pool, air conditioning, and granite countertops. Supposing that the property can be seen as a collection of different characteristics or structural attributes (hedonic pricing method), the property's valuation can be acquired by aggregating the contributory value of every feature [35].

Some of the features that can and are predicted using AI include:

1) Sale prices: Redfin and Zillow utilize machine learning algorithms to make accurate real estate price estimations, according to Soper [36];
2) Rental prices: HomeUnion came up with a tool referred to as RENTestimate for this [37];
3) Temporary rental prices: the pricing system used by Airbnb utilizes mathematical models that learn the likelihood of guests to book certain listings, on a particular date, at an assortment of diverse prices [38].

4 Conclusions

This study looks at how blockchain and AI can be applied in the real estate sector. Automating the various real estate processes using blockchain and AI means less time consumption, lesser human errors, and quality data analysis and predictions. AI improves the quantity and quality of information by efficiently processing it for superior decision-making and valuation purposes.

The combination of blockchain and AI provides several benefits to the real estate sector in securing transactions, extracting vast amounts of related data, analyzing the data, and making accurate assumptions based on the analysis. Enhanced computation power of computers supported with AI can make it simpler to grasp moving parts. Moreover, the integration of blockchain technology, which allows individuals to digitize data assets, can help reduce costs and labor in the real estate industry, through disintermediation. Currently, the sector does not have any standard way of holding data; data is stored in various forms. For instance, commercial real estate markets and lease documents are mostly not standardized, presenting challenges in evaluating information in different files.

Moreover, the discussed technologies can improve the real estate industry through property management, whereby everyday processes done by landlords, property managers, and tenants are streamlined using AI and blockchain capabilities. Landlords can also easily find appropriate tenants, find vendors and offer alerts for regular management and maintenance tasks. From a client's perceptive, these technologies can help them find the suitable properties based on AI-powered recommendations presented through AI algorithms. What's more, payments will be made through blockchains to facilitate safe and secure transactions.

For a future study, a deeper look into the positive and negative implications of the technologies on the firms and customers can further help promote the idea of employing blockchains and AI in real estate.

Funding Acknowledgement. This research was supported by Flexice PC as part of the project "Business Intelligence Network of Real Estate Consultants – BIRN", praxis code KMP6-0286090 and was co-financed by the European Regional Development Fund (ERDF) of the European Union (EE) under the action "Strengthening Research, Technological Development and Innovation under the framework "Investment Innovation Plans" with code OPS 4228 of the Operational Program «Central Macedonia» 2014–2020.

References

1. Treiblmaier, H.: Toward more rigorous blockchain research: recommendations for writing blockchain case studies. In: Treiblmaier, H., Clohessy, T. (eds.) Blockchain and Distributed Ledger Technology Use Cases. PI, pp. 1–31. Springer, Cham (2020). https://doi.org/10.1007/978-3-030-44337-5_1
2. Alladi, T., Chamola, V., Parizi, R.M., Choo, K.-K.R.: Blockchain applications for industry 4.0 and Industrial IoT: a review. IEEE Access **7**, 176935–176951 (2019)
3. Angraal, S., Krumholz, H.M., Schulz, W.L.: Blockchain technology: applications in health care. Circ. Cardiovasc. Qual. Outcomes **10**, e003800 (2017)
4. Bozkir, E., Eivazi, S., Akgün, M., Kasneci, E.: Eye tracking data collection protocol for VR for remotely located subjects using blockchain and smart contracts. In: Proceedings of the 2020 IEEE International Conference on Artificial Intelligence and Virtual Reality (AIVR), pp. 397–401. IEEE (2020)
5. del Castillo, M.: Forbes Blockchain 50 (2022). https://www.forbes.com/sites/michaeldelcastillo/2022/02/08/forbes-blockchain-50-2022/. Accessed 15 Feb 2022
6. Chen, G., Xu, B., Lu, M., Chen, N.-S.: Exploring blockchain technology and its potential applications for education. Smart Learn. Environ. **5**, 1–10 (2018)
7. Chen, J., Lv, Z., Song, H.: Design of Personnel big data management system based on blockchain. Future Gener. Comput. Syst. **101**, 1122–1129 (2019)
8. Bachute, M.R., Subhedar, J.M.: Autonomous driving architectures: insights of machine learning and deep learning algorithms. Mach. Learn. Appl. **6**, 100164 (2021)
9. Mallick, A., Dhara, S., Rath, S.: Application of machine learning algorithms for prediction of sinter machine productivity. Mach. Learn. Appl. **6**, 100186 (2021)
10. Abou Jaoude, J., Saade, R.G.: Blockchain applications-usage in different domains. IEEE Access **7**, 45360–45381 (2019)
11. Aggarwal, S., Chaudhary, R., Aujla, G.S., Kumar, N., Choo, K.-K.R., Zomaya, A.Y.: Blockchain for smart communities: applications, challenges and opportunities. J. Netw. Comput. Appl. **144**, 13–48 (2019)
12. Briner, R.B., Denyer, D.: Systematic review and evidence synthesis as a practice and scholarship tool. In: Oxford Handbook of Evidence-Based Management: Companies, Classrooms and Research, pp. 112–129 (2012)
13. Moher, D., Liberati, A., Tetzlaff, J., Altman, D.G., Group, P.: Preferred reporting items for systematic reviews and meta-analyses: the PRISMA statement. PLoS Med. **6**, e1000097 (2009)
14. Maesa, D.D.F., Mori, P.: Blockchain 3.0 applications survey. J. Parallel Distrib. Comput., **138**, 99–114 (2020)
15. McGhin, T., Choo, K.-K.R., Liu, C.Z., He, D.: Blockchain in healthcare applications: research challenges and opportunities. J. Netw. Comput. Appl. **135**, 62–75 (2019). https://doi.org/10.1016/j.jnca.2019.02.027
16. Honkanen, P., Nylund, M., Westerlund, M.: Organizational building blocks for blockchain governance: a survey of 241 blockchain white papers (2021)
17. Leible, S., Schlager, S., Schubotz, M., Gipp, B.: A review on blockchain technology and blockchain projects fostering open science. Front. Blockchain **16** (2019)

18. Hampton, N.: Understanding the blockchain hype: why much of it is nothing more than snake oil and spin. https://www2.computerworld.com.au/article/606253/understanding-blockchain-hype-why-much-it-nothing-more-than-snake-oil-spin/. Accessed 15 Feb 2022

19. Malhotra, Y.: AI, machine learning & deep learning risk management & controls: beyond deep learning and generative adversarial networks: model risk management in AI, machine learning & deep learning: princeton presentations in AI-ML risk management & control systems (presentation slides). In: Proceedings of the Machine Learning & Deep Learning: Princeton Presentations in AI-ML Risk Management & Control Systems (Presentation Slides). In: Princeton Presentations in AI & Machine Learning Risk Management & Control Systems, 2018 Princeton Fintech & Quant Conference, Princeton University (2018)

20. Sokolov, V.: Discussion of 'deep learning for finance: deep portfolios.' Appl. Stoch. Models Bus. Ind. **33**, 16–18 (2017). https://doi.org/10.1002/asmb.2228

21. Cuturi, M.P., Etchebarne, G.: Real estate pricing with machine learning & non-traditional data sources. https://tryolabs.com/blog/2021/06/25/real-estate-pricing-with-machine-learning-non-traditional-data-sources. Accessed 15 Feb 2022

22. Erika Blockchain In Real Estate: 8 Things (2022) You Should Know. Gokce Cap. We Buy Sell Land (2021)

23. Yadav, A.S., Kushwaha, D.S.: Blockchain-based digitization of land record through trust value-based consensus algorithm. Peer-to-Peer Network. Appl. **14**(6), 3540–3558 (2021). https://doi.org/10.1007/s12083-021-01207-1

24. Blockchain Real Estate: Smart Contracts and Their Potential Impact on RE! Rebellion Res. (2021)

25. Blockchain in Real-Estate: How Technology Can Revolutionize the Industry. https://www.blockchain-council.org/blockchain/blockchain-in-real-estate-how-technology-can-revolutionize-the-industry/. Accessed 16 Feb 2022

26. Dragov, R., Siviero, A., Micheletti, G., Butiniello, L., Magnani, I.: Advanced Technologies for Industry: AT Watch : Technology Focus on Blockchain. Publications Office, LU (2021)

27. PricewaterhouseCoopers Blockchain in Real Estate. https://www.pwc.de/en/real-estate/digital-real-estate/blockchain-in-real-estate.html. Accessed 16 Feb 2022

28. Blockchain in Real Estate: Use Cases and Implementations. https://consensys.net/blockchain-use-cases/real-estate/. Accessed 16 Feb 2022

29. Liebkind, J.: How blockchain technology is changing real estate. https://www.investopedia.com/news/how-blockchain-technology-changing-real-estate/. Accessed 16 Feb 2022

30. Daley, S.: 19 top blockchain real estate companies to know 2022 | built in. https://builtin.com/blockchain/blockchain-real-estate-companies. Accessed 16 Feb 2022

31. Ullah, F., Al-Turjman, F.: A conceptual framework for blockchain smart contract adoption to manage real estate deals in smart cities. Neural Comput. Appl. (2021). https://doi.org/10.1007/s00521-021-05800-6

32. Hayes, A.: Blockchain Explained. https://www.investopedia.com/terms/b/blockchain.asp. Accessed 15 Feb 2022

33. Tajani, F., Morano, P., Ntalianis, K.: Automated valuation models for real estate portfolios: a method for the value updates of the property assets. J. Prop. Invest. Finance **36**, 324–347 (2018). https://doi.org/10.1108/JPIF-10-2017-0067

34. Hoksbergen, M., Chan, J., Peko, G., Sundaram, D.: Asymmetric information in high-value low-frequency transactions: mitigation in real estate using blockchain. In: Doss, R., Piramuthu, S., Zhou, W. (eds.) FNSS 2019. CCIS, vol. 1113, pp. 225–239. Springer, Cham (2019). https://doi.org/10.1007/978-3-030-34353-8_17

35. Abidoye, R.B., Chan, A.P.C.: Improving property valuation accuracy: a comparison of hedonic pricing model and artificial neural network. Pac. Rim Prop. Res. J. **24**, 71–83 (2018). https://doi.org/10.1080/14445921.2018.1436306

36. Soper, T.: Zillow group uses machine learning to improve zestimate algorithm for changing market trends. https://www.geekwire.com/2021/zillow-group-uses-machine-learning-improve-zestimate-algorithm-dynamic-market-conditions/. Accessed 15 Feb 2022

37. RENTestimate: Rent Estimate Calculator by Address. https://www.homeunion.com/rentestimate/. Accessed 15 Feb 2022

38. Constantinescu, M.: Machine-learning real estate valuation: not only a data affair. https://towardsdatascience.com/machine-learning-real-estate-valuation-not-only-a-data-affair-99d36c92d263. Accessed 15 Feb 2022

Modelling the Development and Deployment of Decentralized Applications in Ethereum Blockchain: A BPMN-Based Approach

Nikolaos Nousias⬤, George Tsakalidis⬤, Sophia Petridou⬤,
and Kostas Vergidis(✉)⬤

Department of Applied Informatics, University of Macedonia, Thessaloniki, Greece
{nnousias,giorgos.tsakalidis,spetrido,kvergidis}@uom.edu.gr

Abstract. Decentralized Applications (DApps) have emerged as a new model for building massively scalable and profitable applications. A DApp is a software application that runs on a peer-to-peer blockchain network offering censorship resistance, resilience, and transparency that overcome the challenges of typical centralized architectures. Developing and deploying a DApp in a blockchain network is highly challenging. Developers need to initially decide if developing a DApp is justified, before considering different aspects of blockchain technology (e.g., cryptography, transactions, addresses, etc.). This adversity along with the plethora of previously published works highlight the need for new tools and methods for the development of blockchain-based applications. Throughout literature there is a lack of procedures that can guide practitioners on how to develop and deploy their own applications. This paper aims to address this research gap, by standardizing and modelling such processes, through the employment of the BPMN modelling technique. Initially, a DMN decision model is presented that can facilitate developers to determine whether developing a DApp is justified. Consequently, two BPMN models are introduced, namely the DApp development and the DApp deployment process models. The models can orchestrate new DApp initiatives and facilitate the developers' communication and implementation transparency. We expect that they can serve as a roadmap for enhancing the decision-making in the act of developing a DApp and reducing the implementation time and cost. Finally, we further discuss how the models implement a DApp for the registration and verification of academic qualifications and how BPMN can constitute a powerful tool for the development of DApps.

Keywords: Blockchain · Ethereum · DApp · DApp development · DApp deployment · BPMN · DMN · Modelling · Decision-making

1 Introduction

Nowadays blockchain has attracted a lot of attention in both academia and industry. A blockchain is a digital immutable ledger of transaction data, shared across a network of untrusted users [1]. The ledger is replicated and synchronized across the nodes without the control of any third party [2]. As nodes broadcast transactions to the network,

A. P. Cabral Seixas Costa et al. (Eds.): ICDSST 2022, LNBIP 447, pp. 55–67, 2022.
https://doi.org/10.1007/978-3-031-06530-9_5

they are validated and sealed into blocks using cryptographic primitives to maintain network integrity and avoid data tampering [3]. Once new blocks are appended, a chain of cryptographically linked blocks is established, hence creating the blockchain.

The most prominent application of blockchain is Bitcoin, introduced originally in 2008 by Satoshi Nakamoto [4]. The Bitcoin application constitutes the first generation of blockchains [5] and was initially delimited to the exchange of digital currencies. With the advent of Ethereum [6], the concept of smart contracts was introduced. As a result, the second generation of blockchains emerged, providing a deterministic and secure programming environment for building general-purpose DApps [7]. A DApp is a novel form of the blockchain-empowered software system [8] running on a decentralized peer-to-peer network, such as a blockchain network, and its backend code is employed in smart contracts. The app logic is executed deterministically in the blockchain, while it is guaranteed to be transparent, verifiable, and immutable [9].

As the technology evolves further, more and more applications will be decentralized [7]. However, the development of blockchain-oriented applications poses a new set of challenges that require more sophisticated knowledge compared to the traditional application development approaches [10]. Initially, a decision model is required to determine whether developing a DApp is justified over the development of conventional applications. Moreover, DApps require new ways of thinking about how to build, maintain, and deploy software [9]. Developer support in terms of blockchain applications is limited [11] and thus the development process is considered ambiguous [12] and challenging with a steep learning curve [13]. A plethora of previous works [14–17] highlights the need for specialized tools, techniques, modelling notations, and design patterns for the development of blockchain-based applications.

Traditional software development is enriched with software process models and design decision-making processes [18] that guide developers from the conception of an idea to the realization of the final product. However, to the best of our knowledge, there are no proposed processes and correlation approaches for DApp development and deployment. As of yet, developing a DApp is a composition of decisions which reside in the designers' reasoning and intuition. Hence, we consider the modelling of such processes a novelty and a timely contribution that can serve as a roadmap in new DApp initiatives. By standardizing and modelling such concepts, transparency and communication can be facilitated, resulting in the reduction of the implementation cost and time. In addition, as decision paths are explicitly modeled and documented with model constructs, decision-making can be enhanced. Specifically, developers can decide and enact their following action on the basis of the model logic, circumventing a time-consuming decision of what should be performed next. For this purpose, we employ BPMN as the state-of-the-art process modelling notation [19] and adopt Ethereum as the most popular, and mature blockchain for DApp development [20].

Overall, the purpose of this paper is twofold. Firstly, to propose two standardized processes of developing and deploying a DApp that can facilitate the process-thinking and decision-making of business analysts and software developers alike at their DApp initiatives. Secondly, to shift the discourse towards the applicability of BPMN for designing blockchain-based applications. The rest of the paper is structured as follows. In Sect. 2 we provide the theoretical background of our study. In Sect. 3 and 4, we standardize the processes of developing and deploying a DApp utilizing the BPMN. In Sect. 5, we communicate the advantages of the proposed models and discuss their applicability on real-world applications. Section 6 concludes the paper, while providing directions for future work.

2 Background

In this section, we define the key concepts that will be discussed through the rest of the paper. Initially, we introduce Ethereum as a blockchain platform that enables the autonomous execution of smart contracts. Subsequently, we discuss what a smart contract is and how DApps treat them as first-class elements. Afterwards, we introduce BPMN as the standard process modelling technique that will be utilized to depict the processes of developing and deploying a DApp atop Ethereum. Finally, we present a DMN-based decision model for determining when the DApp development is justified, as a prerequisite decision before the DApp development and deployment processes unfold.

2.1 Ethereum

Ethereum was conceived by Vitalik Buterin in 2013 [6] as a general-purpose blockchain with a built-in Turing-complete programming language and a native cryptocurrency called Ether. Ethereum's vision was to allow anyone to write their own arbitrary rules in the so-called smart contracts, encoding rules for ownership, transaction formats, and state transition functions [6]. Loading and running the contracts in its distributed state machine (i.e., Ethereum Virtual Machine - EVM) results to state changes that are stored in its blockchain. Each node on the network runs a local copy of the EVM to validate the contract execution. To thwart a smart contact's infinite execution when a node attempts to validate it, Ethereum introduces the gas mechanism to limit the resources that any program can consume [7].

   With its deterministic and secure programming environment, the Ethereum platform enables developers to build powerful DApps that constitute the culmination of the Ethereum vision [6]. Ethereum constitutes a protocol that is implemented by independent networks; multiple for testing and one for production. The transactions in a test network do not exchange real-value Ether, making it suitable for initial testing and experimentation. As the most mature Turing-complete programming blockchain, the vast majority of DApps are built atop Ethereum [20].

2.2 Smart Contracts

The concept of smart contracts was introduced by Nick Szabo in 1994 [21], by defining a smart contract as "a computerized transaction protocol that executes the terms of a contract". With the Ethereum foundation, this term was reinforced as "systems that can be autonomously executed and move digital assets according to arbitrary pre-specified rules" [6]. Smart contracts are deployed as data in a transaction and therefore are immutable. Their code can be inspected by every network participant while their execution is deterministic. To trigger their enactment, a message is sent to their address. Their code activation allows to read and write to their internal storage, send other messages or create contracts in turn.

To deploy a smart contract in a blockchain network, developers encode initially their logic in a high-level programming language (e.g., Solidity). Subsequently, the code is translated into bytecode, before being deployed to the network. In case of Ethereum, the bytecode is executed on the EVM as part of the Ethereum network protocol.

2.3 Decentralized Applications (DApps)

The majority of web-based applications are centralized by design. They are based on client-server architecture, which entails that data processing mostly occurs on a single server hosting environment [1]. With the advent of the second generation of blockchains, DApps have emerged. In their most fundamental format, DApps consist of a web user interface (frontend UI) and a distributed backend (smart contract), which are usually bundled via the web3.js Javascript library [7]. Their backend code is distributed to overcome the challenges that arise from having a centralized server [13], such as low transparency or single point of failure [10]. The on-chain nature of DApps allows everyone to audit their code and inspect their functionality.

Blockchain has shown a great potential in enabling a wealth of DApps, related to games, finance, NFTs, health, energy, and supply chain, among others [20]. However, a major consideration remains the immutability of their smart contract code and their challenging development [13], thus necessitating more intricate and secure techniques in designing blockchain applications.

2.4 Business Process Model and Notation (BPMN)

The BPMN standard [22] is a contemporary notation for capturing business processes in a graphical and executable format. Introduced by OMG in 2006, BPMN has been widely adopted as the de facto process modelling notation in both academia and industry. The primary goal is to provide an understandable notation for various business users (i.e., analysts, developers, managers, etc.) [23]. Previous works have employed BPMN for modelling IoT processes [24], RPA initiatives [25], and blockchain-based applications [26], among others.

Beyond its primary goal of modelling business processes, BPMN models serve as inputs to software development projects [27]. Since modelling is an intrinsic part of designing a software [15], BPMN models are handed over to software developers. System requirements, process flow and decision paths, are specified in a graphical representation before developers translate their logic to code execution.

The application of standard BPMN diagrams for designing and developing DApps has evolved as an intriguing challenge in the aspect of existing blockchain limitations [28]. In particular, the usage of BPMN constructs may prove an efficient method in addressing blockchain usability and complexity issues, due to its well-defined steps and comprehensible notation for the communications between project stakeholders. Bearing in mind the emerging interest of the blockchain community in BPMN, we employ BPMN for the modelling of the DApp development and deployment processes, introduced in Sects. 3 and 4.

2.5 A DMN-Based Decision Model for DApp Development

Developing a DApp is a decision-making process towards committing to optimal decisions in specific time frames. Importantly, an initial decision should be taken whether blockchain application is justified, before design decisions emerge during the DApp development and deployment phases. In this regard, a Decision Model and Notation (DMN) - based decision model (Fig. 1) is introduced to guide developers determine whether developing a DApp is a correct decision. DMN [29], emerged as an OMG standard in 2015 for decision modelling, where its primary goal is to provide a common notation for the graphical representation of decisions. The most fundamental constructs are decision nodes, represented by rectangles, and input data, represented by ovals.

In our context, an initial decision path [30] should be followed to justify the blockchain applicability after reviewing the requirements (i.e., use case) and the blockchain peculiarities. Specifically, on the basis of a need for a shared database, the involvement of multiple untrustworthy participants, and the need for disintermediation, the blockchain applicability should be decided. Subsequently, developers need to take design decisions in the act of developing and deploying their own applications. For this purpose, the DApp development and deployment processes unfold in the following sections to standardize the process flow and facilitate the design decision-making.

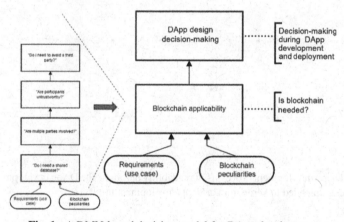

Fig. 1. A DMN-based decision model for DApp development

3 Modelling the DApp Development Process

This section discusses the DApp development process on the Ethereum blockchain and introduces the respective BPMN model. The aim is to model the flow and the decision paths that a developer should follow while developing a DApp, combining blockchain concepts (transactions, cryptocurrencies, public – private keys, addresses, etc.) in a visual and intuitive manner. Thus, the model can shed light on the process of developing a DApp, become a roadmap for DApp development initiatives, and facilitate the decision-making by explicitly determining a sequence of activities and flow paths. Developing a DApp on top of the Ethereum can be regarded as a process with concrete boundaries, a distinct trigger event (e.g., conceptualization of a DApp) and a distinguishable output (e.g., successful DApp development). The DApp development process is modelled in BPMN (Fig. 2) to better conceptualize and standardize the process. Embarking on the DApp development initiative, a developer needs to create an Externally Owned Account (EOA), develop a smart contract, and to configure the interface for the DApp. To communicate better the above three discrete phases, we compartmentalized the process model with BPMN group artifacts. In more detail:

(i)   The Externally Owned Account (EOA) configuration aims at the creation of an account to propagate a valid transaction to the blockchain;
(ii) The Smart Contract configuration aims at the encapsulation and the deployment of the backend application to the Ethereum network;
(iii) The User Interface (UI) configuration aims at the establishment of an interface, facilitating the interaction with a smart contract that is operating on the blockchain.

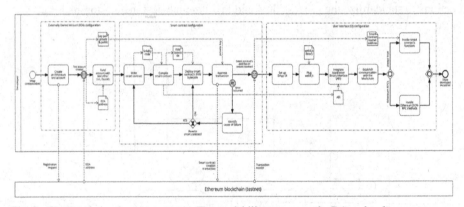

Fig. 2. The DApp development process (For readability purposes, the DApp development process model has been uploaded to verde.uom.gr/dapp/development.html)

3.1 Externally Owned Account (EOA) Configuration

Initializing the development process, a developer should primarily create their own test Ethereum account to be able to interact with the Ethereum blockchain and propagate valid transactions to every node. Specifically, a message (registration request) is propagated to Ethereum, where an EOA is generated (rendered with an intermediate catching message event) and a relative key-pair: private and public (modelled using a data object), is received. Considering that even in a test network, transactions require fees calculated on Ether, a developer is subsequently requested to fund their account. However, due to the testing nature of such networks, developers can reach services (i.e., faucets) that dispense funds in the form of free Ether, instead of buying real-value Ether.

3.2   Smart Contract Configuration

Once the EOA is generated and funded with test Ether, the Smart Contract configuration phase unfolds. At this stage, the developer initially writes a smart contract, typically in Solidity, as the most frequently utilized language for Ethereum smart contracts. Solidity code needs to be further compiled into EVM bytecode to be executed by Ethereum's execution environment, namely the EVM. In this regard, the developer should pass the Solidity code to a Solidity compiler, which in turn produces - as outputs - the EVM bytecode and a contract interface, namely the Application Binary Interface (ABI). Rendered with BPMN data objects, they are further manipulated as the development process unfolds. Thereon, the developer is requested to deploy the previously generated bytecode to the network and approve the smart contract creation transaction. Utilizing their private key, they output a digital signature which verifies that they have the authorization to generate such a transaction. Once successfully created, a transaction receipt is acquired (shown in the model with an intermediate catching message event), indicating the smart contract's address (modelled using a data object) on the Ethereum test network.

However, the propagation of the transaction to the Ethereum network might be interrupted by a plethora of errors. Such errors are mapped with a BPMN error boundary interrupting event, attached to the border of the transaction approval task. The developer should identify the cause of failure and proceed fundamentally either with the code modification or with the gas limit increase.

3.3   User Interface (UI) Configuration

Once the smart contract has been successfully deployed on the Ethereum test network, the configuration of the application's interface is the final step. The developer should establish (task: set-up DApp UI) its interface to the external users and configure its core functionality. Thereafter, the web3 JavaScript library and the previously generated contract's ABI (modelled as BPMN input data objects) should be integrated into the application's logic. Specifically, the former enables the programmatic interaction with the Ethereum blockchain, while the latter is a JSON-based description of the available smart contract's functions. This description defines the methods that the application can invoke so as to interact with the deployed contract [7]. Once successfully integrated, the developer is further requested to formalize the interaction with the blockchain, communicating directly either with the deployed contract or with the blockchain itself. Hence, utilizing the formerly generated smart contract's address, its functions can be invoked, while optionally JSON-RPCs (Remote Procedure Calls) can be conducted to query the blockchain-related information (e.g., current block, current gas price, etc.). For this purpose, an inclusive (OR) gateway is utilized. Importantly, the one sequence flow is always triggered (i.e., condition is always true, considering that the interaction with the smart contract is the developer's ultimate aim), while the other one is an optional flow, indicating the conditional invocation of Ethereum RPCs (i.e., condition is 'Ethereum RPCs'). Once the interaction is successfully established, the DApp development process is completed, triggering at the same time the DApp deployment process. The DApp deployment process unfolds subsequently in Sect. 4.

4   Modelling the DApp Deployment Process

This section introduces the DApp deployment process (Fig. 3), modelled in BPMN. Once the development process is completed, the next step is the DApp migration to the main Ethereum network. The process follows the same process compartmentalization (EOA, Smart Contract and UI configuration). The deployment process should maintain the application's functionality with the minimum number of modifications. For this purpose, the introduced model aims to guide developers on identifying the required changes (e.g., fund account with real Ether, replace smart contract's testnet address with the mainnet one, etc.) and taking consistent decisions, to make their DApps run on a real-value transactions environment.

4.1   Externally Owned Account (EOA) Configuration

With the trigger of the DApp deployment process, the EOA configuration phase is initiated. An Ethereum account is applicable to different networks, maintaining the same address with a different balance. Considering that transactions on the main Ethereum network are executed with real-value Ether, the developer is requested to fund their precedently generated account with real Ether.

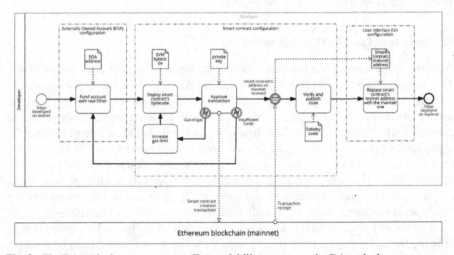

Fig. 3. The DApp deployment process (For readability purposes, the DApp deployment process model has been uploaded to verde.uom.gr/dapp/deployment.html)

4.2   Smart Contract Configuration

Once the EOA is funded with real-value Ether, the developer is requested to deploy the smart contract on the main Ethereum network. At this phase, no code modification is needed given that the smart contract has been successfully developed during the DApp development process. The developer should exclusively deploy the smart contract's bytecode, generated during the development process, on the mainnet, and approve the contract's creation transaction by signing it with the account private key. Intuitively, the transaction (through a BPMN message flow) is propagated to the main Ethereum network, where a contract account and a relative address is generated. At this stage, it is considered as best practice to verify and publish the contract's Solidity source code, inciting the entire network to entrust its encapsulated process logic [7].

In case of an error occurrence during the propagation of the transaction to the entire network, a recovery (i.e., error-handling) procedure is initialized. At this stage, any code-related errors are typically not expected as they are mitigated at the development process. Any transactional-based errors (e.g., out-of-gas, insufficient funds, etc.) are depicted with interrupting error events, attached to the boundary of the transaction approval task. This acts as a warning to modify the transaction details (e.g., increase the transaction's gas limit) or increase the balance of their account, before redeploying the contract's bytecode.

4.3 User Interface (UI) Configuration

Once the smart contract configuration phase is successfully completed, the user interface needs to interact with the contract that is deployed on the mainnet. The process guides the developer to update the smart contract address without modifying neither the application's interface nor its core functionality. As a result, the DApp is able to operate on the main Ethereum network with minimum modifications.

5 Discussion

The process dimension of software engineering is well recognized by researchers and practitioners [18, 31], contrary to the decentralized application software that lacks this perspective. This paper presented the DApp development and deployment process utilizing the BPMN technique. Considering the lack of competing approaches, the paper presents a novelty, offering four major advantages.

First, modelling such processes in BPMN can mitigate any issues arising from their free-form textual description. This approach corroborates Nordsieck's [32] statement that visual models can reveal the notion of a subject matter in a more comprehensive way than any other form of representation. Exploiting the cognitive effectiveness of BPMN [33], developers can intuitively follow the process flow of the models to orchestrate their DApp initiatives. Second, standardizing their flow can make the models serve as an established point of reference, eliminating the necessity of designing, communicating, and agreeing on the software process, each time the development and deployment of a DApp take place. As a result, it is expected that the implementation time and cost can be reduced, while developers' communication and implementation transparency can be improved. Third, decision-making can be facilitated as time-consuming decisions are taken on the basis of the model logic. Being aware of the process control flow, developers identify the forthcoming steps on time, circumventing the need for pondering on their next step. Fourth, the lack of constraints or dependencies in a particular Integrated

Development Environment (IDE) (e.g., Remix, EthFiddle, etc.), or Ethereum client (e.g., Geth, Parity, MetaMask, etc.), enriches the applicability of the proposed processes to all DApp initiatives atop Ethereum. Developers can adhere to their process logic irrespective of the selected tools to implement their applications.

To investigate the applicability of the proposed processes, the authors employed them for the prototype implementation of the VerDe (Verified Degrees) application; a proposed decentralized application for the registration and verification of academic qualifications. As initially presented in [34], VerDe is envisioned as a decentralized application that securely registers and verifies degrees atop Ethereum. The goal is to mitigate fraud and mobility issues inflicted by the current way in which degrees are circulated. Blockchain can serve as a technology enabler for such issues, since it is resistant to the modification of data it holds. Specifically, the VerDe architecture is conceived as a smart contract running on the Ethereum network, offering two distinct user interfaces for writing (i.e., degree registration) and reading (i.e., degree verification) from it. From the conceptual design towards its actual implementation, we followed the previously proposed models. Initially, adhering to the introduced DMN decision model, we decided that developing a DApp is justified, considering that: (i) a shared single source of truth is needed, (ii) universities, students, and companies are involved, (iii) fake degrees are circulated, and (iv) disintermediation from bureaucratic nostrification agencies is required. Subsequently, the introduced BPMN process compartmentalization facilitated the controlled development of the VerDe application in three discrete phases. In detail, we configured our own EOA, developed and deployed the VerDe smart contract, and configured its interfaces to the external world. This approach revealed that planning was promoted ahead of time, allowing the definition and evaluation of each phase's goals. Additionally, issues were detected and fixed quickly, as error-handling procedures were explicitly specified in the models. Thus, implementation time and cost were significantly reduced. Currently, a functional demo of the VerDe platform has been released[1], while the DApp development[1] and deployment[2] processes are publicly available under the same project directory.

Overall, a distinct feature of our work is the employment of BPMN for blockchain modelling. The research conducted in this paper, proved that in contrary to the findings in [28], BPMN diagrams may constitute a useful and efficient method for both the design and development of DApps. What is highlighted is that the interpretation of different blockchain concepts can be achieved through the usage of sophisticated BPMN constructs. Among others, we employed BPMN message flows to model the propagation of transactions to a blockchain network. BPMN error events were introduced to model blockchain failures. Additionally, BPMN message events were utilized to model transaction receipts. The proposed approach can standardize the depiction of such blockchain concepts and inspire researchers to the modelling of their own blockchain-based applications. However, considering that blockchain modelling is recognized as a relatively new research domain, further research is needed to investigate the applicability of BPMN for the modelling of more complex blockchain concepts (e.g., consensus in the distributed network, mining, etc.).

---

[1] A functional demo of the VerDe application can be found on verde.uom.gr.

6   Conclusion

Blockchain opens an opportunity to create DApps that can benefit from its distributed and immutable nature. Compared to traditional software engineering, their development poses new challenges with respect to different blockchain aspects. As DApp software engineering is still a relatively new area, there is a necessity for tools, methods, and design patterns for optimal development and deployment in a blockchain network.

The work presented in this paper allows developers to follow a systematic step-by-step process for developing and deploying a DApp atop the Ethereum network. For this purpose, a DMN decision model was presented to help developers decide whether developing a DApp is justified. Moreover, two BPMN process models were introduced, the DApp development process model and the DApp deployment. By standardizing and modelling their flow, we expect that these models can serve as a roadmap for DApp developers, while eliminating the need to devise and decide on the process flow each time a new DApp initiative unfolds.

To investigate the applicability of our proposed approach, we employed the introduced models for a prototype implementation of a DApp for the registration and verification of academic degrees. Our approach proved to facilitate decision-making and decrease implementation time and cost, advancing further the idea of bringing together process modelling and DApp development.

As future work, we intend to further utilize the BPMN technique for DApp development by exploring how BPMN message flows can define the functionality of smart contracts, as the most critical elements of a DApp. We plan to investigate how the graphical message flows can be translated to Solidity code, thus establishing a sound communication between a DApp's distributed backend and its external environment.

Acknowledgment. This work is part of a project that has received funding from the Research Committee of the University of Macedonia under the Basic Research 2020–21 funding programme.

References

1. Zheng, Z., Xie, S., Dai, H., Chen, X., Wang, H.: An overview of blockchain technology: architecture, consensus, and future trends. In: 2017 IEEE International Congress on Big Data (BigData Congress), pp. 557–564 (2017). https://doi.org/10.1109/BigDataCongress.2017.85
2. Böhme, R., Christin, N., Edelman, B., Moore, T.: Bitcoin: economics, technology, and governance. J. Econ. Perspect. **29**(2), 213–238 (2015). https://doi.org/10.1257/jep.29.2.213
3. Zhang, K., Jacobsen, H.-A.: Towards dependable, scalable, and pervasive distributed ledgers with blockchains. In: 2018 IEEE 38th International Conference on Distributed Computing Systems (ICDCS), pp. 1337–1346 (2018)
4. Nakamoto, S.: Bitcoin: a peer-to-peer electronic cash system (2008). http://bitcoin.org/bitcoin.pdf. Accessed 22 Jan 2022
5. Xu, M., Chen, X., Kou, G.: A systematic review of blockchain. Finan. Innov. **5**(1), 1–14 (2019). https://doi.org/10.1186/s40854-019-0147-z
6. Buterin, V.: A next-generation smart contract and decentralized application platform. Ethereum White Paper (2014). https://ethereum.org/en/whitepaper/. Accessed 22 Jan 2022

7. Antonopoulos, A.M., Wood, G.: Mastering Ethereum: Building Smart Contracts and DApps, 1st edn. O'Reilly Media, Newton (2018)
8. Cai, W., Wang, Z., Ernst, J.B., Hong, Z., Feng, C., Leung, V.C.M.: Decentralized applications: the blockchain-empowered software system. IEEE Access. **6**, 53019–53033 (2018). https://doi.org/10.1109/ACCESS.2018.2870644
9. Karger, E., Jagals, M., Ahlemann, F.: Blockchain for AI data – state of the art and open research, 18 (2021)
10. Cai, C., Duan, H., Wang, C.: Tutorial: building secure and trustworthy blockchain applications. In: 2018 IEEE Cybersecurity Development (SecDev), pp. 120–121 (2018). https://doi.org/10.1109/SecDev.2018.00023
11. Mendling, J., et al.: Blockchains for business process management - challenges and opportunities. ACM Trans. Manage. Inf. Syst. **9**, 4:1–4:16 (2018). https://doi.org/10.1145/318 3367
12. Antal, C., Cioara, T., Anghel, I., Antal, M., Salomie, I.: Distributed ledger technology review and decentralized applications development guidelines. Future Internet **13**, 62 (2021). https://doi.org/10.3390/fi13030062
13. Why Model-Driven Engineering Fits the Needs for Blockchain Application Development - IEEE Blockchain Initiative. https://blockchain.ieee.org/technicalbriefs/september-2018/why-model-driven-engineering-fits-the-needs-for-blockchain-application-development. Accessed 18 Feb 2022
14. Porru, S., Pinna, A., Marchesi, M., Tonelli, R.: Blockchain-oriented software engineering: challenges and new directions. In: 2017 IEEE/ACM 39th International Conference on Software Engineering Companion (ICSE-C), pp. 169–171 (2017). https://doi.org/10.1109/ICSE-C.2017.142
15. Rocha, H., Ducasse, S.: Preliminary steps towards modeling blockchain oriented software. In: 2018 IEEE/ACM 1st International Workshop on Emerging Trends in Software Engineering for Blockchain (WETSEB), pp. 52–57 (2018)
16. AL-Ashmori, A., Basri, S., Dominic, P.D.D., Muneer, A., Al-Tashi, Q., Al-Ashmori, Y.: Blockchain-oriented software development issues: a literature review. In: Silhavy, R., Silhavy, P., Prokopova, Z. (eds.) Software Engineering Application in Informatics, pp. 48–57. Springer, Cham (2021). https://doi.org/10.1007/978-3-030-90318-3_6
17. Koul, R.: Blockchain oriented software testing - challenges and approaches. In: 2018 3rd International Conference for Convergence in Technology (I2CT), pp. 1–6 (2018). https://doi.org/10.1109/I2CT.2018.8529728
18. Sommerville, I.: Software process models. ACM Comput. Surv. **28**, 269–271 (1996). https://doi.org/10.1145/234313.234420
19. Kocbek, M., Jošt, G., Heričko, M., Polančič, G.: Business process model and notation: the current state of affairs. Comput. Sci. Inf. Syst. **12**, 509–539 (2015)
20. State of the DApps. https://www.stateofthedapps.com/. Accessed 1 Feb 2022
21. Szabo, N.: Smart Contracts (1994). http://archive.is/X3lR2. Accessed 10 Feb 2022
22. Business Process Model and Notation Specification Version 2.0.2. https://www.omg.org/spec/BPMN/About-BPMN/. Accessed 1 Feb 2022
23. Chinosi, M., Trombetta, A.: BPMN: an introduction to the standard. Comput. Stand. Interfaces **34**, 124–134 (2012). https://doi.org/10.1016/j.csi.2011.06.002
24. Martins, F., Domingos, D.: Modelling IoT behaviour within BPMN business processes. Procedia Comput. Sci. **121**, 1014–1022 (2017). https://doi.org/10.1016/j.procs.2017.11.131
25. Hindel, J., Cabrera, L.M., Stierle, M.: Robotic process automation: hype or hope? In: WI2020 Zentrale Tracks, pp. 1750–1762. GITO Verlag (2020). https://doi.org/10.30844/wi_2020_r6-hindel

26. Turkanović, M., Hölbl, M., Košič, K., Heričko, M., Kamišalić, A.: EduCTX: a blockchain-based higher education credit platform. IEEE Access **6**, 5112–5127 (2018). https://doi.org/10.1109/ACCESS.2018.2789929
27. Ouyang, C., Dumas, M., Aalst, W.M.P.V.D., Hofstede, A.H.M.T., Mendling, J.: From business process models to process-oriented software systems. ACM Trans. Softw. Eng. Methodol. **19**, 2:1–2:37 (2009). https://doi.org/10.1145/1555392.1555395
28. Udokwu, C., Anyanka, H., Norta, A.: Evaluation of approaches for designing and developing decentralized applications. In: Proceedings of the 2020 4th International Conference on Algorithms, Computing and Systems, pp. 55–62 (2020). https://doi.org/10.1145/3423390.3426724
29. Decision Model and Notation Specification Version 1.3. https://www.omg.org/spec/DMN. Accessed 3 Feb 2022
30. Pedersen, A.B., Risius, M., Beck, R.: A ten-step decision path to determine when to use blockchain technologies. MIS Q. Exec. **18**(2), 99–115 (2019)
31. Fuggetta, A.: Software process: a roadmap. In: Proceedings of the Conference on the Future of Software Engineering. pp. 25–34. Association for Computing Machinery, New York (2000). https://doi.org/10.1145/336512.336521
32. Nordsieck, F.: Die Schaubildliche Erfassung und Untersuchung der Betriebsorganisation. Organisation - Eine Schriftenreihe. C. E. Poeschel Verlag, Stuttgart (1932)
33. Genon, N., Heymans, P., Amyot, D.: Analysing the cognitive effectiveness of the BPMN 2.0 visual notation. In: Malloy, B., Staab, S., van den Brand, M. (eds.) SLE 2010. LNCS, vol. 6563, pp. 377–396. Springer, Heidelberg (2011). https://doi.org/10.1007/978-3-642-19440-5_25
34. Michoulis, G., Petridou, S., Vergidis, K.: Verification of academic qualifications through ethereum blockchain: an introduction to VerDe. In: XIV Balkan Conference on Operational Research (BALCOR 2020), Thessaloniki, Greece, pp. 429–433 (2020)

Decision Support Addressing Business and Societal Needs

Strengthening EU Resilience: Labor Market Integration as a Criterion for Refugee Relocation

Anastasia Blouchoutzi[1]([✉]), Georgios Tsaples[2], Dimitra Manou[3], and Christos Nikas[1]

[1] Department of International and European Studies, University of Macedonia,
54636 Thessaloniki, Greece
ablouchoutzi@uom.edu.gr
[2] Department of Business Administration, University of Macedonia,
54636 Thessaloniki, Greece
[3] Faculty of Law, Aristotle University of Thessaloniki, 54124 Thessaloniki, Greece

Abstract. Migrant labor market integration is one of the key areas mentioned in the new EU Action Plan on Integration and Inclusion. Enhanced resilience of the European economy is envisaged through migrant labor market integration which is considered to generate large economic gains, fiscal profits and contributions to national pension schemes and welfare. In view of the new EU Pact on Migration and Asylum, this paper employs the multiple criteria decision making analysis method PROMETHEE to formulate a relocation model for refugees in the EU28, for a period between 2015 and 2019, based on the labor market integration outcomes of the resident migrant population in the EU. The purpose of this paper is to indicate a relocation plan based on migrant labor market integration prospects that could favor the newcomers' sustainable independent living and social inclusion. Under this lens, the legal commitments, and the actual contributions of the Member States to the EU emergency relocation scheme are observed. The suggested decision making approach to relocation allows policy makers to define the preferences and weights of the criteria so as to assure fair sharing of responsibility among the EU countries. The paper provides evidence that countries opposed to the relocation scheme could have been more favorable destinations for the relocation of migrants since 2015.

Keywords: EU relocation · Migrant integration · PROMETHEE

1 Introduction

The relationship between migration, resilience and labor market integration could be described using three tangent circles. Resilience is understood as "the ability of states and societies to reform, thus withstanding and recovering from internal and external crisis" [1]. For this reason, the concept of resilience fits to the management of migration as well. Migrants' self-reliance through their access to the host country's labor market is distinguished as a crucial element of resilience [2]. However, the employment rate for people between 20 and 64 years old in the European Union of 27 member states has been 64.4% for the people born outside the EU, 73.9% for the native-born population

© Springer Nature Switzerland AG 2022
A. P. Cabral Seixas Costa et al. (Eds.): ICDSST 2022, LNBIP 447, pp. 71–83, 2022.
https://doi.org/10.1007/978-3-031-06530-9_6

and 75.3% for other EU citizens [3]. Although a decrease in the skills gaps and an increase in the dynamism of the EU labor market have been attributed to the legally staying migrants as documented in the recently updated Skills Agenda for Europe [4], the employment gap between natives and migrants remains considerable. Nevertheless, since social inclusion has been one of the targets of the Europe 2020 strategy [5], the effective labor market integration of immigrants is a necessary step to achieve resilience towards migration.

The purpose of the current paper is to utilize the Multiple Criteria Decision Aid (MCDA) method PROMETHEE for a period between 2015 and 2019 to formulate an evidence-based relocation model for refugees including labor market integration indicators. In this way, this paper indicates a dispersal plan of refugees among the EU 28 member states that could facilitate migrants' sustainable independent living and social inclusion and analyses the legal commitments and the actual contributions of the Member States to the implemented relocation scheme under this perspective. Moreover, the application of the method allows the policy makers to formulate the decision making analysis under dynamic preferences and weights so as to assure fair sharing of responsibility among the EU member states.

The paper is structured as follows: Sect. 2 provides a short overview of the benefits of migrants' labor market integration in the host country as summarized in the relevant literature. In Sect. 3, the methodology is presented while in Sect. 4 the results are displayed and analyzed. Conclusions and future research avenues are discussed in Sect. 5.

2 Literature Review

The New Pact on Migration and Asylum currently under consideration by the EU leaders with regard to the reform of the Common European Asylum System launches a system of permanent and effective solidarity among EU member states abolishing the Dublin regulation and replacing it by the Asylum and Migration Management Regulation. The new migrant relocation mechanism will replace the one of September 2015 in an effort to resolve the disagreements between EU member states caused by the deficiencies in the planning and implementation of the EU asylum policy. Member States will be distinguished to the benefitting, the contributing and the sponsoring ones promoting a fair sharing of responsibility and a balance of efforts among the 27 EU countries. The population and the GDP of each member state will define the distribution key for their contributions to the mechanism [6].

The ad hoc decision of the EU for the first relocation emergency mechanism followed the arrival of over one million people to Europe in 2015 and escalated the public debate over the dispersal quotas and the impact of migration in the European countries [7]. Greece, Italy and Spain in the Eastern, Central and Western Mediterranean migration route accordingly, have experienced massive inflows of migrants and asylum seekers from the Middle East, South East Asia and Africa during the last years. The unprecedented flows of migrants and asylum seekers in the frontline European Union Member States led to the activation of the emergency response system envisaged under Article 78(3) of the Treaty on the Functioning of the European Union [8] including the distribution among the EU Member States of persons in need of international protection commonly known as "Relocation".

The initial relocation mechanism was based on a decision of the Home Affairs Council of the EU to alleviate the pressure of massive migrant flows in Italy and Greece by distributing them to other Member States into a sharing responsibility framework and entered into force in 15 September 2015 [9]. Apart from the size of the host country's population and its GDP, the relocation mechanism proposed in the Agenda on Migration [10] was also based on two quantifiable and verifiable indicators that reflected the capacity of member states to integrate the refugee population, the unemployment rate and the size of the asylum applications over the previous four years.

The scheme was voluntary with two years duration and referred to applicants that entered the EU borders after 15 August 2015 till 17 September 2017 and came from states with an asylum recognition rate more than 75%. The Asylum, Migration and Integration Fund provided a lump sum of six thousand Euros to the receiving Member States for each relocated person. Denmark and the UK did not participate while Ireland kept the opt in possibility and Norway, Switzerland and Liechtenstein volunteered to the program. In addition to the distribution keys, an extra matching between the applicants' qualifications and cultural and social ties with the Member States was requested [11]. Even so, the mechanism failed to overcome the lack of solidarity within the Dublin system.

Due to the intensification of the migrant flows over the summer 2015, the Commission proposed a second relocation program including people seeking international protection from Italy, Greece and Hungary which had 98,072 asylum applications in 2015 [11]. However, Hungary did not want to participate as a beneficiary to the program. Table 1 presents the legal commitments of the Member States and their actual contribution to the relocation scheme in the framework of responsibility sharing.

Table 1. Member states' contributions to the emergency relocation mechanism [12]

	Legal commitment	Total relocations by 14 November 2017
Germany	27536	9169
France	19714	4699
Spain	9323	1301
Poland	6182	0
Netherlands	5947	2551
Romania	4180	728
Belgium	3812	1059
Sweden	3766	2851
Portugal	2951	1507
Czech Rep.	2691	12
Finland	2078	1980
Austria	1953	15
Bulgaria	1302	50

(*continued*)

Table 1. (*continued*)

	Legal commitment	Total relocations by 14 November 2017
Hungary	1294	0
Croatia	968	78
Slovakia	902	16
Lithuania	671	384
Ireland	600	646
Slovenia	567	232
Luxembourg	557	482
Latvia	481	321
Estonia	329	141
Cyprus	320	143
Malta	131	168
Liechtenstein	–	10
Norway	–	1509
Switzerland	–	1421

As of November 2017, 31,473 people in need of international protection were relocated. The number was much lower than predicted due to the effect of the EU-Turkey statement on the irregular flows in Greece and the eligibility of the asylum seekers arriving in Italy. As it is portrayed in Table 1, there are EU Member States that have not met their obligations. Czech Republic, Poland and Hungary have been referred to the EU Court of Justice in December 2017 due to their non-compliance with the relocation responsibilities [13]. However, all Member States have been encouraged to continue relocations from Italy and Greece besides their legal obligations which extended for a reasonable timeframe after the end of the emergency scheme in September 2017. Till April 2018, the number of relocations increased to 34,563.

Consequently, the issue of migrants' relocation drew the attention of researchers. However, the potential of relocation under the lens of labor market integration hasn't been adequately covered. Moraga and Rapoport [13] suggested the use of a Tradable Refugee Quotas system along with a matching mechanism between refugees or asylum seekers and EU member states that deals with heterogeneity in preferences. Altemeyer-Bartscher et al. [14] argued that the migrant distribution criteria should reflect the cost of their integration in the host countries, efficient distribution keys would balance the marginal cost of integration and compensation payments should be allocated through the EU budget. Carlsen [15] followed a partial order methodology on various combinations of the adjusted net national income, the population size, the unemployment rate and the fragile state index to conclude on the distribution keys for relocation of refugees in the EU. Denmark, Germany, Netherlands, Sweden and UK are in the top-10 list of countries to accommodate larger shares of the newcoming migrant population in the EU according to Carlsen's findings. Embarking upon the conclusion of Carlsen that indicators such as the unemployment rate should be part of the distribution criteria because they indicate the host country's potential for absorption and integration of refugees, we enrich the multiple criteria decision making model with such indicators.

The net fiscal contribution of an immigrant is strongly determined by his/her labor market integration which is usually a win-win situation for the immigrants and for the host country [16]. Migrant labor market integration has been one of the key areas upon which the EU has given emphasis on. In fact, one of the first actions towards fulfilling the commitments of the New Migration Pact, which mentions that there is a necessity for attracting talented people in the EU due to the ageing and shrinking population and the skills shortages, was the adoption of the new Action Plan on Integration and Inclusion 2021–2027 [2], which explains that labor market integration could create large economic and fiscal profits and support national welfare. However, migrant households are considered to be among the most vulnerable and severely hit by the crisis despite their critical role in performing basic functions in EU societies during the pandemic [17]. To this background, this research focuses on illuminating the relocation planning under the labor market integration perspective as one of the most important aspects for effective social inclusion. The indicators about the employment status of the migrant population illustrate the effectiveness of migrant labor market integration reflecting the contribution of other parameters examined in the literature such as the migrants' preferences, their social ties, the fragility of the host country and the fiscal cost of integration.

Multi-criteria decision methods have been employed in migration governance literature and particularly in the area of migrant settlement. Drakaki et al. [18] combined Fuzzy Analytical Hierarchy Process and Fuzzy Axiomatic Design Approach with risk factors as an intelligent multi-agent system to evaluate refugee settlement sitting in Greece. Kuttler et al. [19] focused on the resettlement of environmental migrants across multiple planning periods with the technique for order preference to similarity (TOPSIS). Blouchoutzi et al. [20] employed the PROMETHEE method in policy making to assess the effectiveness of EU member states in the field of social inclusion in the EU as well as in the field of migrant labor market integration [21].

Among the various MCDA methods that have been employed in migration governance, PROMETHEE appears to be particularly suitable; its friendliness-of-use and richness of information that entails mean that the method can be used by policy makers at the higher level to design, structure and justify policies regarding migration. Moreover, the availability of software means that the results are reproducible, increasing their robustness. Finally, decision making on migration is inherently ill-defined, involving multiple stakeholders with diverging objectives, which makes PROMETHEE a natural candidate to use. Consequently, PROMETHEE was used in the context of the current paper and the following sections illustrate those characteristics that support the choice of the method for a refugees' relocation problem.

3 Methodology

PROMETHEE [22] is one of the most widely used outranking MCDA methods. Similar to other methods, it includes a set of alternatives $\{a_1, a_2, \ldots a_i, \ldots a_n\}$ and a set of criteria $\{g_1(*), g_2(*), \ldots g_j(*), \ldots g_m(*)\}$ upon which the alternatives are evaluated.

The alternatives and the criteria form the evaluation table. To represent the preferences of the decision maker, relations are defined as follows:

$$j : g_j(a) \geq g_j(b) \Leftrightarrow aPb \tag{1}$$

$$\exists k : g_k(a) > g_k(b) \Leftrightarrow aPb \tag{2}$$

$$\forall j : g_j(a) = g_j(b) \Leftrightarrow aIb \tag{3}$$

$$\exists s : g_s(a) > g_s(b) \Leftrightarrow aIb \tag{4}$$

P stands for preference, I stands for indifference and R stands for incomparability, where no decision can be made between two alternatives. The upkeep of incomparabilities is one of the characteristics of PROMETHEE and its differentiation element [23].

Apart from the alternatives and the criteria, the decision maker needs to assign weights indicating the relative importance of the criteria, along with the level of deviations between the evaluation of the alternative for each criterion. These deviations are those that determine the preference functions (1)–(4) and are expressed with the following sets of functions:

$$P_j(a, b) = F_j[d_j(a, b)], \forall a, b \in A \tag{5}$$

$$where, d_j(a, b) = g_j(a) - g_j(b) \tag{6}$$

$$and \ for \ which, \ 0 \leq P_j(a, b) \leq 1 \tag{7}$$

Consequently, each criterion is accompanied by information on the preference function that results in a more enriched process. For more information on the preference functions the reader is referred to [22].

The process continues with the aggregation of the preference indices as:

$$\pi(a, b) = \sum_{j=1}^{k} P_j(a, b)w_j \tag{8}$$

$$\pi(b, a) = \sum_{j=1}^{k} P_j(b, a)w_j \tag{9}$$

where a, b belong to the set of alternatives. As it can be observed the value $\pi(a, b)$ is expressing the degree to which alternative a is preferred to alternative b over all the criteria and $\pi(b, a)$ the reverse. The assumption is made that $\pi(a, b) \sim 0$ implies a weak global preference of alternative a over alternative b and $\pi(a, b) \sim 1$ implies a strong global preference of alternative a over alternative b.

This seven steps process [24] concludes with the calculation of the following flows:

$$\varphi^+(a) = \frac{1}{n-1} \sum_{x \in A} \pi(a, x) \tag{10}$$

$$\varphi^-(a) = \frac{1}{n-1} \sum_{x \in A} \pi(x, a) \tag{11}$$

$$\varphi(a) = \varphi^+(a) - \varphi^-(a) = \frac{1}{n-1} \sum_{j=1}^{k} \sum_{x} \left[P_j(a, x) - P_j(x, a)\right]w_j \tag{12}$$

Equation (10) represents the positive outranking flow that expresses how an alternative is outranking all the others (the higher the better). Equation (11) represents the negative outranking flow that expresses how an alternative is outranked by all the others (the lower the better). Finally, Eq. (12) represents the global flow that expresses an overall assessment of an alternative compared to the rest.

In the context of the current paper, the model constructed provides a ranking of the EU 27 member states plus the UK during a five year period, between 2015 and 2019, for the relocation of refugees. The methodology included both the distribution criteria for the EU relocation scheme implemented including population size, GDP and the number of asylum applications submitted in the EU member state under consideration as well as the employment rate, the unemployment rate, the activity rate and self-employment of the foreign (non-EU) persons in private households of the reference member state aged 15–64 years old and they are available in Eurostat [25]. Population refers to the total citizen population of the reference country, GDP is measured in market prices and the asylum applications is the sum of the applications submitted in the previous four years in the reference country as calculated by the authors. Employment rate is the percentage of employed people compared to the total working population, unemployment rate refers to the percentage of unemployed people to the labor force and activity rate indicates the percentage of economically active population including employed and unemployed people to the comparable working population. Self-employment refers to the number of sole or joint owners of unincorporated enterprises that are not at the same time in paid employment, the unpaid family members, the outworkers and the workers producing goods or services for their own final use of capital formation individually or collectively. The labor market integration indicators added in the empirical model are included in the Zaragoza Declaration which was adopted in April 2010 by the EU Ministers responsible for integration [26].

The preferences set in the model include minimum unemployment rate, maximum employment and activity rate, maximum self-employment, maximum population size and GDP and minimum asylum applications per country as portrayed in Table 2. The weights of all the criteria are equal for the purpose of this paper but since they are dynamic, in a deeper policy analysis they could receive different values indicating the most important criterion among them for the policy maker. The function chosen is the Linear one, which requires an indifference threshold q and a preference threshold p. The thresholds in this case were defined following the values of the data.

Table 2. Criteria and information

	Employment rate	Unemployment rate	Activity rate	Self-employment	Population	GDP	Asylum applications
Min/Max	Max	Min	Max	Max	Max	Max	Min
Weight	1	1	1	1	1	1	1
Preference function	Linear	Linear	Linear	Linear	Linear	Linear	Linear
Thresholds	Absolute	Absolute	Absolute	Absolute	Absolute	Absolute	Absolute
Q:indifference	3	3	3	10	1000	50	5000
P:preference	7	7	7	50	5000	150	15000

4 Results

The calculation of the global flows from 2015 to 2019 leads to the preference rankings that are displayed in Table 3 below.

Table 3. Global flows of the PROMETHEE method

2015	2016	2017	2018	2019
Czech Rep.	Czech Rep.	Czech Rep.	Czech Rep.	Poland
UK	UK	Poland	Romania	Czech Rep.
Spain	Italy	UK	UK	UK
Slovakia	Spain	Portugal	Poland	Portugal
Italy	Portugal	Romania	Portugal	Germany
Germany	Poland	Italy	Slovakia	Romania
Romania	Romania	Spain	Italy	Italy
Portugal	Germany	Germany	Spain	Spain
Lithuania	Malta	Malta	Germany	Ireland
Estonia	Ireland	Estonia	Ireland	Lithuania
Slovenia	Estonia	Ireland	Malta	Slovakia
Cyprus	Slovenia	Slovenia	Estonia	Estonia
Hungary	Lithuania	Slovakia	Lithuania	Malta
Poland	Latvia	Latvia	Netherlands	Netherlands
Latvia	Slovakia	Lithuania	Slovenia	Slovenia
Ireland	Netherlands	Netherlands	Latvia	Latvia
Netherlands	France	France	France	France
France	Cyprus	Cyprus	Austria	Hungary

(continued)

Table 3. (*continued*)

2015	2016	2017	2018	2019
Malta	Greece	Denmark	Cyprus	Cyprus
Bulgaria	Denmark	Austria	Denmark	Denmark
Austria	Austria	Greece	Sweden	Austria
Greece	Hungary	Sweden	Croatia	Luxembourg
Denmark	Luxembourg	Hungary	Greece	Sweden
Luxembourg	Sweden	Luxembourg	Luxembourg	Greece
Sweden	Bulgaria	Bulgaria	Hungary	Croatia
Finland	Belgium	Finland	Finland	Belgium
Belgium	Croatia	Belgium	Bulgaria	Finland
Croatia	Finland	Croatia	Belgium	Bulgaria

The most interesting outcomes provided by the ranking are the places received by the Czech Republic and Poland. Although these countries failed to meet their legal obligations following the Council's decision on relocations and adopted a negative stance towards the quotas mechanism proposed, the model introduced in this paper suggests that both countries were favorable places to relocate migrants based on the combination of the EU relocation scheme criteria with the labor market integration outcomes of the already established population in these countries. As portrayed in Table 3, Czech Republic receives the highest place in the ranking for four out of the five years examined. Slovakia, which voted against the second relocation decision, has an above average place for four out of five years examined. On the other hand, Hungary, also a member of the Visegrad 4 rejecting the compulsory relocation mechanism [27], has a below average position after 2015. As regards Austria, whose 18th place in 2018 has been the highest one received in the ranking between 2015 and 2019, the country had an exemption from the emergency mechanism till 2017 due to the 90,000 refugees accepted in the country in 2017.

The case of the Nordic countries is also an interesting one. Finland abstained from voting. Both Finland and Sweden took the necessary actions to receive the relocated migrant population though. Actually, Sweden fulfilled 80% and Finland 95% of their legal obligations as presented in Table 1. However, their place in the ranking from 2015 to 2019 hasn't been satisfying. They are actually among the least preferable alternative countries in the model. Denmark, which reserved the opt out possibility of the emergency scheme under the Treaty, has a higher rank than Finland and Sweden for most of the years but a below average position among the 28 countries.

The UK didn't participate in the scheme either, but it maintains a place high in the ranking. On the other hand, Ireland, with the opt in possibility and an above average position in the ranking after 2015, accepted more people than originally agreed. Slovenia's rank has worsened since 2015 but the government also accepted part of its share in the scheme. Romania achieves a higher rank than Bulgaria. Romania's commitment has been three times higher than Bulgaria's and managed to meet a greater percentage of the relocations expected although it had also voted against the second relocation decision. Croatia being among the least preferable countries in the ranking also participated in the mechanism but in a much lower share than the one committed to. As regards the Baltic countries' ranks, they don't demonstrate large deviations during the years compared to the other EU member states. It should be mentioned that the Baltic countries have fulfilled above 40% of their relocation commitments.

With regard to the European Union founding countries, Germany, which has had an integration strategy since the late 1970s, stands in the first ten places of the ranking. Hence it is reasonable that it accepted the main bulk of the relocations. On the other hand, the score of France, which is considered the oldest European immigration country and second in line receiving a large share of people in need of international protection under the EU emergency relocation scheme, is below average after 2015 and remains consistent. Netherlands, whose integration vision puts the responsibility of integration on the immigrants and accepted the fifth largest share of relocations, has also a low but improving rank. Luxembourg and Belgium do not fulfill the necessary criteria based on their position in the ranking but they have accepted their legal commitments for relocation.

The Mediterranean countries, which have been the main entrance of immigrants to the European Union, have also been included in the model. Greece's and Italy's ranks have worsened after the peak of the migrant crisis in 2015 but Italy has a far better place than Greece besides its restrictive strategy as regards its migration policy. Spain, where migration is considered as generally open and committed to integration [28], also receives a high but downgrading rank. Portugal, being among the ten first countries with the largest relocation commitments, has improved its position since 2015 while the rank of Malta, whose first integration program was launched just in 2018, demonstrates some slight ups and downs. Malta actually received a larger share of migrants than the one committed to while Cyprus, the other big Mediterranean island, admitted half the share it was obliged to. Cyprus's position in the ranking has been downgraded between 2015 and 2019.

Both the mixture of the weights among the criteria and their degrees of preference in PROMETHEE remain upon the choice of the decision maker. As a result the comparative ranking is vulnerable to changes outside certain stability intervals. Table 4 portrays the stability intervals of this model for which the results remain unaffected as produced by a sensitivity analysis which is valuable for policy makers to assess their strategy. In this case study, the intervals are not wide, probably due to the lack of large deviations among the values of the data inserted with each other.

Table 4. Sensitivity analysis

	2015	2016	2017	2018	2019	All
Employment rate	14,20–15,38	13,66–14,36	14,07–14,88	14,02–14,55	12,70–14,38	13,95–14,44
Unemployment rate	12,96–14,29	12,56–14,38	14,21–15,33	14,15–15,16	14,12–14,48	13,87–14,54
Activity rate	14,23–15,47	13,94–14,40	14,13–14,40	13,60–14,51	13,59–14,36	14,02–14,38
Self-employment	14,27–15,77	14,19–14,59	13,62–15,14	13,18–15,12	13,26–14,81	14,11–15,70
Population	14,27–14,75	14,24–14,78	13,89–14,67	13,90–14,59	14,21–14,81	14,20–14,48
GDP	14,18–14,55	14,23–14,49	13,86–14,42	14,14–14,61	14,23–14,59	13,63–14,47
Asylum applications	13,50–14,39	14,14–14,34	12,79–14,36	14,11–14,39	14,00–14,36	14,06–14,75

5 Conclusions

In a period of a polarised political debate in the European Union on the direction of the revised migration governance, this paper suggests an evidence-based decision making approach to the migrants' relocation issue driven, apart from the current criteria, also by labor market integration ones, so as to facilitate the social inclusion of the newcomers and enhance the resilience of the EU towards migration. Combining the preference ranking of the 27 EU Member States and the UK provided by the PROMETHEE method with the decision on the legal obligations for relocations as well as the actual relocations happened in the EU between 2015 and 2019, the paper provides a ground for further research and discussion with regard to the assessment of EU migration governance.

Since employment is a crucial parameter for the social inclusion of people and the employment of the migrants is a priority area for the EU, migrant relocation decisions could be made considering the effectiveness of the member states in integrating the migrant population into their labor markets. The findings suggest that the countries opposed to the relocation scheme could have been more favorable destinations for the relocation of migrants since 2015 if considering also labor market integration criteria. The case study confirms the importance of Germany's contribution in the scheme. However, it doesn't come in accordance with the share attributed to France, Belgium, and Netherlands. Comparing this paper's findings with the previous literature, it should be noticed that the high ranks of Czech Republic and UK are in accordance with the PROMETHEE results in the field of social inclusion provided by Blouchoutzi et al. [20]. On the other hand, the position of Germany in this paper's PROMETHEE ranking is better that it is in the paper of Blouchoutzi et al. [21] which included a preference model constructed only with migrant labor market integration criteria. Both the positions of Germany and UK in the top-10 list of favorable migrant relocation destinations provided in this paper are consistent with the outcomes of Carlsen's methodology [15], but the places of Denmark, Sweden and Netherlands in the ranking do not comply between the two papers.

This paper suggested an analytical approach which allows for the application of dynamic preferences and weights in criteria that serve the EU's policy priorities and a sensitivity analysis to calculate the stability of the policy models. Following such an approach with accurate and updated data inputs from the available EU toolbox could effectively support sound and smart EU migration governance.

Future directions of the research include the analysis of the data with different MCDA and/or Operational Research methodologies, along with the inclusion of different criteria that are not focused on labor market integration such as the preferences of migrants, existing networks in host countries etc. Finally, the combination of these methodologies with different scenaria of migration flows could facilitate policy makers to design robust policies that would anticipate the events.

References

1. European Commission and High Representative of the Union for Foreign Affairs and Security Policy: A Strategic Approach to Resilience in the EU's External Action, JOIN (2017) 21 final, Brussels 7/6/2017
2. European Commission: Action Plan on Integration and Inclusion 2021–2027, COM (2020) 758 final, Brussels 24/11/2020
3. European Commission: Statistics on Migration to Europe. https://ec.europa.eu/info/strategy/priorities-2019-2024/promoting-our-european-way-life/statistics-migration-europe_en. Accessed 04 May 2021
4. European Commission: EUROPE 2020: A strategy for smart, sustainable and inclusive growth, COM (2010), 2020 final, Brussels, 3 March 2010
5. European Commission: European skills agenda for sustainable competitiveness, social fairness and resilience, COM (2020) 274, Brussels, 1 July 2020
6. European Commission: New Pact on Migration and Asylum, COM (2020) 609 final, Brussels, 23 September 2020
7. IOM: Mixed Migration Flows in the Mediterranean and Beyond. Compilation of Available Data and Information. Reporting Period 2015. https://www.iom.int/sites/default/files/situation_reports/file/Mixed-Flows-Mediterranean-and-Beyond-Compilation-Overview-2015.pdf. Accessed 04 May 2021
8. European Union: Consolidated Version of the Treaty on the Functioning of the European Union. Official Journal of the European Union, C326/47 (2012)
9. Council Decision (EU) 2015/1523 of 14 September 2015 establishing provisional measures in the area of international protection for the benefit of Italy and of Greece
10. European Commission: A European Agenda on Migration. COM (2015) 240 final. Brussels, 13 May 2015
11. European Parliament. https://www.europarl.europa.eu/legislative-train/theme-towards-a-new-policy-on-migration/file-1st-emergency-relocation-scheme. Accessed 5 May 2021
12. European Commission: https://ec.europa.eu/home-affairs/sites/default/files/what-we-do/policies/european-agenda-migration/20171114_relocation_eu_solidarity_between_member_states_en.pdf. Accessed 04 May 2021
13. Fernández-Huertas Moraga, J., Rapoport, H.: Tradable refugee-admission quotas and EU asylum policy. CESifo Econ. Stud. **61**(3–4), 638–672 (2015)
14. Altemeyer-Bartscher, M., Holtemöller, O., Lindner, A., Schmalzbauer, A., Zeddies, G.: On the distribution of refugees in the EU. Intereconomics **51**(4), 220–228 (2016). https://doi.org/10.1007/s10272-016-0606-y
15. Carlsen, L.: An alternative view on distribution keys for the possible relocation of refugees in the European Union. Soc. Indic. Res. **130**(3), 1147–1163 (2017)
16. European Commission Directorate General for Economic and Financial Affairs: An Economic Take on the Refugee Crisis - European Economy Institutional Paper 033, Luxembourg (2016)
17. OECD: OECD Employment Outlook 2020: Worker Security and the COVID-19 Crisis, Paris (2020)

18. Drakaki, M., Gören, H.G., Tzionas, P.: An intelligent multi-agent based decision support system for refugee settlement siting. Int. J. Disaster Risk Reduction **31**, 576–588 (2018)
19. Kuttler, E., Cilali, B., Barker, K.: Destination selection in environmental migration with TOPSIS. In: 2021 Systems and Information Engineering Design Symposium (SIEDS), pp. 1–6. IEEE (2021)
20. Blouchoutzi, A., Manou, D., Papathanasiou, J.: A PROMETHEE MCDM application in social inclusion: the case of foreign-born population in the EU. Systems 9 (2021)
21. Blouchoutzi, A., Digkoglou, P., Papathanasiou, J., Nikas, C.: An evaluation on the effectiveness of labor market integration policies in EU member states using PROMETHEE. Int. J. Oper. Res. Inf. Syst. **12**(1), 73–84 (2021)
22. Brans, J.-P., Mareschal, B.: PROMETHEE methods. In: Multiple Criteria Decision Analysis: State of the Art Surveys. ISORMS, vol. 78, pp. 163–186. Springer, New York (2005). https://doi.org/10.1007/0-387-23081-5_5
23. Mareschal, B., Tsaples, G.: The history and future of PROMETHEE. In: Papathanasiou, J., Zaraté, P., Freire de Sousa, J. (eds.) EURO Working Group on DSS. ISIS, pp. 259–272. Springer, Cham (2021). https://doi.org/10.1007/978-3-030-70377-6_14
24. Papathanasiou, J., Ploskas, N.: Multiple Criteria Decision Aid. Methods, Examples and Python Implementations. Springer Optimization and its Applications, vol. 136. Springer, Cham (2017). https://doi.org/10.1007/978-3-319-91648-4
25. Eurostat. https://ec.europa.eu/eurostat/statistics-eplained/index.php?title=Migrant_integra tion_statistics_%E2%80%93_labour_market_indicators. Accessed 04 May 2021
26. Council of the European Union, Declaration of the European Ministerial Conference on Integration. Zaragoza 15–16 April 2010
27. Šabić, S.Š.: The relocation of refugees in the European Union. Friedrich Ebert Stiftung, Zagreb (2017)
28. Arango, J.: Exceptional in Europe? Spain's experience with immigration and integration. Migration Policy Institute, Washington, DC (2013)

Towards an Inclusive Europe: Ranking European Countries Based on Social Sustainability Indicators

Jelena J. Stanković[✉] [iD], Marija Džunić [iD], and Ivana Marjanović [iD]

Faculty of Economics, University of Niš, Trg kralja Aleksandra Ujedinitelja 11, Niš, Serbia
jelena.stankovic@eknfak.ni.ac.rs

Abstract. The aim of the paper is to assess the state of social sustainability throughout European countries, based on the inclusion of various indicators that reflect the social dimension of sustainable growth. Using the methods for creating composite indexes combined with official social statistics, the ranking of European countries based on poverty and social exclusion indicators is provided. The terms poverty and social exclusion refer to various types of social disadvantages, related to the problems such as unemployment, income inequality, material deprivation and the inability to participate in social and political activities. Our analysis enables the evaluation of social sustainability, at the country level, through formation of a composite index that includes all observed indicators. The indicators included in the analysis are classified into three groups: (1) income distribution and monetary poverty, (2) living conditions (health, labour, and housing) and (3) material deprivation. Research is based on the data provided by European Union (EU) statistics on income and living conditions, a comparative statistic on income distribution and social inclusion for EU countries as well as accession candidate countries. The results are based on analysis that includes 33 countries. For the assessment of social sustainability, a multi-criteria analysis model is developed, combining the CRITIC method (CRiteria Importance Through Intercriteria Correlation) for determining the relative importance of criteria and PROMETHEE (Preference Ranking Organization METHod for Enrichment Evaluation) method for ranking countries. The results clearly indicate that candidate countries have a lower level of social sustainability compared to EU countries.

Keywords: Social sustainability · Multi-criteria analysis · Poverty · Social exclusion · Material deprivation

1 Introduction

The problem of measuring poverty and social exclusion is contemporary task among academic researchers and at the same time analytically and operationally relevant topic at all levels of policymaking. The design of indicators is one of the crucial parts in measuring poverty and social exclusion, because of their ability to include all relevant aspects and provide comparability of data both at the regional and at the state level.

© Springer Nature Switzerland AG 2022
A. P. Cabral Seixas Costa et al. (Eds.): ICDSST 2022, LNBIP 447, pp. 84–96, 2022.
https://doi.org/10.1007/978-3-031-06530-9_7

This approach was proposed by [1] in their study on European Union (EU) indicators for social inclusion. In order to make indicators consistent with their purpose, their design needs to be based on a set of following principles: (i) indicators should identify the essence of the problem and have an agreed normative interpretation, (ii) indicators should be robust and statistically validated, (iii) indicators should be interpretable in an international context, (iv) indicators should reflect the direction of change and be susceptible to revision as improved methods become available and (v) the measurement of an indicator should not impose too large a burden on countries, on enterprises, nor on citizens and the design of social indicators should use already available information, wherever possible [2].

A concept that meets all requirements mentioned above and it is accepted by the EU Commission is EU Statistics on Income and Living Conditions (EU-SILC) as an EU survey aiming at collecting timely and comparable cross-sectional and longitudinal multidimensional micro data on income, poverty, social exclusion and living conditions. The main indicator people at risk of poverty or social exclusion (AROPE), consists of the three sub-indicators: (i) monetary poverty, (ii) severe material deprivation and (iii) very low work intensity. Despite the methodological objections that are present in scientific and professional literature in the field of statistics and sampling [3], EU-SILC is still the main, practically the unique, data source for constructing indicators of poverty and social exclusion in the multi-country comparative context of the EU. It is also important to emphasize that EU-SILC, like most other complex population-based surveys, is primarily designed to be representative at the country (rather than at the subnational or regional) level [3].

The aim of this paper is to compare and rank European countries from the aspect of indicators that show measures of poverty, social exclusion and material deprivation. The countries will be ranked according to three groups of criteria, representing different aspects of income distribution and monetary poverty, living conditions such as health, labour, and housing, as well as material deprivation, based on indicators contained in EU-SILC survey. As a result, a country ranking list will be created, pointing to main strengths and difficulties regarding social sustainability in analysed countries.

The structure of the paper includes a brief literature overview of the issues related to measuring social sustainability, after which methodology and data used in the paper are explained. The subsequent section presents the baseline results in the form of a ranking list, while the last section offers some concluding remarks.

2 Literature Review

Social sustainability issues have marked the last decade of policy making, as social environment has become one of the essential determinants of human prosperity. However, there is no generally accepted definition of social sustainability [4]. The lack of a uniform definition of social sustainability stems from the fact that social sustainability has often been seen as an adjunct to economic and environmental sustainability, which have long been considered priority aspects of sustainability. According to [5], the definition of social sustainability must be based on the fundamental values of democracy and equality with respect for all human rights. Social sustainability reflects the possibility of achieving the development goals of a society based on the interconnectedness of all individuals within society, taking into account spatial constraints and the natural environment [6]. Within the concept of sustainable competitiveness, The World Economic Forum defines social sustainability as the set of policies and factors that enable individuals to contribute and benefit from the economic prosperity of the society they live in [7]. Furthermore, social sustainability is closely related to economic sustainability, since the realization of a broader set of human rights is one of the determinants of foreign direct investment, and consequently economic growth [8]. The new approach to economic growth – inclusive growth, insists on its sustainability over decades, its cross-sectoral foundations, creation of new employment and reducing poverty [9]. More specifically, economic growth ought to be cohesive, sustainable, and inclusive and be supposed to ensure prosperity for the whole of Europe [10].

Even though initially neglected, in recent years social sustainability has become particularly important, especially having in mind the growing number of inhabitants on the planet. However, measuring progress towards social sustainability is a challenging task. Namely, in addition to the difficulties in defining social sustainability, there are ambiguities about the criteria that should be taken into account when assessing the concept of social sustainability [11]. The evaluation of sustainability policies in most countries is mainly based on the assessment of individual indicators, which almost inevitably makes it impossible to compare the overall performance with other countries. This is due to the fact that in the case of evaluation of individual indicators, one country may be better than another in one indicator, but worse in another indicator, and it is not possible to objectively compare the two countries. If there is no objective measure that encompasses all dimensions of the multidimensional phenomenon, there is a danger that excessive public attention will be focused on only one or several dimensions [12], which would lead to an utterly erroneous strategic direction of policies [13]. A solution for evaluating multidimensional phenomena can be found in creating composite indices. Composite indices can aggregate several dimensions of data that characterize a complex, multidimensional phenomenon into a single indicator. This makes it possible to compare several countries, as well as to monitor the evolution of an individual country over time. There have been many attempts of constructing aggregate, single measure indicators, based on a number of indicators [14]. Evaluation of different aspects of sustainability was performed using different techniques [15–21], where the main focus of these research is on the evaluation of the economic and environmental dimension of sustainability. However, in the last decade there has been a noticeable increase in the number of studies evaluating the social dimension of sustainability. Including different aspects of social environment is most often achieved by the use of multi-criteria assessment methods [22, 23]. Therefore, in this paper, the sustainability assessment of European countries will be performed using a non-compensatory multicriteria method, the PROMETHEE method.

3   Model Development and Methodology

The paper is aimed to explore and asses social sustainability, at the country level, through formation of a composite measure that includes all various social indicators. The sample of countries included in the research encompasses the EU27 countries, Switzerland,

Norway and four candidate countries for EU accession: North Macedonia, Montenegro, Albania and Serbia. The indicators included in the analysis are grouped into three key areas in relevant for measuring poverty and social exclusion: (1) income distribution and monetary poverty, (2) living conditions (health, labour, and housing) and (3) material deprivation. Each area includes a set of indicators and a total number of observed indicators/criteria is 15 (Fig. 1). Indicators were selected based on a review of the literature, taking into account leading European policies and the availability of data. Research is based on the data provided by Eurostat database and the last year for which complete data are available for all countries in the sample (2019) is used [24]. In addition to the Eurostat database, there are other open databases available online, such as the database of Organization for Economic Co-operation and Development (OECD. Stat) or the World Bank datasets (for example World Development Indicators), however, due to the comprehensiveness, uniformity and greater availability of the data, the authors opted to use only data from the Eurostat database.

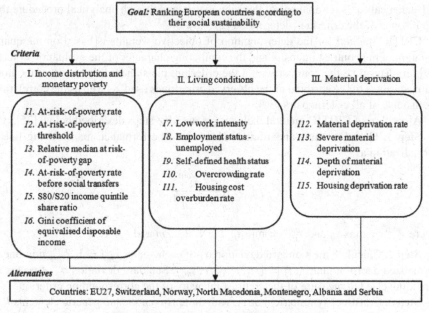

Fig. 1. Hierarchical structure of the model

The creation of composite measures of social sustainability of the observed 33 countries, based on 15 indicators of poverty and social exclusion, is achieved by solving a proposed multi-criteria model. The model is solved by the integrated approach of the CRITIC method for determining the weight coefficients and the PROMETHEE II method for determining the final rank of alternatives.

3.1 Objective Approach to Weights Determination Using CRITIC

The creation of composite measures of social sustainability of the observed 33 countries, based on 15 indicators of poverty and social exclusion, is achieved by solving a proposed multi-criteria model. The model is solved by the integrated approach of the CRITIC method for determining the weight coefficients and the PROMETHEE II method for determining the final rank of alternatives.

CRITIC method (CRiteria Importance Through Intercriteria Correlation) is an objective weight determination method, founded by [25], that belongs to the group of correlation methods and is based on the analytical examination of the decision-making matrix in order to determine the information contained in the criteria for evaluating the alternatives.

The assessment of weights in multi-criteria decision-making problems is a key stage of the whole decision-making process [26]. All weighting coefficients can be classified into two basic groups: subjective methods, based on the modelling of subjective preferences of the decision-maker and objective, based on the application of mathematical and statistical tools for analysis of decision matrix and though analytical procedure the significance of the criteria is determined [27, 28].

CRITIC method for the determination of objective weights is based on the quantification of the contrast intensity and the conflicting character of the evaluation criteria [29]. To determine the contrast within the criterion, the standard deviation of the normalized values of the attribute of the observed criterion is used, as well as the correlation coefficients of all criteria pairs [30].

Algorithm of CRITIC method includes six iterative steps described below [25]:

Step 1. Calculate the standardized values r_{ij} of performance matrix using linear normalization as

$$r_{ij} = \frac{x_{ij} - x_{ij}^{min}}{x_{ij}^{max} - x_{ij}^{min}} \tag{1}$$

where $x_{ij}^{max} = \max_i x_{ij}$ and $x_{ij}^{min} = \min_i x_{ij}$, $i = 1, 2..., m$ and $j = 1, 2..., n$.

Step 2. Calculate the standard deviation σ_j of each vector $r_j, j = 1, 2..., n$ in linear normalized decision matrix, $r_j = (r_{1j}, r_{2j}, ..., r_{mj})$. Standard deviation σ_j of vector r_j is nothing else but measure of the contrast intensity of the corresponding criterion.

Step 3. Construct symmetric matrix, with dimension $n \times n$ and generic elements R_{ij}, which are the linear correlation coefficients between each pair of normalized criteria in the model.

Step 4. Calculating measure of the conflict between criteria through the aggregation formula

$$\sum_{j=1}^{n} (1 - R_{ij}) \tag{2}$$

Step 5. Calculation of amount of information C_j emitted by the jth criterion.

$$C_j = \sigma_j \sum_{j=1}^{n} (1 - R_{ij}) \tag{3}$$

Step 6. Determination of and relative importance, i.e. weight W_j of jth criterion based on C_j values using additive normalization

$$W_j = \frac{C_j}{\sum_{j=1}^{n} C_j} \tag{4}$$

The most commonly used criteria in economics are in the field of finance, or ratio analysis, as well as in all problems where there is a relatively significant correlation between the coefficients of the performance matrix. As indicators of poverty and material deprivation are often relative numbers, the performance matrix of the problem that is solved in this paper fits into the description for the application of the CRITIC method.

3.2 PROMETHEE Outranking Method

PROMETHEE (Preference Ranking Organization METHod for Enrichment Evaluation) is a well-known family of multiple-criteria decision making methods founded by [31]. It is a group of widely applied outranking methods based on pair-wise comparison of the alternatives in accordance to each separate criterion [32].

The algorithm of PROMETHEE method consists from five iterative steps [33]:

Let's assume again the same multi-criteria problem that can be described as

$$\text{Max/Min} \{f_1(a), f_2(a), \dots, f_n(a) | a \in K\}, \tag{5}$$

where K is a finite set of alternatives and $f_j, j = 1, 2, \dots, n$, are k criteria to be maximized or minimized.

Step 1. Determination of deviation between two alternatives a and b $(a, b \in K)$ through the pairwise comparison.

$$d_j(a, b) = f_j(a) - f_j(b), \tag{6}$$

where $d_j(a, b)$ is the difference between the evaluation of alternative a and b on each criterion $j, j = 1, 2, \dots, n$.

Step 2. Application of the preference function

$$P_j(a, b) = F_j[d_j(a, b)], j = 1, 2, \dots, k \tag{7}$$

where $P_j(a, b)$ denotes the preference of alternative a regarding to alternative b on each criterion, as a function of $d_j(a, b)$.

Step 3. Calculation of an overall preference index $\pi(a, b)$, $\forall a, b \in K$

$$\pi(a, b) = \sum_{j=1}^{n} P_j(a, b) w_j \tag{8}$$

Preference index $\pi(a, b)$ of alternative a over alternative b is defined as weighted sum of preference functions $P_j(a, b)$. Relative importance of each criterion in the model is denoted as $w_j, j = 1, 2, \dots, k, \sum_{j=1}^{n} w_j = 1$.

Step 4. Calculation of positive and negative outranking flows φ^+ and φ^- and determination of partial ranking (PROMETHEE I)

$$\varphi^+(a) = \frac{1}{m-1} \sum_{x \in A} \pi(a, x) \tag{9}$$

$$\varphi^-(a) = \frac{1}{m-1} \sum_{x \in A} \pi(x, a) \tag{10}$$

Number of alternatives in the model is denoted as m.

Step 5. Calculation of complete ranking (PROMETHEE II) as a net outranking flow

$$\varphi(a) = \varphi^+(a) - \varphi^-(b) \tag{11}$$

Three PROMETHEE software packages, including PROMCALC, DECISION LAB and Visual PROMETHEE, have been developed to facilitate the implementation of PROMETHEE method. In this paper, all the calculations are performed using Visual PROMETHEE software, academic edition, developed by Bertrand Mareschal.

4　Empirical Data and Analysis

As the sample covers 33 European countries, it is a heterogeneous sample, with substantial disparities in both macroeconomic and social indicators, which are the subject of analysis in this paper. Also, the data included in research include a wide range of data on poverty, material deprivation, and living conditions, so it is needed to present more detailed description and range of values of these data.

When it comes to macroeconomic data, significant differences can be observed between member states and candidate countries. Regarding unemployment rates, average unemployment rate in the sample is 4.5%, and the most of EU27 countries are below or on sample's average when it comes to unemployment data, while candidate countries are quite above the average, with unemployment rates ranging from 6.3% (Serbia) up to 11.5% (Albania). However, even some EU15 countries such as Spain (9.1%) and Greece (10.7%) have unemployment rates in the range of unemployment rates characteristic for candidate countries. When youth unemployment is observed, the average of the sample is 27.5%, with youth unemployment again being highest in the candidate countries. High unemployment rates are characteristic of the labour markets of transition countries and affect older workers with outdated skills and young people alike, as indicated by especially high youth unemployment rates [34]. Unemployment has a certain social cost, which is reflected in many ways [35]: in addition to loss of income, the consequence of lack of employment is reflected in the interruption in the productive role of individuals, and consequently leads to loss of social status and social legitimacy because social contacts and social interaction are developed mainly through participation in the labour market. The problems of unemployment and deprivation became especially pronounced due to the COVID-19 pandemic, during which many temporary and low-skilled workers lost their jobs. The consequences of the pandemic will most likely be reflected in a further increase in inequality and unemployment, and the focus of European countries must be on reducing poverty and social exclusion, as well as providing quality jobs and conditions for training and retraining. Prior to the pandemic, 91 million people were at risk of poverty or social exclusion, but that number rose to 96.5 million in 2020 [36].

Average employment rate in the sample is 72.9% and it is evident that candidate countries North Macedonia, Albania, Montenegro and Serbia, are far below the average of the sample with employment rates ranging from 55.2% (Montenegro) up to 65.9%

(Serbia). On the other hand, the highest employment rates refer to Switzerland (82.5%), the Netherlands (80%) and Nordic countries (Denmark, Sweden and Norway).

The most significant disparities in the sample are visible in the data on median equivalised net annual income (in €), where the ratio between the highest value in Switzerland and the lowest in Albania is almost 18.5. Finally, when it comes to gross domestic product presented as GDP per capita in PPS, (EU27 = 100) it could be concluded that the candidate countries are far below the sample average, with GDP per capita PPS less than 50% of sample average. However, even some member states such as Bulgaria and Greece are quite below the sample average, with GDP per capita PPS less than 70% of sample average. On the other hand, non-EU countries (Norway and Switzerland) are far above the sample average.

Differences are evident in both economic and social indicators in the sample, and the application of the multi-criteria approach allows the aggregate analysis of these indicators and the comparison of countries based on all observed parameters at the same time.

5 Results and Discussion

The first part of the results refers to determining the weight coefficients in the multi-criteria model, i.e., to determining the relative importance of each of the indicators of poverty and social exclusion included in the model. For the purpose of weights determination, the algorithm of CRITIC method is applied.

The results of weights determination based on CRITIC method are given in Table 1. The criterion with highest relative importance is I_2, At-risk-of-poverty threshold ($W_2 = 0.139$), followed by I_9, Self-defined health status and I_4, At-risk-of-poverty rate before social transfers.

Table 1. Relative importance W_j of jth criterion

Indicator	I_1	I_2	I_3	I_4	I_5	I_6	I_7	I_8
W_j	0.061	0.139	0.061	0.083	0.050	0.047	0.067	0.063
Indicator	I_9	I_{10}	I_{11}	I_{12}	I_{13}	I_{14}	I_{15}	
W_j	0.094	0.059	0.067	0.051	0.050	0.051	0.057	

Source: Authors' calculations.

According to PROMETHEE II algorithm, ranking is conducted through calculation of net outranking flow φ as the difference between positive and negative outranking flows φ^+ and φ^- (Table 2).

Table 2. PROMETHEE flow table

Rank	Country	Composite index (φ)	Rank	Country	Composite index (φ)
1	Norway	0.2527	18	Austria	0.0334
2	Slovenia	0.2182	19	Luxembourg	0.0318
3	Czech Republic	0.2153	20	Germany	0.0116
4	Malta	0.1973	21	Croatia	0.0013
5	Finland	0.1501	22	Lithuania	−0.0010
6	Cyprus	0.1317	23	Spain	−0.0020
7	Netherlands	0.1271	24	Sweden	−0.0084
8	France	0.1033	25	Latvia	−0.0284
9	Slovakia	0.1031	26	Italy	−0.0541
10	Estonia	0.0996	27	North Macedonia	−0.2219
11	Switzerland	0.0767	28	Greece	−0.2480
12	Portugal	0.0740	29	Montenegro	−0.2765
13	Poland	0.0577	30	Bulgaria	−0.3009
14	Belgium	0.0569	31	Romania	−0.3010
15	Hungary	0.0527	32	Albania	−0.3162
16	Denmark	0.0450	33	Serbia	−0.3215
17	Ireland	0.0402			

Source: Authors' preview of results generated using Visual PROMETHEE.

Results presented in Table 2 indicate that the highest ranked country with the highest social sustainability is Norway and in context to the previous literature the results is confirming findings given in Global Inequality by [37]. The most of old member states (EU15) have positive values in net outranking flow φ (composite index) according to poverty and social exclusion indicators, which points out their steadily social sustainability. However, several countries in the EU15 group have a negative outranking flow, among which are Italy, Spain, and Greece. At the very bottom of the list there are EU candidate countries, Albania and Serbia, whose data on poverty and social exclusion are the worst and point to seriously high poverty rates, poor living conditions and material deprivation of a significant part of the population. The countries that joined the EU in 2004 have satisfactory results, except two of the Baltic countries that have negative results (Latvia and Lithuania). Member states that have joined the EU in 2007 (Bulgaria and Romania) are at the bottom of the list, which indicates a very low level of social sustainability in these countries. Finally, some relatively good results when it comes to reducing poverty and social exclusion are recorded in Croatia, that has joined the EU in 2013.

The relatively low level of social sustainability of European countries, and especially the old EU member states, is a consequence of the fact that in the previous decades the social dimension of European integration was severely neglected, resulting in harsh and serious social difficulties [38]. Therefore, nowadays EU policies are aimed at eradicating sources of social instability, preventing and eradicating poverty and reducing the development gap [39]. Europe's strategic orientation towards achieving a strong social protection system and improving employment is reflected in the priority areas of the new cohesion policy. One of the main policy objectives of 2021–2027 EU cohesion policy is a more social and inclusive Europe. However, creating a universal policy to reduce poverty and social exclusion is difficult to do due to the specifics of individual countries [40]. Policies need to be adapted to the local level, as it is then possible to make the widest impact [39].

In 2017, the European Commission introduced the European Pillar of Social Rights, which entails a set of social rights and principles and was complemented by a package of proposals to improve social policy and eradicate poverty and social exclusion. It is believed that the application of the European Pillar of Social Rights principles will improve living standards, increase employment and alleviate social difficulties [41]. However, in order to achieve social sustainability, strategies must be aimed at strengthening social policy and social infrastructure, improving labour market conditions, providing trainings for adult population, providing adequate housing conditions, improving access to quality healthcare and access to basic services of sufficient quality [42].

6 Conclusion

Social sustainability is characterized by multidimensionality, which, for policy purposes, is useful to synthesize in one measure on the basis of which it would be possible to quantify the progress of countries towards social sustainability. In this paper, ranking of 33 European countries based on their indicators of poverty and social exclusion was performed. In contrast to the previous literature, our empirical results are obtained using integrated approach of two multi-criteria decision-making methods – CRITIC and PROMETHEE II.

There are significant conclusions drawn in the fact that country of the best social sustainability is not EU country, but Norway, the fact that the process of European integration, do not necessarily mean reducing poverty and social exclusion (Bulgaria, Latvia, Romania, etc.), as well as the fact that candidate countries have a very pronounced problem of social unsustainability. The results further indicate the importance of inclusive growth, since it can be noticed that a high level of economic development is not a necessary precondition for achieving a high level of social sustainability. The obtained results can be the basis for further creation of policies in the social sphere aimed at achieving social sustainability and reducing poverty and social exclusion. Creating adequate policies in the social sphere aimed at reducing poverty, encouraging employment, securing quality health care, providing adequate living conditions and reducing inequality must be a priority of European countries. The introduction of the European Pillar of Social Rights represents a positive step towards achieving social sustainability and, if implemented in compliance with planned legislative measures, can enhance the EU's social image and contribute to improving the social situation of the population [38].

The contribution of the paper is twofold. In theoretical terms, it contributes to the literature on social sustainability, with special emphasis on issues of poverty and social exclusion. The contribution in methodological terms is reflected in the application of the well-known family of ranking methods, PROMETHEE for solving a new kind of problem - the creation of composite indexes of social sustainability, which is a step forward in applying PROMETHEE II method for solving socio-economic problems.

The research faces some limitations. Firstly, the ranking has been conducted based only on data from one year. Further research will focus on analysis that includes longer period of observation, in order to determine the trends of changing individual social policies of countries in the sample and to see the direction of their social (un)sustainability. Secondly, although when choosing the indicators, the authors took into account the availability of data and current European policies, it should be noted that it is important to include a wider range of institutional, social and economic factors in the composite indicator in future research such as [35]: the integration of vulnerable social groups, literacy, education, et cetera.

References

1. Atkinson, T., Cantillon, B., Marlier, E., Nolan, B.: Social Indicators: The EU and Social Inclusion. Oxford University Press, Oxford (2002)
2. Marlier, E., Atkinson. A.B.: Indicators of poverty and social exclusion in a global context. J. Policy Anal. Manag. **29**(2), 285–304 (2010). Special Issue on Poverty Measurement
3. Verma, V., Lemmi, A., Betti, G., Gagliardi, F., Piacentini, M.: How precise are poverty measures estimated at the regional level? Reg. Sci. Urban Econ. **66**, 175–184 (2017)
4. Vallance, S., Perkins, H.C., Dixon, J.E.: What is social sustainability? A clarification of concepts. Geoforum **42**(3), 342–348 (2011)
5. Sachs, I.: Social sustainability and whole development: exploring the dimensions of sustainable development. In: Egon, B., Thomas, J. (eds.) Sustainability and the Social Sciences: A Cross-Disciplinary Approach to Integrating Environmental Considerations into Theoretical Reorientation. Zed Books, London (1999)
6. Colantonio, A.: Social sustainability: exploring the linkages between research, policy and practice. In: Jaeger, C., Tàbara, J., Jaeger, J. (eds.) European Research on Sustainable Development, pp. 35–57. Springer, Heidelberg (2011). https://doi.org/10.1007/978-3-642-19202-9_5
7. Corrigan, G., Crotti, R., Drzeniek Hanouz, M., Serin, C.: Assessing progress toward sustainable competitiveness. In: Schwab, K. (ed.) The Global Competitiveness Report 2014–2015: Full Data Edition, World Economic Forum, Geneva (2014)
8. Lobanova, J.Z., Lobanov, M., Zvezdanović, M.: Governance and civil and political rights as FDI determinants in transition countries. Zbornik Radova Ekonomski Fakultet u Rijeka **39**(1), 59–86 (2021)
9. Ianchovichina, E., Lundstrom, S.: Inclusive growth analytics: framework and application. In: Policy Research Working Paper No. 4851. World Bank, Washington DC (2009)
10. Bachtler, J., Martins, J.O., Wostner, P., Zuber, P.: Towards Cohesion Policy 4.0: Structural Transformation and Inclusive Growth. Routledge (2019)
11. Shirazi, M.R., Keivani, R.: Critical reflections on the theory and practice of social sustainability in the built environment–a meta-analysis. Local Environ. **22**(12), 1526–1545 (2017)
12. Micklewright, J.: Should the UK government measure poverty and social exclusion with a composite index? Centre for Analysis of Social Exclusion, Indicators of Progress: A Discussion of Approaches to Monitor the Government's Strategy to Tackle Poverty and Social Exclusion, CASE Report (13), pp. 45–50 (2001)

13. Rogge, N.: EU countries' progress towards 'Europe 2020 strategy targets.' J. Policy Model. **41**(2), 255–272 (2019)
14. Hak, T., Moldan, B., Dahl, A. (eds.): Sustainability Indicators: A Scientific Assessment, SCOPE, vol. 67. Island Press (2007)
15. Stanković, J.J., Marjanović, I., Papathanasiou, J., Drezgić, S.: Social, economic and environmental sustainability of port regions: MCDM approach in composite index creation. J. Mar. Sci. Eng. **9**(1), 74 (2021)
16. Lindfors, A.: Assessing sustainability with multi-criteria methods: a methodologically focused literature review. Environ. Sustain. Indic. **12**, 100149 (2021)
17. Neto, J., Cunha, M.: Agricultural sustainability assessment using multicriteria indicators and hierarchical tools-a review. Int. J. Sustain. Agric. Manage. Inf. **6**(4), 381–400 (2020)
18. Tian, N., Tang, S., Che, A., Wu, P.: Measuring regional transport sustainability using super-efficiency SBM-DEA with weighting preference. J. Clean. Prod. **242**, 118474 (2020)
19. Dalampira, E.S., Nastis, S.A.: Back to the future: simplifying sustainable development goals based on three pillars of sustainability. Int. J. Sustain. Agric. Manag. Inf. **6**(3), 226–240 (2020)
20. Tajbakhsh, A., Shamsi, A.: Sustainability performance of countries matters: a non-parametric index. J. Clean. Prod. **224**, 506–522 (2019)
21. Rashidi, K., Cullinane, K.: Evaluating the sustainability of national logistics performance using data envelopment analysis. Transp. Policy **74**, 35–46 (2019)
22. Rafiaani, P., et al.: Identifying social indicators for sustainability assessment of CCU technologies: a modified multi-criteria decision making. Soc. Indic. Res. **147**(1), 15–44 (2020)
23. Sierra, L.A., Yepes, V., Pellicer, E.: A review of multi-criteria assessment of the social sustainability of infrastructures. J. Clean. Prod. **187**, 496–513 (2018)
24. Eurostat. The European Union Statistics on Income and Living Conditions (EU-SILC), database 2019. https://ec.europa.eu/eurostat/web/microdata/european-union-statistics-on-income-and-living-conditions. Accessed 20 Jan 2022
25. Diakoulaki, D., Mavrotas, G., Papayannakis, L.: Determining objective weights in multiple criteria problems: the CRITIC method. Comput. Oper. Res. **22**(7), 763–770 (1995)
26. Petrović, J., Radukić, S., Radović, M.: A multicriteria analysis on regional disparity of economic and demographic development in the Republic of Serbia. Econ. Themes **58**(3), 327–342 (2020)
27. Stanković J., Džunić M., Džunić Ž., Marinković S.: A multi-criteria evaluation of the European cities' smart performance: economic, social and environmental aspects. Proceedings of Rijeka Faculty of Economics. J. Econ. Bus. **35**(2), 519–550 (2017)
28. Vasilić, N., Semenčenko, D., Popović-Pantić, S.: Evaluating ICT usage in enterprises in Europe: Topsis approach. Econ. Themes **58**(4), 529–544 (2020)
29. Rostamzadeh, R., Ghorabaee, M.K., Govindan, K., Esmaeili, A., Khajeh Nobar, H.B.: Evaluation of sustainable supply chain risk management using an integrated fuzzy TOPSIS- CRITIC approach. J. Clean. Prod. **175**, 651–669 (2018)
30. Milićević, M.R., Župac, G.Ž: Objektivni pristup određivanju težina kriterijuma. Vojnotehnički glasnik **60**(1), 39–56 (2012)
31. Brans, J.P.: L'ingénierie de la décision; Elaboration d'instruments d'aide à la décision. La méthode PROMETHEE. In: Nadeau, R., Landry, M. (eds.) L'aide à la décision: Nature, Instruments et Perspectives d'Avenir, pp. 183–213. Presses de l'Université Laval, Québec, Canada (1982)
32. Stanković, J.J., Janković-Milić, V., Marjanović, I., Janjić, J.: An integrated approach of PCA and PROMETHEE in spatial assessment of circular economy indicators. Waste Manage. **128**, 154–166 (2021)
33. Brans, J.P., Vincke, P., Mareschal, B.: How to select and how to rank projects: the PROMETHEE method. Eur. J. Oper. Res. **24**(2), 228–238 (1986)

34. Stanković, J.J., Džunić, M., Marinković, S.: Urban employment in post-transition economies: skill mismatch in the local labor market. Zbornik Radova Ekonomski Fakultet u Rijeka **39**(2), 279–297 (2021)
35. Rogge, N., Self, R.: Measuring regional social inclusion performances in the EU: looking for unity in diversity. J. Eur. Soc. Policy **29**(3), 325–344 (2019)
36. Eurostat: One in five people in the EU at risk of poverty or social exclusion. https://ec.eur opa.eu/eurostat/web/products-eurostat-news/-/edn-20211015-1. Accessed 20 Jan 2022
37. Milanovic, B.: Global Inequality - A New Approach for the Age of Globalization. Harvard University Press (2015)
38. Garben, S.: The European pillar of social rights: effectively addressing displacement? Eur. Const. Law Rev. **14**(1), 210–230 (2018)
39. Łuczak, A., Kalinowski, S.: Assessing the level of the material deprivation of European Union countries. PLoS ONE **15**(9), e0238376 (2020)
40. Carella, B., Graziano, P.: Back to the future in EU social policy? Endogenous critical junctures and the case of the European pillar of social rights. JCMS: J. Common Market Stud. (2021)
41. Hacker, B.: A European social semester? The European pillar of social rights in practice. The European Pillar of Social Rights in practice (June 12, 2019). ETUI Research Paper-Working Paper (2019)
42. EPSR: The European pillar of social rights action plan. https://op.europa.eu/webpub/empl/european-pillar-of-social-rights/en/#chapter2. Accessed 30 Jan 2022

Decision Support Ecosystems: Definition and Platform Architecture

Jonas Kirchhoff[✉], Christoph Weskamp, and Gregor Engels

Department of Computer Science, Paderborn University, Paderborn, Germany
{jonas.kirchhoff,christoph.weskamp,engels}@upb.de

Abstract. Decision support systems are crucial in helping decision makers to quickly identify optimal business decisions in increasingly volatile and complex business environments. However, the ideal DSS for one decision maker may not optimally address the requirements for decision support of another decision maker. This is due to differences between decision makers in business goals, regulatory restrictions or availability of resources such as data. By using a suboptimal DSS, decision makers risk implementing suboptimal decision recommendations which endanger the success of their business. This presents DSS developers with the challenge to implement a customizable DSS which can be tailored to the individual requirements for decision support of a single decision maker. In order to address this challenge, we suggest a *decision support ecosystem* in which DSS developers, decision makers and other domain experts collaborate using a shared platform to provide and combine reusable decision support services into a tailored DSS. The contribution of our paper is twofold: First, we define the concept of a decision support ecosystem with respect to existing digital business ecosystems and discuss expected benefits and challenges. Second, we present a reference architecture for a shared platform supporting the realization of a decision support ecosystem. We demonstrate our contributions in the example application domain of regional energy distribution network planning.

Keywords: Decision support ecosystem · Ecosystem platform · DSS generator · Multi-enterprise DSS · Collaborative DSS

1 Introduction

Business environments exhibit an increasing volatility, uncertainty, complexity and ambiguity (VUCA). Decision makers must therefore consider frequent, unpredictable change in many influencing factors with unknown cause-effect relationships when making a decision [1,13]. This circumstance creates a demand for interactive computer-based decision support systems (DSS) to help decision makers quickly identify optimal decisions [16,20,23].

Partially supported by the European Regional Development Fund (ERDF) through grant EFRE-0801186 and the North Rhine Westphalian Ministry of Economic Affairs, Innovation, Digitalisation and Energy (MWIDE) through grant 005-2011-0022.

© Springer Nature Switzerland AG 2022
A. P. Cabral Seixas Costa et al. (Eds.): ICDSST 2022, LNBIP 447, pp. 97–110, 2022.
https://doi.org/10.1007/978-3-031-06530-9_8

In the context of an interdisciplinary research project for decision support in the domain of regional energy distribution network planning with industry partners [10], we observed that the requirements for decision support vary between individual decision makers. For instance, decision makers can only leverage a cross-sectoral planning approach when they actually manage distribution networks for multiple energy sectors. Decision makers furthermore may have different targets with respect to metrics such as network reliability and network reinforcements costs. Moreover, decision makers have different access to resources such as forecast data or time available to identify an optimal decision. Similar observations can be made in the domain of supply chain management [23,25] and business model development [8]. A misalignment in the requirements for decision support derived from the situational context of an individual decision maker and the decision support provided by a DSS is expected to result in suboptimal decision recommendations. The implementation of those recommendations can endanger the competitiveness of the associated business or even negatively impact society as a whole in case the business manages critical infrastructure. Consequently, DSS developers need to implement each DSS so that it can be tailored to the individual requirements of decision makers derived from business goals, constraints and availability of resources. However, such customization is often lacking in existing "off-the-shelf" DSS and retrospective extensions are usually a cost- and time-intensive undertake. This circumstance raises the research question: *How to provide decision makers with decision support systems tailored to their individual requirements for decision support in a timely manner?*

Existing state of the art in the domain of decision support and software engineering is only partially suitable for the adhoc creation of tailored DSS (cf. Sect. 2). In this paper, we therefore propose the concept of a *decision support ecosystem* in which decision makers, DSS developers and domain experts collaborate using a shared platform to document individual requirements for decision support functionality and to provide reusable software and data services that can be combined to implement such functionality without extensive software development knowledge. By assembling reusable services without software development knowledge, we expect decision makers to be able to quickly create tailored DSS themselves. Our contribution towards such decision support ecosystem is twofold: First, we provide a definition for decision support ecosystems and discuss their expected benefits and challenges with respect to existing digital business ecosystems (cf. Sect. 3). Second, we describe a reference architecture for the shared platform of a decision support ecosystem (cf. Sect. 4) and explain future research that is required to implement such a platform and other aspects of decision support ecosystems (cf. Sect. 5).

2   State of the Art and Related Work

A **DSS generator** is an "environment for developing an application-specific DSS" by providing "tools that make it easier and faster to develop models, data, and user interfaces that are customized to the application's requirements" [2].

DSS generators historically require knowledge in mathematical modeling [2] which cannot be expected from decision makers and domain experts [20], thereby leaving any tailoring up to the DSS developer. A search on Clarivate's *Web of Science* for publications implementing DSS generators throughout the last ten years reveals a narrow focus on maps [11], spreadsheets [20] or software developers [12]. **Adaptive DSS** adapt support to "the high-level cognitive needs of the users, task characteristics, and decision contexts" [7]. While this adaptation can consider a decision maker's situational requirements for decision support, the run-time adaptation only works to the extent that was considered up-front by the DSS developer during design-time. **Multi-Enterprise Collaborative DSS** aim to provide decision makers with "decision making components (e.g., data, models, solvers and data and process visualizations)" across multiple enterprises [23]. However, existing approaches either focus on a single application domain (e.g., [26]), the selection of data sources or software functionality without recombination (e.g., [23,24]) or uniting decision makers from multiple enterprises without any customization of decision support [6]. **Service-oriented DSS** [5] provide a conceptual framework for DSS development that targets software engineers, not decision makers or domain experts with limited to no software development knowledge (although these stakeholders may be partially supported using automated service composition [16]). **LowCode- and NoCode-platforms** have emerged as model-driven approaches to enable non-developers to create software applications [19], but without a specific focus on decision support.

3   Decision Support Ecosystem Concept

In this section, we derive the concept of a *decision support ecosystem (DSE)* from existing digital business ecosystems and discuss expected benefits and challenges of DSEs in providing tailored decision support in a timely manner.

3.1   Decision Support Ecosystem Definition

A *digital business ecosystem* is a "socio-technical environment of individuals, organisations and digital technologies with collaborative and competitive relationships to co-create value through shared digital platforms" [22]. The socio-technical entities of a digital business ecosystem are visualized in Fig. 1: A *platform provider* provides and maintains a *shared digital platform* on which *service providers* offer their services. *Service consumers* query the platform to obtain and combine services into a *product* which satisfies the demands of *end users*. In this setting, value (i.e., any financial or nonfinancial benefit [22]) is created for service providers by allowing them to advertise their services via the shared platform, for service consumers by discovering and combining services to implement business ideas more quickly [22], and for end users by being provided with products that satisfy their (individual) demands.

The concept of a digital business ecosystem can be refined based on the types of services which are exchanged via the shared platform. For instance, in

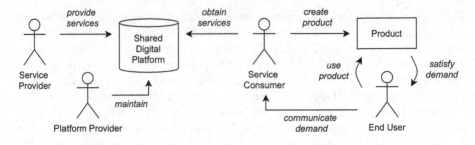

Fig. 1. Overview of entities in a digital business ecosystem

software ecosystems, the services can be software components or applications
using a common technology. An example is the *Microsoft Windows* operating
system, where developers can provide frameworks utilized by other developers
for the development of applications used by end users [3]. In a *data ecosystem*,
the primary resource exchanged between platform users is data, but also related
resources such as software for data manipulation or infrastructure for data per-
sistency and software execution [18]. Data ecosystems are for instance used in a
governmental context to support regulators in policy making [17,18].

The concept of a digital business ecosystem can be applied to the domain of
decision support as follows: The product is a *DSS* which is tailored according
to the requirements of an individual end user, i.e., *decision maker*. The DSS
is assembled using *decision support services* provided by *decision support service providers*. Similar to the previous explanation of data ecosystems, we expect
decision support services to include data, software and computing infrastructure.
In the exemplary domain of energy distribution network planning, data might be
a forecast of electric vehicle market shares, software might be an algorithm for
load forecasting or the optimization of network reinforcements, and infrastructure a high-performance cluster to execute the optimization algorithm. The role
of the *service provider* can be assumed by DSS developers who extract reusable
functionality from their existing DSS, but also from domain experts such as
research institutions or consulting agencies for software and data services as well
as cloud providers for infrastructure services. The role of the *service consumer*
should ideally be assumed by decision makers using an "end user programming"
approach [3] to ensure timeliness of decision support. Assuming that decision
makers can communicate their requirements for decision support, the role could
also be assumed by DSS developers or domain experts to establish best practices.

As a consequence of the previous explanations and our initially formulated
research question, we define a *decision support ecosystem* as follows:

*A decision support ecosystem (DSE) is a network of decision makers, DSS
developers and domain experts who share requirements for decision support and decision support services (including software, data and computing infrastructure) via a shared digital platform which enables the adhoc
composition and execution of decision support services without extensive*

software development knowledge to quickly and optimally address an individual decision maker's requirements for decision support.

3.2   Expected DSE Benefits and Challenges

By deriving our concept of a decision support ecosystem from digital business ecosystems, in particular software and data ecosystems, we can expect some of their benefits and challenges to translate to DSEs as well.

Benefit 1 – Mass-Customization: By combining existing services into a DSS, the DSE concept shares similarities with software product lines [3] and enables the development of "a diversity of similar applications" at "lower cost, in shorter time, and with higher quality when compared with the development of single systems" [14]. Combining services offered via the shared platform ensures that all companies, regardless of their research and development budget, can cooperate to fulfill the high demand for customization by users [3].

Benefit 2 – Faster Time-to-Market: The combination of existing services does not only lower development costs, but also results in a faster time-to-market [14]. Consequently, decision makers are able to use the DSS sooner. This benefit is increased when decision makers can apply the customizations themselves, e.g., following an end-user programming approach [3].

Benefit 3 – Innovation: Digital business ecosystems foster innovation [9]. When decision makers and DSS developers exchange their challenges and solution approaches for decision making, we can expect decision makers to profit from new, innovative decision support services. Simultaneously, decision support service providers can receive feedback for their services and use it to improve services or identify new business opportunities [18]. Furthermore, decision makers do not only profit from newly developed services, but also from discovering existing services, especially data, which they can utilize for decision making [18].

These benefits immediately align with our initially formulated research question of providing decision makers with tailored decision support in a timely manner. Nevertheless, an ecosystem approach also introduces challenges:

Challenge 1 – Participation: Value creation based on providing and consuming services in ecosystems only works when enough stakeholders participate in the ecosystem [3,9,17]. This requires low entry barriers to encourage participation in the ecosystem [9]. In case of supporting customization by end users, this also includes identifying sufficient abstractions to ensure that end users can intuitively create service-based applications without being limited in the complexity of the applications [3,18]. Moreover, a governing entity is needed to support service quality [17] and to ensure the sustainability of the ecosystem [9]. A further concern, especially with respect to data, is the consideration of privacy and confidentiality as not every service provider may want to make all of their services publicly available [17].

Challenge 2 – Platform Design: The underlying shared platform of an ecosystem is a deciding factor to what extent the aforementioned ecosystem benefits can be utilized while minimizing the effects of the described challenges [22]. Unfortunately, there is still a lack of technical knowledge and resources to implement such platform [17,22], especially in the context of decision support.

4   DSE Platform Architecture

The previous section introduces the concept of a decision support ecosystem and discusses its potential benefits and challenges. A particular challenge is the design of the shared platform as key enabler of any ecosystem [22]. In this section, we therefore propose a technological reference architecture for a shared DSE platform. We expect this reference architecture to guide DSE platform implementation in multiple application domains, thereby proving the technical feasibility of DSEs and encouraging future DSE research, e.g., DSE governance.

4.1   Research Approach

We document our reference architecture for a shared DSE platform in form of design principles, i.e., propositions for platform components, user roles and their interactions which can be tailored to a specific application domain. We use the supportive approach described by Möller et al. [15] for the identification of design principles. For this purpose, we first collect meta-requirements which document fundamental functionality requirements of any DSE platform regardless of a specific application domain. We use our experience from the aforementioned research project and the discussion of the DSE concept in the previous sections as a knowledge base for meta-requirement identification. The design principles are subsequently derived as a response to address the meta-requirements. For evaluation purposes, we subsequently demonstrate the design principles in the exemplary application domain of energy distribution network planning.

4.2   DSE Platform Meta-requirements

We identified the following meta-requirements for the shared DSE platform:

MR1 – *Common Terminology*. The ambiguity of VUCA business environments [1,13] creates the need to establish a common terminology across ecosystem participants. It must therefore be possible to document the entities of the associated application domain as well as potential alternatives among decision makers' goals, restrictions and resources when making a decision. For the exemplary domain of energy distribution network planning, an entity would be a regional electricity network which incurs investment and operating costs that should be minimized while power outages must be avoided. In addition to its primary purpose of establishing a common understanding, the documentation can also be used by ecosystem participants to identify decision making use cases.

MR2 – *Individuality of Decision Support Requirements.* The requirements for decision support vary between individual decision makers, even for the same type of decision within an application domain [10,23]. It is therefore necessary to document and consider the individual requirements of decision makers throughout the DSE.

MR3 – *Discoverability of Decision Support Services.* The fundamental idea of business ecosystems is to co-create value by providing and consuming services [22]. In the DSE context, service discoverability helps to find those decision support services that best align with an individual decision maker's requirements for decision support. From a service provider's point of view, the visibility of an offered decision support service likely results in economic gain. The technical platform of a DSE must therefore support the discoverability of decision support services, i.e., software, data, infrastructure. However, limiting discoverability can also be desired in certain cases, either to ensure privacy and confidentiality to avoid the misuse of personal data [17] (e.g., historical electricity consumption per household), or to delay access to innovative decision support services as a means to keep an advantage over direct competitors.

MR4 – *Holistic Decision Support Process.* Due to the complexity of business environments [1,13], identifying a decision recommendation is a multi-stage process with potentially multiple activities for the selection, preparation, manipulation, analysis and visualization of data. By definition, a single decision support service can and should not cover all of these activities to foster reusability. Consequently, multiple "single-purpose" decision support services must be combined to represent a holistic decision support process. In this context, it is important to ensure the correctness of information exchange between decision support services, otherwise the decision support may fail due to technical errors.

MR5 – *Timeliness of Decision Support.* The volatility of business environments requires decision makers to identify optimal decisions in a short amount of time [23]. The available time should therefore not be spent waiting for the individualized DSS, but instead actually using the DSS. Consequently, both the previously mentioned assembly of decision support services into an individualized decision support process as well as its subsequent utilization must be fast. From a decision maker's point of view, participation of other ecosystem stakeholders such as DSS developers should be minimized for this purpose.

MR6 – *Experience & Innovation.* Once the tailored decision support has been used by a decision maker, it can be rated considering for instance alignment with requirements for decision support, quality of decision recommendations or quality of individual decision support services. On the one hand, such feedback helps selecting a decision support service among multiple alternatives or identifying which service assemblies best address certain requirements for decision support. This naturally requires some kind of traceability to track which decision support services were selected based on which requirements. On the other hand, the feedback can be used by service providers to improve their decision support services [18] or identify functionality gaps to be filled by additional services.

4.3   DSE Platform Design Principles

We identified the following DSE platform design principles for architectural components, user roles and their interaction as a response to address the previously described meta-requirements. An overview of the reference architecture is given in Fig. 2. Note that each DSE participant can potentially assume multiple roles.

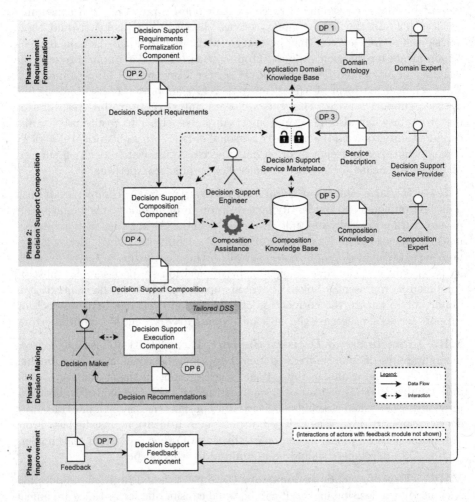

Fig. 2. Proposed reference architecture for the shared platform of a DSE

DP1 – *Application Domain Knowledge Base.* We expect *domain experts* to capture entities of the application domain and decision making characteristics with respect to these entities in the form of formal *domain ontologies*. The domain ontologies are aggregated into a *application domain knowledge base* to establish a common terminology between ecosystem participants for other architecture components, thereby addressing MR1 – *Common Terminology*.

DP2 – *Decision Support Requirements Formalization*. Individual decision makers use the *decision support requirements formalization component* to formally document their individual requirements for decision support based on the *application domain knowledge base*. The requirements documentation is used in other components to ensure that the created decision support aligns with a decision maker's requirements, thereby partially addressing MR2 – *Individuality of Decision Support Requirements*.

DP3 – *Decision Support Service Marketplace*. *Decision support service providers* make their *decision support services* available via a central *service marketplace*. For this purpose, they have to provide a *service description*. Based on the *application domain knowledge base*, the service description includes information about the service's functionality, resource requirements, guarantees (i.e., with respect to availability) and how to invoke the service. The service marketplace is divided into a *public* and a *private* section to control whether a service is available to all or just a limited subset of ecosystem participants. The service marketplace addresses MR3 – *Discoverability of Decision Support Services*.

DP4 – *End-User Decision Support Composition*. A *decision support composition* describes how to integrate multiple decision support services to address all activities of a decision support process. The composition is created using the *decision support composition component* based on the requirements for decision support specified by an individual decision maker and the decision support services made available via the *decision support service marketplace*. The *composition component* is primarily operated by a *decision support engineer*. Despite the reference to "engineer" in the role title, we do not expect this actor to have a software engineering or software development background. Instead, we suggest to design the composition in a way that allows end-user programming, following a low-code or no-code development paradigm [19]. The role of the *decision support engineer* could thereby be assumed by decision makers or other domain experts. The decision support composition addresses MR2 – *Individuality of Decision Support Requirements*, MR4 – *Holistic Decision Support Process* and MR5 – *Timeliness of Decision Support*.

DP5 – *Knowledge-Based Composition Assistance*. The *composition assistance* is a digital assistance system that also interacts with the *decision support composition component* in order to support the *decision support engineer* during service composition. The composition assistance may ensure the consideration of best practices or anti-patterns for decision support in the application domain. For this purpose, it utilizes a *composition knowledge base* which is filled by domain experts. The knowledge-based assistance partially addresses MR5 – *Timeliness of Decision Support* and MR6 – *Experience & Innovation*.

DP6 – *Decision Support Execution*. The created *decision support composition* is forwarded to the *decision support execution component*. The component orchestrates the services as specified by the composition. By automating this orchestration, the invocation of the included services is transparent to the decision maker, i.e., from the point of a decision maker, they still interact with a "traditional" DSS. This includes the decision maker specifying assumptions or being able to inspect decision recommendations, e.g., by using interactive visualizations. The automated execution addresses MR4 – *Holistic Decision Support Process* and MR5 – *Timeliness of Decision Support*.

DP7 – *Decision Support Feedback*. Before, during or after execution of a decision support composition, the decision maker may provide *feedback* for the provided decision support. All stakeholders can view this feedback via the *feedback module* and use it to improve their contribution to the DSE. Most importantly, domain experts can identify new composition knowledge. Service providers can analyze room for improvements in their provided decision support services or identify a demand for new services. Decision support engineers can update a composition if they failed to address a requirement for decision support or decision makers can update their requirements if they misunderstood the requirements formalization – an indicator for domain experts to improve the descriptions in the *application domain knowledge base*. These feedback-based improvements address MR6 – *Experience & Innovation*.

4.4   Demonstration for Energy Distribution Network Planning

Ideally, one would implement the platform reference architecture described by the previous design principles for a concrete application domain to evaluate its practicability (cf. "field-testing" in [15]). However, this requires additional refinement of individual architecture components, e.g., (1) adapting existing approaches for the formalization of requirements, services and service compositions to decision support, (2) assessing and adapting low-code platforms for the use of these formalizations, and (3) the formalization, extraction and consideration of composition knowledge via the composition assistance. As these research problems are out of scope for this paper, we defer the field-test to future work and instead demonstrate the application of platform components with an experience-based example in the domain of energy distribution network planning.

In our example application derived from [10], we consider decision recommendations for the reinforcement of regional electricity distribution networks. With respect to **DP1 – *Application Domain Knowledge Base***, an electricity network is characterized by capital and operational costs, electrical loads of buildings connected to the network, and a redundancy strategy which describes how many transformers in the network may simultaneously fail without impacting the functionality of the network. Building loads can describe historical or expected future loads. With respect to **DP3 – *Decision Support Service Marketplace***, we consider the following services:

1. `LF-Scale`: Computes expected future building loads by multiplying current loads with a constant scaling factor.

2. `LF-Extrapolation`: Computes expected future building loads by extrapolating the historical loads of the last 5 years.
3. `LF-Technology`: Computes expected future building loads by predicting which building might adopt which consumer technology (e.g., electric vehicle, charging station, heat pump). Has a longer runtime than other LF services.
4. `Marketshares`: Data with expected future consumer technology market shares.
5. `OPT-Exact`: Receives an electricity network with expected future loads and uses a mathematical exact optimization algorithm to recommend transformers which should be replaced to support loads while minimizing costs. Considers network redundancy, i.e., one transformer might fail without impacting network reliability. Requires a high-performance cluster to be executed. Runtime scales exponentially in the number of loads to consider. Guarantees that the found optimum equals the theoretical optimum (100% optimality).
6. `OPT-Heuristic`: Similar to `OPT-Exact`, but uses a heuristic optimization algorithm which runs on commodity hardware bundled with the service. Does not support redundant network design. Runtime scales linearly in the number of building loads to consider. Only guarantees 80% optimality.
7. `HPC`: High-Performance Cluster inducing high costs when used.
8. `NR-Reduce` Reduces the size of a provided electricity network by intelligently aggregating building loads.
9. `NR-Revert` Reverts a network reduction by translating all reinforcement recommendations from the reduced network to the original electricity network.

With respect to **DP2 – *Decision Support Requirements Formalization***, we consider two distribution network operators (DNOs) who want to optimize their electricity network. The first DNO documents that they want a cost-minimizing, redundant electricity network and are not constrained in monetary or temporal resources. The second DNO documents that they also want a cost-minimizing, redundant network but are very limited in resources. With respect to **DP4 – *End-User Decision Support Composition***, the first DNO might initially combine the services `LF-Extrapolation` and `OPT-Exact` services. With respect to **DP5 – *Knowledge-Based Composition Assistance***, the composition assistance might point out that the `OPT-Exact` service is missing the `HPC` service and that experience shows that the `LF-Technology` service, albeit more expensive, provides a better load forecast than the `LF-Extrapolation` service. The first DNO can accept these improvements and the composition can be executed automatically. The second DNO might initially combine the `LF-Extrapolation` and `OPT-Heuristic` services to not violate any resource constraints. The composition assistance might point out that the decision maker is missing the historical load data required for the `LF-Extrapolation` service and that the `LF-Scaling` service could be used instead. Furthermore, the `OPT-Heuristic` service does not align with the documented requirement of network redundancy. Instead, the second DNO can apply a network reduction with the `NR` services and utilize the `OPT-Exact` service. **DP6 – *Decision Support Execution*** may be automated by providing the services as web services and invoking them via a workflow engine. In the context of **DP7 – *Decision Support Feedback***, the second DNO may have forgotten to revert the network reduction and the composition knowledge can be updated to reflect that the use of the NR-Reduce service implies that the NR-Revert service must be invoked sometime later. Any DNO may communicate demand for decision support functionality which is currently not considered, e.g., the identification of robust reinforcement recommendations across multiple potential future load scenarios.

5   Summary and Future Work

Decision support systems are crucial in helping decision makers to quickly identify optimal decisions in VUCA business environments. However, the identification of optimal decisions requires decision support that is quickly tailored to the individual requirements of decision makers with consideration of their goals and constraints during decision making. The state of the art in decision support and software engineering only partially supports the creation of tailored decision support in a timely manner. We therefore discussed the concept of a decision support ecosystem which allows DSS developers, decision makers and domain experts to collaborate using a shared platform to provide and consume digital decision support services, i.e., software, data and infrastructure. In this context, we presented a reference architecture for the shared platform of a DSE characterized by the assisted end-user composition of decision support services which are available from a central service marketplace.

During the demonstration of the reference architecture, we already presented aspects of individual architecture components that require additional research before the platform can be implemented for a concrete application domain. In future research, we want to address these research questions and subsequently evaluate our presented DSE concept in form of a field-test by implementing the reference architecture for energy distribution network planning. Inspired by digital business ecosystems, additional future work may focus on transitioning into a DSE (cf. [3,22]), governing a DSE to ensure its health and sustainability (cf. [9,18,21,22]) or supporting DSE research, e.g., by modeling DSEs (cf. [4]).

References

1. Bennett, N., Lemoine, G.J.: What a difference a word makes: understanding threats to performance in a VUCA world. Bus. Horiz. **57**(3), 311–317 (2014)
2. Bhargava, H., Sridhar, S., Herrick, C.: Beyond spreadsheets: tools for building decision support systems. Computer **32**(3), 31–39 (1999)
3. Bosch, J.: From software product lines to software ecosystems. In: Proceedings of the 13th International Software Product Line Conference, pp. 111–119. Carnegie Mellon University (2009)
4. Boucharas, V., Jansen, S., Brinkkemper, S.: Formalizing software ecosystem modeling. In: Proceedings of the 1st International Workshop on Open Component Ecosystems, IWOCE 2009, pp. 41–50. ACM (2009)

5. Demirkan, H., Delen, D.: Leveraging the capabilities of service-oriented decision support systems: putting analytics and big data in cloud. Decis. Support Syst. **55**(1), 412–421 (2013)
6. Drissen-Silva, M.V., Rabelo, R.J.: A collaborative decision support framework for managing the evolution of virtual enterprises. Int. J. Prod. Res. **47**(17), 4833–4854 (2009)
7. Fazlollahi, B., Parikh, M.A., Verma, S.: Adaptive decision support systems. Decis. Support Syst. **20**(4), 297–315 (1997)
8. Gottschalk, S., Yigitbas, E., Nowosad, A., Engels, G.: Situation- and domain-specific composition and enactment of business model development methods. In: Ardito, L., Jedlitschka, A., Morisio, M., Torchiano, M. (eds.) PROFES 2021. LNCS, vol. 13126, pp. 103–118. Springer, Cham (2021). https://doi.org/10.1007/978-3-030-91452-3_7
9. Jansen, S., Cusumano, M.A.: Defining software ecosystems: a survey of software platforms and business network governance. In: Software Ecosystems. Edward Elgar Publishing (2013)
10. Kirchhoff, J., Burmeister, S.C., Weskamp, C., Engels, G.: Towards a decision support system for cross-sectoral energy distribution network planning. In: Energy Informatics and Electro Mobility ICT (2021)
11. Kita, P., Szczyrba, Z., Fiedor, D., Letal, A.: Recognition of business risks when purchasing goods on the internet using GIS: experience from Slovakia. Electron. Commer. Res. **18**(3), 647–663 (2017)
12. Liang, Z., Jia, X.: The technical system establishment and application of decision support system generator based on component coordination. In: 2014 Seventh International Symposium on Computational Intelligence and Design, vol. 1, pp. 229–233 (2014)
13. Mack, O., Khare, A.: Perspectives on a VUCA world. In: Mack, O., Khare, A., Krämer, A., Burgartz, T. (eds.) Managing in a VUCA World, pp. 3–19. Springer, Cham (2016). https://doi.org/10.1007/978-3-319-16889-0_1
14. Metzger, A., Pohl, K.: Software product line engineering and variability management: achievements and challenges. In: Future of Software Engineering Proceedings, pp. 70–84. ACM (2014)
15. Möller, F., Guggenberger, T.M., Otto, B.: Towards a method for design principle development in information systems. In: Hofmann, S., Müller, O., Rossi, M. (eds.) DESRIST 2020. LNCS, vol. 12388, pp. 208–220. Springer, Cham (2020). https://doi.org/10.1007/978-3-030-64823-7_20
16. Mustafin, N., Kopylov, P., Ponomarev, A.: Knowledge-based automated service composition for decision support systems configuration. In: Silhavy, R., Silhavy, P., Prokopova, Z. (eds.) CoMeSySo 2021. LNNS, vol. 231, pp. 780–788. Springer, Cham (2021). https://doi.org/10.1007/978-3-030-90321-3_63
17. Oliveira, M.I.S., de Fátima Barros Lima, G., Lóscio, B.F.: Investigations into data ecosystems: a systematic mapping study. Knowl. Inf. Syst. **61**(2), 589–630 (2019)
18. Oliveira, M.I.S., Lóscio, B.F.: What is a data ecosystem? In: Proceedings of the 19th Annual International Conference on Digital Government Research: Governance in the Data Age, dg.o 2018. ACM (2018)
19. Sahay, A., Indamutsa, A., Di Ruscio, D., Pierantonio, A.: Supporting the understanding and comparison of low-code development platforms. In: 2020 46th Euromicro Conference on Software Engineering and Advanced Applications (SEAA), pp. 171–178 (2020)
20. Savió, D.A., Bicik, J., Morley, M.S.: A DSS generator for multiobjective optimisation of spreadsheet-based models. Environ. Modell. Softw. **26**(5), 551–561 (2011)

21. Schwichtenberg, B., Engels, G.: SecoArc: a framework for architecting healthy software ecosystems. In: Muccini, H., et al. (eds.) ECSA 2020. CCIS, vol. 1269, pp. 95–106. Springer, Cham (2020). https://doi.org/10.1007/978-3-030-59155-7_8
22. Senyo, P.K., Liu, K., Effah, J.: Digital business ecosystem: literature review and a framework for future research. Int. J. Inform. Manage. **47**, 52–64 (2019)
23. Shafiei, F., Sundaram, D., Piramuthu, S.: Multi-enterprise collaborative decision support system. Expert Syst. Appl. **39**(9), 7637–7651 (2012)
24. Stănescu, I.A., Ştefan, A., Filip, F.G.: Cloud-based decision support ecosystem for renewable energy providers. In: Camarinha-Matos, L.M., Baldissera, T.A., Di Orio, G., Marques, F. (eds.) DoCEIS 2015. IAICT, vol. 450, pp. 405–412. Springer, Cham (2015). https://doi.org/10.1007/978-3-319-16766-4_43
25. Weskamp, C., Koberstein, A., Schwartz, F., Suhl, L., Voß, S.: A two-stage stochastic programming approach for identifying optimal postponement strategies in supply chains with uncertain demand. Omega **83**, 123–138 (2019)
26. Zha, X.F., Sriram, R.D., Fernandez, M.G., Mistree, F.: Knowledge-intensive collaborative decision support for design processes: a hybrid decision support model and agent. Comput. Ind. **59**(9), 905–922 (2008)

A Systematic Research Methodology for Business Model Decision Making in Commercialising Innovative Healthcare Diagnostic Technologies

Aira Patrice R. Ong[1]([⊠]), Shaofeng Liu[1], Genhua Pan[2], and Xinzhong Li[3]

[1] Plymouth Business School, University of Plymouth,
Drake Circus, Plymouth, Devon PL4 8AA, UK
{aira.ong,shaofeng.liu}@plymouth.ac.uk
[2] School of Computing Electronics and Mathematics, University of Plymouth,
Drake Circus, Plymouth, Devon PL4 8AA, UK
[3] School of Science, Engineering & Design, Teesside University, Middlesbrough TS1 3BX, UK

Abstract. Business models and decision making play a vital role in the delivery and implementation of technological innovations in the healthcare industry, especially for entrepreneurs, healthcare providers, managers, researchers and policy makers. However, despite its significance, current conceptualisations of business models do not adequately guide in designing business models particular to the complex and dynamic healthcare environment. With the exploratory nature and lack of research in this area, this paper aims to design a new methodology to develop business models incorporating multidimensional implications of various stakeholder perspectives. A systematic literature review of existing methods in business models and decision making has been done and a new methodology has been proposed, entitled Thematic + TISM + MICMAC = TTM methodology. An application of this method has been tested with empirical findings from the healthcare diagnostics value chain to establish the key factors of innovative business model development in healthcare decision making. Limitations, future directions and challenges in the proposed methodology are also discussed. It is hoped that this study will guide practitioners in future work towards advancement of these techniques and will help the managers to select better decisions by making use of these methodologies.

Keywords: Business model · Decision making · Healthcare value chain ·
Innovative diagnostics · Medical device · Success factors

1 Introduction

Healthcare is a very dynamic and innovative field despite its bureaucratic nature. The innovation ranges from new medical technologies to clinical services emerging from a wide range of inputs and stakeholders such as scientists, engineers, clinicians and most importantly, patients. Technological advances, disease outbreak, demographics

© Springer Nature Switzerland AG 2022
A. P. Cabral Seixas Costa et al. (Eds.): ICDSST 2022, LNBIP 447, pp. 111–123, 2022.
https://doi.org/10.1007/978-3-031-06530-9_9

and patient demands are main drivers of innovations in this segment. However, due to the complex nature of the healthcare environment including technical, societal, institutional, and political considerations creates difficulties for diffusion of innovations [1–3] and change initiatives intended to make improvements [4, 5]. To understand why this happens, it is essential to examine the implicit and explicit business models (BM) and understand how innovation actually takes place.

BM design and innovation are crucial for a firm's performance and success [6–8] and to adapt to changing environments [9, 10]. In every business venture established, it either explicitly or implicitly employs a particular BM [11], and for a venture to become viable, a sound BM is required [12]. A BM can be defined as "the logic of how an organisation creates, delivers, and captures value" [13]. BM design and innovation are crucial for a firm's performance and success [6–8] and to adapt to changing environments [9, 10]. 'Designing' a business is an iterative task that shall be flexible and adaptive to the competitive environment [11]. While the BM concept first became popular in the Internet bubble era in the late 1990s and has rapidly been researched in a wide range of businesses, it was rarely studied in the healthcare industry.

With the exploratory nature and lack of research in this area, this paper aims to design a new methodology to develop business models incorporating multidimensional implications of various stakeholder perspectives. Specific objectives include:

- Identification of factors influencing BM design for innovative healthcare technologies
- Establishment of factor relations and ranking using TISM methodology
- Classification of factors based on their driving and dependence power using MICMAC analysis
- Derivation of practical implications

A systematic literature review of existing methods in BM healthcare and decision making has been done and a new methodology has been proposed, entitled Thematic + TISM + MICMAC = TTM methodology. An application of this method has been tested with empirical findings from the healthcare diagnostics value chain to establish the key factors of innovative business model development in healthcare decision making.

1.1 Research Context

As the healthcare value chain is a complex web of interconnected entities working collaboratively to develop and link the medical diagnostic device to patients, a comprehensive and deep understanding of the medical device business model can only be reached by probing healthcare value chain stakeholders' thoughts, values, prejudices, views, feelings and perspectives. In this study, the motivation comes from the EU Horizon 2020 Project entitled, AiPBAND (An Integrated Platform for Developing Brain Cancer Diagnostic Techniques), which aims to advance the early diagnosis of brain tumours using molecular biomarkers in the blood with state-of-the-art technologies.

Brain Cancer Market, Research and Developments

Treatments for cancer have been advancing at an accelerated pace in recent years, offering clinical progress, as well as increased specificity through selection according to biomarkers, or through engineered cell or gene therapies. Drivers of diagnostic technology innovation and adoption includes (1) Rapid and significant advances in test technologies and related bioinformatics and connectivity capabilities, (2) Increases in numbers of tests performed and (3) Pressure from patients and carers for more accurate and rapid diagnosis [9]. By 2023, it is estimated that the brain tumour therapeutics market globally will grow at a compound annual growth rate (CAGR) of 12.9%. Global spending on cancer therapies and supportive care drugs exceeds £100 ($133) billion, as the value of these medicines is recognized and a greater share of drug budgets is allocated to these products. AiPBAND Project is an example of this initiative that focuses on brain cancer diagnostic technologies, where the researcher is also involved as the BM researcher. It is crucial to integrate BM thinking towards commercialisation and linking the value created to the key beneficiaries especially in these types of research collaborations. BM concept has become a popular tool in business practice because it can help to successfully analyse and handle these complexities. Therefore with the reduction of complexity and the resulting focus on essential information, the quality of decision-making can be enhanced [14].

Figure 1 presents a general flow of healthcare innovations in medical technology development from discovery to market.

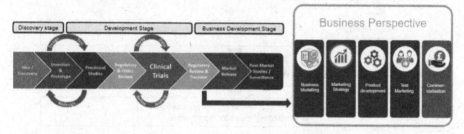

Fig. 1. The stages of medical technology development.

The first two stages are focused on the life sciences perspective, which includes the discovery and clinical validation. In the development of these devices, collaborations are necessary between academia, healthcare providers (e.g. hospitals, clinicians) and industry in the development of these devices. Medical and information technology adoption decisions differ when made by individuals or organisations. Beyond that distinction, the number of stakeholders potentially affected by any technology adoption decision varies greatly. Once a clinician decides to use a new device or piece of technology, the clinician must often consider not only the impact on the patient and on the practice but also what it means for reimbursement, health care policy, and the organisation in which the clinician works.

2   Review of Literature in Healthcare BM

A systematic literature review (SLR) has been conducted to explore the current BM applications in healthcare decision making. The method allows answering a specific research question adopting an evidence-based approach [14, 15]. SLR approach performs a key role in identifying, selecting and analysing the most relevant papers in the research area [16]. Systematic reviews differ from traditional narrative reviews in that they adopt a replicable, scientific and transparent process, intended to minimise bias through extensive searches and by providing an audit trail of the reviewers' steps, strategies, procedures and decisions [17]. The SLR phases used are shown in the diagram below (see Fig. 2).

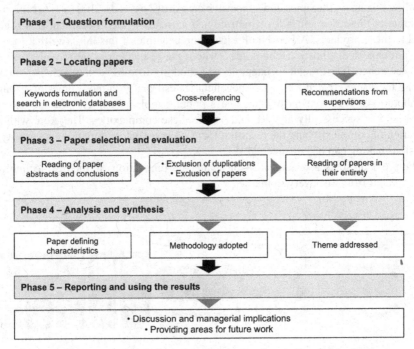

Fig. 2. The process of systematic literature review (adopted from [14])

According to a systematic review done by the authors, 38 papers are conceptual studies while 12 are empirical papers. All papers selected for this study were compiled using Mendeley reference manager by Elsevier then imported to NVivo 12 software, version 12.1.1.256 by QSR International to qualitatively review and analyse the studies in a more organised manner. The papers were coded and classified according to the following criteria:

- Defining characteristics: the selected contributions were classified according to their general details – year of publication, first authors' country/nationality.
- Classification of papers: two research methodologies were distinguished: conceptual papers and empirical papers case studies/interviews. In the case of multiple methodologies, each paper was classified according to the primary methodology used.
- Themes addressed: finally, the collected papers were classified according to the focus of each study and the key issues investigated.

The conceptual studies consist mainly of author perspectives based on their expert opinion and literature, while empirical papers adopted case study and interviews. It means that Majority of the publications are from the USA (26), followed by Netherlands (5), Canada (3), France (2), Sweden (2), then each of the following countries have one: UK, Switzerland, South Korea, India, Iran, Ireland, Malaysia, Australia, Austria, Belgium and 2 not specified. Value based healthcare models have been distinguished as a trend in the BM of innovative treatments/diagnostics. While its mostly on a conceptual basis, its adoption in the healthcare setting is a challenge. This calls for a dynamic perspective in designing business models, taking into account the different healthcare stakeholders such as the patients, care professionals, care providers, technology companies, payers, and the society.

2.1 Thematic Analysis: Identifying Value Components of the Business Model

Several definitions for the business model exist in the literature. The interest of academia and practitioners in the field of novel business models is ever-increasing. This is evidenced by the numerous definitions provided in scientific journals such as Journal of Cleaner production, Long Range planning, Journal of business models, etc.

Based on the systematic literature review and thematic analysis, four value components form a business model: the (1) value offering, (2) value delivery, (3) value network, (4) value capture as visualised in the BM full value circle in Fig. 3.

Building on the BM, the 10 key factors of each component have been identified, shown in the outer layer of the BM circle.

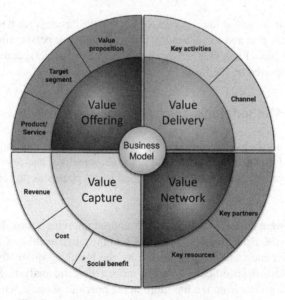

Fig. 3. Business model full value circle (by authors).

Value Offering
The value offering in a business model includes the product or service offered, identification of target segment and value proposition. Product or service offered entails solutions that may address needs in the current standard of care, enable innovation and offer innovativeness. Target segment is the customer of the new value proposition who receives the value but also may contribute by co-creating or delivering information. Value propositions are used to describe what value an organisation creates for its customers by providing goods or services, and how important that value is to the customer that helps customers get a job done more effectively, conveniently, and affordably.

Value Delivery
The value delivery is how the value is delivered to customers and it comprises the key activities and channel. The key activities involve the main activities necessary for a business to provide its offerings while the channel. BMs not only serve their target customers but also improve the entire healthcare system in the respective target market [18].

Value Network
Typically involve different stakeholders with different needs, hence value propositions are required to create value for the network of participating organisations. Key partners and resources build up the value network component. Particularly in healthcare supply chains, processes that integrate a smooth and continuous flow of materials, information and services are crucial. This sector stems from the complexity of technologies and the multiple stakeholders aspects such as building relationships.

Value Capture
Answers the question how value is generated back to the business for it to be sustainable in terms of revenue, cost and social benefit. From an economic perspective, value capture includes revenue model and cost structure, while in a social perspective, it entails the social benefits captured by the firm.

3 Research Methodology

This section comprehensively describes and justifies the methodological framework used for this study in order to achieve the research objectives and answer the research questions. The overall research design is divided into 3 phases as presented in Fig. 4.

Phase 1
Qualitative data were collected using semi-structured interviews regarding the interviewees' opinion on the aspects of designing BM for innovative healthcare technologies. In order to obtain accurate and meaningful results, the matching qualitative data analysis technique was adopted, specifically by performing a thematic analysis. Several BM factors have been identified from the literature in the previous section, which will be used during the empirical stage (such as product/ service, target segment, value proposition, channel, key activities, key partners, key resources, revenue, cost and social benefit),

newly identified factors in this stage were categorised into either existing or new groups, depending on whether the existing BM value component encompassed the new factors. If new categories emerged during the interviews, they were noted and eventually added to the theoretical framework via coded data, and categorised as appropriate. 30 interviews have been conducted from companies/firms, research institutions and healthcare organisations involved in the biomedical industry. Profiles of the interviewees are 12 top level management (CEO, Founder, Cofounder, Professors), 8 middle management level (project managers, team lead) and 10 low management level (researchers, staff). Data was gathered from across the EU (Germany, Italy, Netherlands, Slovenia, Switzerland and UK) and Asia (India, Philippines and Turkey). Interviews have been transcribed, consent form and proper ethical documentation have been followed.

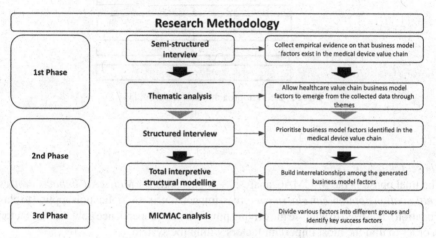

Fig. 4. Research design.

Phase 2
After identifying and validating the BM factors in Phase 1, a structured interview has been done to prioritise and understand the interrelationships among the 34 BM factors. Interviewees from the Phase 1 and other recommended references were invited and 5 experts agreed to participate. The TISM methodology adopted in the study is an extension of interpretive structural modelling (ISM) [19], which explicitly captures the causal thinking behind the interrelationship during data collection. Flowchart of the TISM is visualised in Fig. 5.

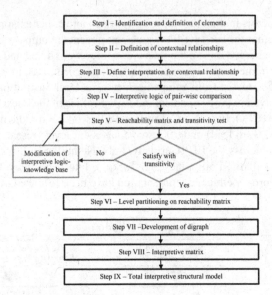

Fig. 5. TISM approach. Adopted from [19].

Phase 3

The final phase is the MICMAC analysis, which stands for *Matrice d'Impacts croises-multipication appliqu´ean classment* (cross-impact matrix multiplication applied to classification). It is used to analyse the driving power and the dependence power of the factors in order to find the most important factors within the system.

4   Data analysis and Findings

4.1   Thematic Analysis

34 factors have been identified which are relevant to the study as enumerated in Table 1. Categorising these factors back to the BM value components: factors 1 to 9 are in Value Offering, 10 to 23 for Value Delivery, 24 to 30 in Value Network and 31 to 34 in Value Capture.

Table 1. BM factors identified based on empirical data

No	BM factor	No	BM factor
1	Addresses needs in the current standard of care	18	Clear customer needs
2	Enabling innovation	19	R&D sustaining innovations
3	Innovativeness	20	Regulatory approval
4	Identified market based on health focus	21	Timely delivery of value
5	Early detection	22	Training support (internal)
6	Ease of use	23	Awareness initiatives
7	Cost effective	24	Health champions for technology adoption
8	Platform for collaboration	25	Outsourcing value creation
9	Portability	26	Sustaining value ecosystem
10	Satisfied regulatory clearance	27	Team expertise
11	Earning trust of stakeholders	28	Culture and values
12	Adoption of innovation	29	Intellectual property
13	Satisfying customer requirement	30	Funding
14	Managing collaborations	31	Adaptive revenue stream
15	Training and support provided	32	Investors support
16	Onboarding customers	33	Knowledge exchanges
17	Effective sales channel	34	Managing costs

4.2 TISM Results

All 34 elements from empirical data have been considered for TISM evaluation. Here, the contextual relationships among the various BM factors have been studied. For the present study, the following structure for defining the contextual relationships among various BM factors has been considered: "Whether one BM factor influences the other one?" Fig. 6 showcases the final TISM model of the 34 factors with 11 levels and 93 links.

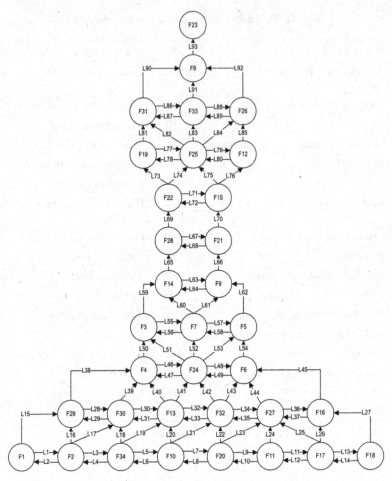

Fig. 6. TISM model for the BM factors. (11 levels)

4.3 MICMAC Analysis

The factor dependencies are established using Total Interpretive Structural Modelling (TISM) methodology. MICMAC analysis is used to classify the factors based on their ability to influence other factors. The output of TISM forms the input for MICMAC analysis. Based on their driving power and dependence power, the factors have been classified into four categories shown in Fig. 7.

(a) First quadrant (Quadrant I): This is an autonomous quadrant. The factors placed in this quadrant have less driving power and dependents and because they do not have much influence on the system. In the present study the absence of factors in the first quadrant shows that all considered enablers are significant. Therefore, all selected 34 factors have an important influence in designing BM for innovative diagnostic devices.

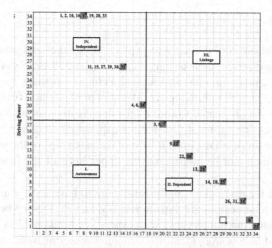

Fig. 7. MICMAC diagram of BM factors

(b) Second quadrant (Quadrant II): This is a dependent quadrant with low driving power and high dependence. According to the present study, seventeen BM factors, including F1 Addresses needs in the current standard of care, F2 Economic and political consideration, F10 Regulatory approval, F16 Effective sales channel, F17 Earning trust of stakeholders, F19 Clear customer needs, F20 Satisfied regulatory clearance, F33 Managing costs, F11 Satisfying customer requirement, F15 Onboarding customers, F27 Team expertise, F29 Intellectual property, F30 Funding, F32 Investors support, F4 Identified market based on health focus, F6 Ease of use, F24 Health champions for technology adoption, F3 Innovativeness, F5 Early detection, F7 Cost effective, F9 Portability, F12 Managing collaborations, F22 Timely delivery of value, F28 Culture and values, F13 Training support (internal), F21 Training and support provided, F14 R&D sustaining innovations, F18 Adoption of innovation, F25 Outsourcing value creation, F26 Sustaining value ecosystem, F31 Adaptive revenue stream, F34 Knowledge exchanges, F8 Platform for collaboration and F23 Awareness initiatives. In the TISM model, these factors form the top levels which need other BM factors that collectively act to influence BM design.

(c) Third quadrant (Quadrant III): This quadrant is known as linkage. Factors with high driving power and high dependence fall in this quadrant. No factors fell in this cluster.

(d) Fourth quadrant (Quadrant IV): This is an independent quadrant which has strong driving power but weak dependence power. According to this study, 17 factors appear in this quadrant including F3 Innovativeness, F5 Early detection, F7 Cost effective, F9 Portability, F12 Managing collaborations, F22 Timely delivery of value, F28 Culture and values, F13 Training support (internal), F21 Training and support provided, F14 R&D sustaining innovations, F18 Adoption of innovation, F25 Outsourcing value creation, F26 Sustaining value ecosystem, F31 Adaptive revenue stream, F34 Knowledge exchanges, F8 Platform for collaboration and F23 Awareness initiatives.

5 Conclusion

Business models allow entrepreneurs to explore the market and commercialise their innovations [20] and hence, their design is critical [21, 22]. Business model design is a key decision for a new firm entrepreneur and a crucial - perhaps more difficult - task for managers charged with rethinking an old model to make their firm fit for the future [22]. A business model is geared toward total value creation for all parties involved. It lays the foundations for the focal firm's value capture by co-defining (along with the firm's products and services) the overall 'size of the value pie,' or the total value created in transactions, which can be considered the upper limit of the firm's value capture potential.

It is important for researchers and practitioners to have a deep understanding and knowledge of interrelationships among different BM factors. This has been achieved with 30 in-depth semi-structured interviews with experienced stakeholders in the healthcare value chain. 34 BM factors were identified through thematic analysis. After that, another round of data collection with structured interviews were applied to TISM to uncover the potential interrelationships among the identified BM factors. Finally, MICMAC analysis to identify the key factors in various categories. The results indicate that the following factors were the key elements for the healthcare BM: Addresses clinical need, Satisfied regulatory clearance, Earning trust of stakeholders, Effective sales channel, Regulatory approval, Managing costs, and Economical, political environment have the highest driving power and lie at the lowest level of the TISM hierarchy; thus, they should be given top priority.

This study contributes to research on decision support for designing BM incorporating healthcare stakeholders' views. The TTM methodology proposed in this study can also be used by academic researchers and managers to identify the most important factors and determine the dependencies of factors among themselves. Other sectors and industries can also adopt this systematic methodology for establishing relationships among factors and prioritising them. The limitations of the study offer several future research avenues to explore and validate the outcomes.

Acknowledgements. This project has received funding from the European Union's Horizon 2020 research and innovation programme under grant agreement No 764281.

References

1. Berwick, D.M.: Disseminating innovations in health care. JAMA **289**(15), 1969–1975 (2003)
2. Plsek, P.E., Wilson, T.: Complexity science: Complexity, leadership, and management in healthcare organisations. BMJ **323**(7315), 746–749 (2001). https://doi.org/10.1136/bmj.323.7315.746
3. Greenhalgh, T., Papoutsi, C.: Studying complexity in health services research: desperately seeking an overdue paradigm shift. BMC Med. **16**(1), 95 (2018)
4. Glouberman, S., Zimmerman, B.: Complicated and complex systems: what would successful reform of medicare look like? (2002). Accessed 15 Jul 2020
5. Braithwaite, J.: Changing how we think about healthcare improvement. BMJ **361**, k2014 (2018)

6. Kesting, P., Günzel-Jensen, F.: SMEs and new ventures need business model sophistication. Bus. Horiz. **58**(3), 285–293 (2015)
7. Zott, C., Amit, R.: Business model design and the performance of entrepreneurial firms. Organ. Sci. **18**(2), 181–199 (2007). https://doi.org/10.1287/orsc.1060.0232
8. Zott, C., Amit, R.H., Massa, L.: The business model: recent developments and future research. J. Manag. (2011). https://doi.org/10.2139/ssrn.1674384
9. Gioia, D.A., Schultz, M., Corley, K.G.: Organizational Identity, Image, and adaptive Instability. Acad. Manag. Rev. **25**(1), 63–81 (2000). https://doi.org/10.5465/amr.2000.279 1603
10. Bohmer, R.M., Edmondson, A.C.: Organizational learning in health care. Health Forum J. **44**(2), 32–35 (2001)
11. Teece, D.J.: Business models, business strategy and innovation. Long Range Plan. **43**(2–3), 172–194 (2010)
12. Magretta, J.: Why business models matter. Harv. Bus. Rev. **80**(5), 86–92, 133 (2002)
13. Osterwalder, A., Pigneur, Y.: Business Model Generation: A Handbook for Visionaries, Game Changers, and Challengers. Wiley, Hoboken (2010)
14. Denyer, D., Tranfield, D.R.: Doing a Literature Review in Business and Management. SAGE Publications, Thousand Oaks (2016)
15. Tranfield, D., Denyer, D., Smart, P.: Towards a methodology for developing evidence-informed management knowledge by means of systematic review **14**, 207–222 (2003). https://doi.org/10.1111/1467-8551.00375
16. Denyer, D., Tranfield, D.: Producing a systematic review. In: Buchanan, D.A. (ed). The Sage Handbook of Organizational Research Methods, vol. 738, pp. 671–689 (2009)
17. Rousseau, D.M.: Is there such a thing as 'evidence-based management'? Acad. Manag. Rev. **31**(2), 256–269 (2006). https://doi.org/10.5465/amr.2006.20208679
18. Winterhalter, S., Zeschky, M.B., Neumann, L., Gassmann, O.: Business models for frugal innovation in emerging markets: the case of the medical device and laboratory equipment industry. Technovation **66–67**, 3–13 (2017)
19. Sushil.: Interpreting the interpretive structural model. Glob. J. Flex. Syst. Manag. **13**(2), 87–106 (2012)
20. Doganova, L., Eyquem-Renault, M.: What do business models do?: Innovation devices in technology entrepreneurship. Res. Policy **38**(10), 1559–1570 (2009)
21. Morris, M., Schindehutte, M., Allen, J.: The entrepreneur's business model: toward a unified perspective. J. Bus. Res. **58**(6), 726–735 (2005)
22. Zott, C., Amit, R.: Business model design: an activity system perspective. Long Range Plann. **43**(2–3), 216–226 (2010)

A DSS Based on a Control Tower for Supply Chain Risks Management

Chenhui Ye[1](✉) ⓘ, Pascale Zaraté[1] ⓘ, and Daouda Kamissoko[2] ⓘ

[1] IRIT, Toulouse Université, 2 rue du Doyen Gabriel Marty, 31042 Toulouse Cedex 9, France
{Chenhui.YE,Pascale.Zarate}@irit.fr
[2] Ecole Des Mines d'Albi, All. des sciences, 81000 Albi, France
Dadouda.Kamissoko@mines-albi.fr

Abstract. Propose: This paper presents a supply chain control tower deployed with a decision support system for supply chain risk management in a multi-source data and risk environment. The study provides a digital risk management process and a group decision making approach for companies to improve their supply chain resilience in a supply chain risk environment. We have designed the system from two perspectives. Supply Chain Control Tower and Supply Chain Risk Management. Supply chain risks are mainly all the risks faced in the process from product design to delivery to customers. Supply chain risk management is a very complex activity that requires assessing the vulnerability of all participants in the supply chain. It is a multi-step process. The Supply Chain Control Tower is a dashboard that integrates information from across the supply chain. The supply chain control tower integrates multiple data sources, key performance indicators and activity sources in the supply chain. The control tower should include an intelligent decision support system that uses decision support models and technologies, such as machine learning, to provide decision support and ranking of alternative strategies for supply chain managers.

Results. In this paper, a decision support system-based supply chain control tower is designed to support supply chain decision makers in selecting the most appropriate alternative strategies to reduce the risk impact and enhance the resilience of the supply chain.

Keywords: Supply chain risk management · Multiple-criteria decision-making · Database · Group decision support system · Supply chain control tower

1 Introduction

A supply chain may be defined as an integrated process wherein a number of various business entities (i.e., suppliers, manufacturers, distributors, and retailers) work together in an effort to: (1) acquire raw materials, (2) convert these raw materials into specified final products, and (3) deliver these final products to retailers [1]. The Supply Chain (SC) is an essential activity in our societies, related to the production and development of human society. From 1913, when Ford applied the concept of the assembly line to T-model cars, to the birth of Tesla's electric car super factory in 2016, supply chain 4.0 has

© Springer Nature Switzerland AG 2022
A. P. Cabral Seixas Costa et al. (Eds.): ICDSST 2022, LNBIP 447, pp. 124–136, 2022.
https://doi.org/10.1007/978-3-031-06530-9_10

become the current trend. Industry and supply chain 4.0 are basically oriented to the use of mechanization, automation, Internet of things (IoT), Decision software aided tools, etc. [2]. Under the trend of globalization, companies need to open up markets, purchase raw materials, produce, and transportation in different countries to reduce costs and expand profits. The trend of globalization has made the supply chain more complex and fragile than ever. Economic and political instability has brought diverse and complex risk issues to the supply chain under the background of globalization. Hence, Supply Chain Risk Management (SCRM) is necessary. SCRM is a very complex activity that requires assessing the vulnerability of all actors in the supply chain. It's a multi-step process. In the era of globalization, the security of the supply chain is not just an issue for an enterprise. The supply chain network links all enterprises together, so the spread of risks becomes stronger. Resisting supply chain risks is no longer a company's sole activity, but so far, the following three obstacles are still difficult to resolve: 1. Information sharing between companies, 2. Risk-sharing between companies, 3. Enterprises group decision-making to face the risk problem.

By the early 1970 s, the concept of decision support systems had been conceived through the work of Scott Morton [3]. Decision support systems use algorithms and computer science to help decision-makers find the most suitable alternative strategies, the goal of the decision support system is not to replace humans in making decisions, but to assist human judgments. There are usually three fundamental components of DSSs. Firstly; there is database management system (DBMS) which serves as a data bank for the DSS. The second component is Model-based management system (MBMS). The role of MBMS is to storage several models of problem to solve and, finally the method of dialog generation management system (DGMS) which is in charge of make the interactions between the end-user and the system as clear as possible [4].

With the continuous development of DSS theoretical research for decades, the relationship between DSS and supply chain risk management has been valued by scientists. Several DSS methods have been developed in the literature to assist organizations in managing supply chain risks. However, they do not incorporate all the commonly accepted steps of SCRM. In addition, there is little empirical work to test the proposed SCRM models on real study cases. So far, the main scientific issues identified in this work are the following: (1) identification of a typology of sensors and data sources (2) use of artificial intelligence to interpret data and determine risk situations (3) analyse the indicators to determine feasible and realistic alternative decision plans (4) definition of the criteria of evaluation of these alternatives according to the objective and relative dimensions (preferences), (5) study of the methods combination and aggregation of these criteria to obtain the qualification of the alternatives, their choice and their classification, and (6) investigation of the immersive decision making tools making it possible to better support decision-makers. With the evolution of information technologies, the availability of increasingly voluminous data (Big Data) has been witnessed from diverse sources.

This paper proposes a System for supply chain risk management by deploying a supply chain control tower based on a decision support system to solve the six main scientific issues that currently exist and break the barriers between enterprises in the supply chain network.

2 Literature Review and Related Works

2.1 Supply Chain Risk Management (SCRM)

Brenchley and Walker (2003) define risk as a chance of danger, damage, loss, injury, or any other undesired consequences [5], the core of the supply chain is to create the greatest benefits for the enterprise, and supply chain risk management (SCRM) aims to provide a structured approach to achieve the aforementioned benefits [6]. SCRM is a multifaceted concept and scholars diverge widely regarding its definition. For the most part, SCRM practices seek to reduce SC vulnerability and mitigate disruptions impacts [7]. Generally, based on different sources of supply chain risk, it can usually be divided into 8 categories: operations risk, demand risks, security risks, macroeconomic risks, policy risks, competitive risks, and resource risks [5]. According to Christopher and Peck (2004) [8] in Jörn-Henrik Thun and DanielHoenig (2011) [9], risks driving the vulnerability of supply chains are discussed based on an approach distinguish between external and internal supply chain risks. In terms of internal supply chain risks, cross-company-based risks and internal company risks can be differentiated. Internal company risks deal with disruptions caused by problems within the organizational boundaries of the company such as machine breakdowns or IT problems [9]. The external risk of the supply chain usually comes from the uncertainty of demand and sudden changes in the external environment, such as Covid-19 in 2020. The drastic changes in demand have a strong impact on the stability of the supply chain. According to Fortune (2020), more than 94% of top 1000 companies have been negatively affected by this outbreak [10]. Drawing on extant literature, Fan and Stevenson (2018) provide a comprehensive framework of SCRM comprising the identification, assessment, treatment, and monitoring of SC risks [11]. Nevertheless, the keypoint for companies is to find a way for resilience when they face unforeseen events.

2.2 Supply Chain Resilience

The risks of the supply chain are divided into certain risks and uncertain risks. I. Manuj and J.T. Mentzer in 2008 categorized risks according to different sources, where risks with identifiable sources are defined as certain risks, such as supply risk, demand risk, operational risk, etc. [12]. Whereas, risks of unanticipated resource are defined as uncertain risks. With the development of globalization, the sources of risks are becoming more and more diverse and unavoidable. In order to reduce risks, supply chains must be designed to incorporate event readiness, provide an efficient and effective response, and be capable of recovering to their original state or even better post the disruptive event. This is the essence of supply chain resiliency [13]. Craighead, Rungtusanatham and Handfield proposed in 2007 that all supply chains have inherent risks and the risk of interruption cannot be avoided. The severity of supply chain disruption is closely related to (i) the three supply chain design characteristics of density, complexity, and node criticality and (ii) two supply chain mitigation capabilities of recovery and warning [14]. So before the risk comes, Mainly through three supply chain design characteristics (1. density, 2. complexity, 3. node criticality) to evaluate the supply chain resilience. When a risk occurs, the supply chain resilience should be evaluated in two dimensions:

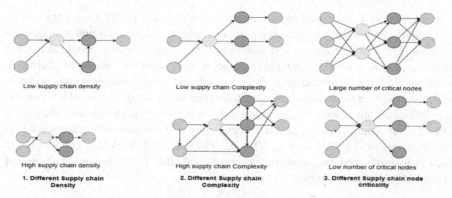

Fig. 1. Three supply chain design characteristics

1.the impact of the supply chain performance and 2 Recovery time for supply chain performance to return to normal levels.

As shown in Fig. 1, in order to better understand the three design characteristics of the supply chain, we need to abstract the supply chain as a process composed of countless events, and each event is represented by a node. Different colors in the Fig. 1 represent different components of the supply chain, for example: red for suppliers, yellow for factories, blue for warehouses, and green for distribution centers.

The density of the supply chain is mainly manifested in two aspects: the number of nodes in the supply chain and the physical distance between each node [15]. The closer physical distance between each node indicates that the density of the supply chain is greater, and it also means that the supply chain is more likely to encounter uncertain risk or regional risk events. The number of nodes will also affect the supply chain resilience. When a risk occurs, more nodes mean more alternative options, but the complexity of the supply chain will also increase.

The complexity of the supply chain is related to the number of nodes in the supply chain, and the connection between the nodes in the supply chain [15]. A highly complex supply chain has more nodes and more connections between nodes. The increase in complexity is conducive to the generation of alternative solutions. When a node is interrupted due to risk issues, it is easier to find alternatives. In general, the increase in the complexity of the supply chain has a certain positive impact on the supply chain resilience.

Node criticality is defined as the relative importance of a given node or set of nodes within a supply chain [14]. Node criticality is connected to multiple nodes as the core component of the supply chain in the supply chain, and often plays a key role in linking the upstream and downstream of the supply chain. A supply chain that contains a large number of critical nodes would have a greater potential for disruption than one within which support for critical processes is distributed among several different nodes [15].

2.3 Decision Support System and MCDM

In 1971. Gorry and Morton defined a decision support system as: systems that assist decision-makers in semi-structured and unstructured decision problems [16]. DSS is a

computer-based decision-making system that uses data and model knowledge to discover and analyses the problem in a particular area of information and management
systems [17]. The decision support system is not created to replace people in making
decisions, but to assist decision-makers to get a more scientific ranking of alternative
solutions. With the continuous improvement of information technology, the development
of decision support software has emerged. Computer-based decision support tools use the
capabilities of interactive software to assist decision-makers to gain useful information
from a combination of raw data sets by employing a logical scientific framework [18]
Decision-making software such as VISUAL PROMETHEE [19] have been maturely
used in industry, medical, environment, energy and other fields. In the Fig. 2, we list
several MCDA methodologies.

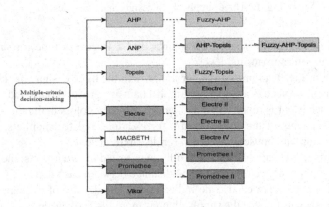

Fig. 2. Multiple-criteria decision-making models

Multiple criteria decision-making (MCDM) was introduced as a promising and
important field of study in the early 1970s. Since then the number of contributions
to theories and models, which could be used as a basis for more systematic and ratio-
nal decision-making with multiple criteria, has continued to grow at a steady rate [20].
Multi-criteria decision making has aided academics and industrial practitioners in their
decisions in such fields from economy and management to engineering and manufacturing [21]. In recent years, more than a dozen classic MCDM models have been widely
used in many fields, such as: Topsis [3]. With the development of Fuzzy theory, the
combined model of Fuzzy and MCDM is also used more in the decision-making field.

3   The Concept of Using Supply Chain Control Towers for Supply Chain Risk Management

The concept of supply chain control tower (SCCT) provides a new direction for the
combination of DSS and supply chain risk management. Every enterprise operates under
its own risk and should manage the risk on its own. Since the interconnectedness of
enterprises in the network makes them depend on each other, it is useful to partially share
the risk management process and develop collaborative methods to manage risk [22]. As

the information management and decision-making center of the supply chain, the core role of the control tower is: 1. Break down the barriers of information exchange between enterprises, more effectively transmit key information and data sharing, 2. Predict and warn of risks, and optimize the efficiency of risk management, 3. All enterprises in the supply chain share risks together, 4. All companies in the supply chain make group decisions together.

Similar to the role of the control tower in the airport, the Supply chain control tower (SCCT), as the most central part of supply chain information, controls the various sub-databases in the supply chain and records the latest data updated from various supply chain software in real time. These data include KPIs, key business, logistics, distribution centers etc. Data sensors distributed in the information flow of the supply chain transmit real-time data to the dashboard of the control tower, and the data analysis center of the control tower will use new technologies such as machine learning to predict time series data to warn.

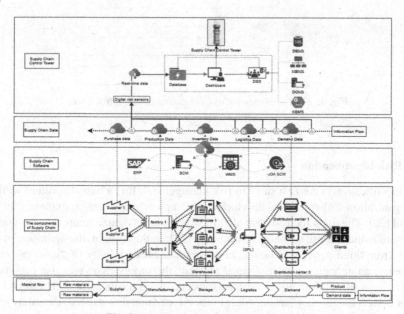

Fig. 3. The structure of the control tower

Figure 3 shows the conceptual diagram after the deployment of the control tower. The supply chain is composed of five parts. The information flow is transmitted from the downstream to the upstream. On the contrary, the material flow is transmitted from the upstream to the downstream, which corresponds to the various components of the supply chain. Every enterprise has its own supply chain management software, such as SAP-ERP. The information flow is saved and recorded in each software, and the digital risk sensor is deployed in each software, and the key data is transmitted to the database of the supply chain control tower in real time. The key information is analyzed and displayed on the dashboard in the form of icons. The control tower also contains a decision support system, which consists of four parts, a knowledge base management system, a model bases management system, a database management system and an Interactive interface.

4 Risk Management of Supply Chain Control Tower

A typical risk management process of an enterprise consists of: 1. risk identification, 2. risk assessment, 3. decision and implementation of risk management actions (risk response), 4. risk monitoring [22]. As shown in Fig. 4, the control tower will lead the four processes of risk management to resist the negative impact of risks to restore supply resilience. Supply chain Control Tower as a new technology does not change the risk management process, but rather digitizes all the steps in the process.

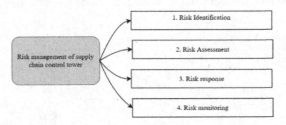

Fig. 4. Four activities for risk management of control towers

4.1 Risk Identification

Risk identification is the first stage in risk management. It is a basis for future work of the organization with regards to developing and implementing new programmes for risk control [22]. The main focus of risk identification is to recognize future uncertainties to be able to manage these scenarios proactively [22]. In this system, the definition of risk comes from three parts: 1. When a certain component or activity of the supply chain encounters an uncertain sudden disaster or event, the supply chain manager reports the event to the control tower, and the control tower conducts the incident. 2. The digital risk sensor detects that the key business data in the information flow exceeds the safety range and triggers an alarm. The risk signal is transmitted to the cloud database of the supply chain control tower and displayed on the dashboard. 3. Use machine learning to analyze time-series data in the supply chain to achieve the effect of risk prediction. When the algorithm predicts the upcoming risk, a risk prediction report will be generated and sent to the control tower.

When the control tower receives the risk signal, as shown in Fig. 5, the work of risk identification mainly consists of the following steps: 1. According to the source of the risk signal, determining the risk comes from which part of the supply chain, 2.According to the location of the risk, use the node model to infer which related businesses and enterprises will be affected, 3. According to the risk information and location, find the specific classification and description of the risk in the knowledge base management system, and finally define the code of the risk, 4. Transmit risk code to all companies.

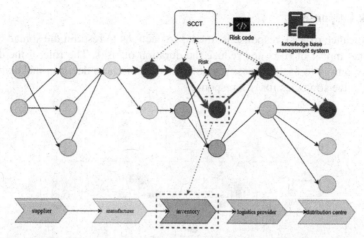

Fig. 5. Use the node model to infer which related businesses and enterprises will be affected

4.2 Risk Assessment

Risk assessment and prioritization are needed to be able to choose suitable management actions for the identified risk factors according to the situation at both company and network level [22]. As shown in Fig. 6, after the risk definition step, the risk code has been determined, and the knowledge base management system starts to work. KBMS will output key data such as the frequency of the risk and the impact it has caused. At the same time, the knowledge base will output a list of alternative emergency strategies, various criteria that need to be considered, and a list of decision-makers who need to make decisions on this risk. The main purpose of this step is to provide an information basis for the work of the "decision support system" in the next step. The knowledge base management system can greatly shorten the time of risk analysis and quickly determine the preparations required for decision support. Therefore, the risk knowledge management system can greatly improve the agility of the supply chain.

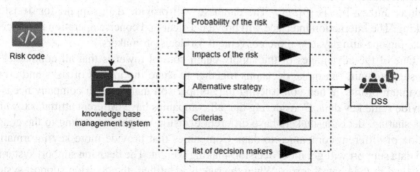

Fig. 6. The knowledge base management system outputs the information for decision support

4.3   Risk Response

The significance of Risk response is to take key actions to restrain the spread of risks, weaken the impact of risks and reduce the duration of risks. The role of the decision support system is to use the most scientific methods to help decision-makers find the best alternative strategies for risk response.

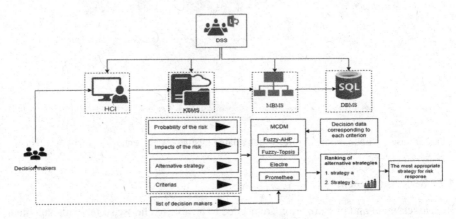

Fig. 7. Decision support system provides decision-makers with alternative strategy ranking

The decision support system in the control tower consists of four systems: knowledge base management system, group decision model base management system, database and human-computer interaction interface.

As shown in Fig. 7, the decision-makers provided by the knowledge base management system will use the human-machine interface to complete the group decision-making process. The role of the knowledge base is to output alternative strategies that can resist the risks, the criteria that need to be considered in decision-making, and the list of decision-makers. The model bases management system will recommend a most suitable multi-criteria decision support model to decision-makers based on the number of decision-makers, the number of criteria, and the characteristics of alternative strategies such as: Fuzzy-Topsis [3], etc. The database will provide data support for decision-making. The interaction interface will provide a clear and concise operation interface to make the operating system more convenient for decision-makers.

One of the advantages of the supply chain control tower is that all companies in the supply chain can make decisions together to share the impact of risks and create maximum profits. When constructing the comparison matrix, each company needs to provide some key data. Considering that all companies have different attitudes towards data sharing, decision-makers have different decision weights according to the contribution of different companies to data. Companies that provide more key information and data support will get more decision-making weight. The decision support system is deployed in the control tower. When the risk is identified, the decision support system will play a role to help the decision-makers of the emergency decision team use the most appropriate group multi-criteria decision support model to compare various alternative strategies. In the end, the decision-maker completes the decision-making process through DSS and gets a ranking of alternative strategies. The strategy will be sent to all relevant organizations to deal with risks.

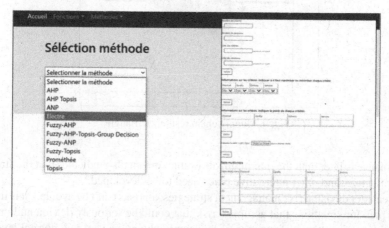

Fig. 8. Program "Module d'aide à la décision" and input screen for the decision data

So far, we have developed a decision-support system called "Module d'aide à la décision". As shown in Fig. 8 is the main interface and data input interface of the DSS. This decision support system can support decision calculations for ten different MCDM models. Four of these models support group decisions. The DSS can import decision data in three ways: manual input, table (*.csv) input and import information from an external service. In subsequent work, we will be adding five more group multi-criteria decision support models to address different group-decision scenarios. This system will be part of the supply chain control tower and connected to the database of the control tower in the future.

4.4 Risk Monitoring

After the strategy generated by the decision support is implemented, the impact of the risk may still exist, so it is necessary to monitor the risk. As shown in Fig. 9, according to the supply chain resilience triangle concept, risks should be monitored from two perspectives: the impact of supply chain performance and the time it takes for supply chain performance to recover to a normal level. The effectiveness of the strategy is reflected in the area of the resilience triangle. If the effect is better, the area of the triangle is smaller.

Therefore, when the strategy is implemented, according to the current situation of the supply chain, the effectiveness of the strategy needs to be judged from two aspects: 1. The lowest point where the supply chain performance can fall, 2. The longest time for the supply chain performance to return to normal levels. If the performance of the supply chain continues to fall below the minimum allowable value after the strategy is implemented, it means that the strategy is invalid and it is necessary to go back to the third step to formulate a new strategy. Similarly, if the recovery time of the supply chain

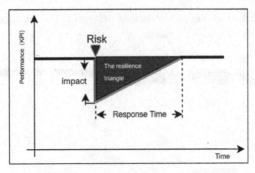

Fig. 9. Supply chain resilience triangle

performance is later than the maximum allowable time, it also indicates that the strategy is not effective, and other alternative plans need to be developed.

Even after devising risk management strategies, all risks can't be avoided, it is important to plan for situations that assume a risk that could be seriously detrimental may be realized [5]. When the performance of the supply chain recovers to a normal level, all risk-related data will be recorded in the database and knowledge bases management system to provide data support for the next decision.

5   Conclusion and Perspectives

This article proposes a DSS based on a control tower for risk management. The control tower uses digital risk sensors to solve the problem of risk identification; uses a knowledge base management system to manage supply chain risk strategies; uses a decision support system to rank alternative strategies. This system also solves the three major problems in the cooperation of various companies in the supply chain network. The DSS-based control tower can predict risks faster, strengthen the efficiency of information transmission between companies, and help companies share risks and group decisions.

This paper is a theoretical framework for future work. In the future, we will continue to develop and program the DSS-based supply chain control tower system. In the future, experiments will be designed to verify the effect of this system: use real enterprise data for simulation, and invite 10–20 supply chain managers to participate in the experiment. Simulate the risk management and decision-making of each decision-maker in the traditional supply chain network scenario and the scenario with the DSS control tower system, and finally compare the performance of the supply chain, supply chain resilience and various indicators. If the supply chain performance is better and the supply chain resilience is stronger in the scenario with the DSS control tower system, it proves that this research can effectively optimize the risk management problems in the context of multi-source data and risk environments.

A limitation of this paper is that there is a realistic constraint on information sharing between companies, and not all companies are willing to share data with their upstream and downstream partners. One of the challenges of the framework is the amount of information that companies are willing to share. Therefore, designing a fair and effective collaboration regulation, as well as using the advantages of control towers to increase profits, is an important prerequisite to motivate companies to participate in the control tower framework, which is also one of the directions of our future work.

References

1. Beamon, B.M.: Supply chain design and analysis: models and methods. Int. J. Prod. Econ. **55**(3), 281–294 (1998)
2. Dossou, P.-E.: Impact of sustainability on the supply chain 4.0 performance. Procedia Manuf. **17**, 452–459 (2018). https://doi.org/10.1016/j.promfg.2018.10.069
3. Yazdani, M., Zarate, P., Coulibaly, A., Zavadskas, E.K.: A group decision making support system in logistics and supply chain management. Exp. Syst. Appl. **88**, 376–392 (2017)
4. Erfani, M., Afrougheh, S., Ardakani, T., Sadeghi, A.: Tourism positioning using decision support system (case study: Chahnime—Zabol, Iran). Environ. Earth Sci. **74**(4), 3135–3144 (2015). https://doi.org/10.1007/s12665-015-4365-z
5. Manuj, I., Mentzer, J.T.: Global supply chain risk management strategies. Int. J. Phys. Distrib. Logist. Manag. **38**(3), 192–223 (2008). https://doi.org/10.1108/09600030810866986
6. Zsidisin, G.A., Henke, M. (eds.): Revisiting Supply Chain Risk. SSSCM, vol. 7. Springer, Cham (2019). https://doi.org/10.1007/978-3-030-03813-7
7. Wieland, A., Wallenburg, C.M.: Dealing with supply chain risks: linking risk management practices and strategies to performance. Int. J. Phys. Distrib. Logist. Manag. **42**, 887–905 (2012). https://doi.org/10.1108/09600031211281411
8. Christopher, M., Peck, H.: Building the resilient supply chain. Int. J. Logist. Manag. **15**(2), 1–14 (2004). https://doi.org/10.1108/09574090410700275
9. Thun, J.-H., Hoenig, D.: An empirical analysis of supply chain risk management in the German automotive industry. Int. J. Prod. Econ. **131**(1), 242–249 (2011). https://doi.org/10.1016/j.ijpe.2009.10.010
10. El Baz, J., Ruel, S.: Can supply chain risk management practices mitigate the disruption impacts on supply chains' resilience and robustness? Evidence from an empirical survey in a COVID-19 outbreak era. Int. J. Prod. Econ. **233**, 107972 (2021). https://doi.org/10.1016/j.ijpe.2020.107972
11. Fan, Y., Stevenson, M.: A review of supply chain risk management: definition, theory, and research agenda. Int. J. Phys. Distrib. Logist. Manag. **48**(3), 205–230 (2018). https://doi.org/10.1108/IJPDLM-01-2017-0043
12. Manuj, I., Mentzer, J.T.: Global supply chain risk management. J. Bus. Logist. **29**(1), 133–155 (2008)
13. Ponomarov, S.Y., Holcomb, M.C.: Understanding the concept of supply chain resilience. Int. J. Logist. Manag. **20**(1), 124–143 (2009). https://doi.org/10.1108/09574090910954873
14. Craighead, C.W., Blackhurst, J., Rungtusanatham, M.J., Handfield, R.B.: The severity of supply chain disruptions: design characteristics and mitigation capabilities. Decis. Sci. **38**(1), 131–156 (2007). https://doi.org/10.1111/j.1540-5915.2007.00151.x
15. Falasca, M., Zobel, C., Cook, D.: A decision support framework to assess supply chain resilience. In: Proceedings of ISCRAM 2008 - 5th International Conference on Information Systems Crisis Response Management, January 2008
16. Gorry, G.A., Scott Morton, M.S.: A framework for management information systems, Cambridge, M.I.T., Working Paper, 1971. Accessed 12 Oct 2021. https://dspace.mit.edu/handle/1721.1/47936

17. Goswami, R., Barua, P.: Web-based decision support system: concept and issues. In: Handbook of Computational Intelligence in Manufacturing and Production Management 2008. https://www.igi-global.com/chapter/web-based-decision-support-system/www.igi-global.com/chapter/web-based-decision-support-system/19365. Accessed 28 Sep 2021

18. Marto, M., et al.: Web-based forest resources management decision support system. Forests **10**(12), 1079 (2019). https://doi.org/10.3390/f10121079

19. Mareschal, B., De Smet, Y.: Visual PROMETHEE: developments of the PROMETHEE & GAIA multi criteria decision aid methods. In: 2009 IEEE International Conference on Industrial Engineering and Engineering Management, pp. 1646–1649, December 2009. https://doi.org/10.1109/IEEM.2009.5373124

20. Carlsson, C., Fullér, R.: Fuzzy multiple criteria decision making: recent developments. Fuzzy Sets Syst. **78**(2), 139–153 (1996). https://doi.org/10.1016/0165-0114(95)00165-4

21. Carvalho, J.B., Varela, M.L.R., Putnik, G.D., Hernández, J.E., Ribeiro, R.A.: A web-based decision support system for supply chain operations management towards an integrated framework. In: Dargam, F., et al. (eds.) Decision Support Systems III - Impact of Decision Support Systems for Global Environments. EWG-DSS EWG-DSS 2013 2013. Lecture Notes in Business Information Processing, vol. 184, pp. 104–117. Springer, Cham (2014). https://doi.org/10.1007/978-3-319-11364-7_10

22. Hallikas, J., Karvonen, I., Pulkkinen, U., Virolainen, V.-M., Tuominen, M.: Risk management processes in supplier networks. Int. J. Prod. Econ. **90**(1), 47–58 (2004). https://doi.org/10.1016/j.ijpe.2004.02.007

Multiple Criteria Approaches

Using the FITradeoff Method for Solving a Truck Acquisition Problem at a Midsize Carrier

Mariana Wanderley Cyreno, Lucia Reis Peixoto Roselli[(✉)] [ORCID],
and Adiel Teixeira de Almeida [ORCID]

Center for Decision Systems and Information Development (CDSID), Universidade Federal de
Pernambuco, Recife, PE, Brazil
{lrpr,almeida}@cdsid.org.br

Abstract. The study demonstrates the flexible functioning of the FITradeoff method that integrates the Holistic Evaluation with the Elicitation by Decomposition. For that purpose, the new features of the FITradeoff method in which integrates the two paradigms of preference modeling have been explored to solve a real multi-criteria decision problem. In this paper, a truck acquisition problem, at a midsize carrier faced with an uncertain and turbulent scenario due to the Coronavirus pandemic, was solved using the FITradeoff method. In this problem, seven criteria were considered to represent the Decision-Maker objectives. Also, six trucks (alternatives) have been examined by the Decision-Maker (Financial Director). The FITradeoff DSS supported the company as to obtain, through the combination of Holistic Evaluation and Elicitation by Decomposition, a ranking of all the trucks based on the preferences expressed during the decision process to ensure lower costs and higher profits in the long run, also guaranteeing a quicker (more efficient) resolution of the problem.

Keywords: FITradeoff method · Elicitation process · Holistic evaluation · Multi-criteria decision making/Aiding (MCDM/A) · Truck acquisition

1 Introduction

In general, organizations are constantly faced with the necessity of choosing, among a set of alternatives, the one that best satisfies different and often conflicting objectives. In other words, these companies need to solve numerous Multi-Criteria Decision problems. In this regard, the Muti-Criteria Decision Making/Aiding (MCDM/A) [1–4] presents itself as a strong ally to ensure that these institutions optimize their results, through the accurate definition of decision-making as a process characterized by various analysis and mathematical foundations and not only on previous personal experiences of executives and managers [4]. In the literature, there is a wide range of examples of MCDM/A problems that are present in the most diverse areas of society, all of which were solved with the help of decision support methods. In this respect, Supplier Selection problems are among the main challenges faced by organizations today [5–8]. For this

A. P. Cabral Seixas Costa et al. (Eds.): ICDSST 2022, LNBIP 447, pp. 139–150, 2022.
https://doi.org/10.1007/978-3-031-06530-9_11

reason, numerous studies focus on concrete situations in which these problems are solved using decision support methods, as in [9], where the MCDM approaches between 2000 and 2008 are reviewed specifically in problems of this category, among several other situations and applications discussed in a vast and deep way in the literature.

Also, it is important to emphasize that there are numerous methods capable of assisting the decision-making process, each appropriate for a different circumstance [4]. Among them, the most used in the context of the Multi-Attribute Theory of Value (MAVT) and, more specifically, for a discrete set of alternatives is the additive aggregation model [1, 2].

Hence, it is possible to state that this study aims to delve further into additive aggregation models, more specifically into the FITradeoff method [10, 11]. After all, the main goal is to demonstrate the effectiveness of the new features of FITradeoff, which allows the combination between Holistic Evaluation and Elicitation by Decomposition, consequently providing improvements in the consistency of the preference modeling process [11]. For this, a ranking problematic in a medium-sized carrier was chosen. It is necessary to point that the main objective of the organization is to define a ranking of the trucks' possibilities to be acquired by the company, all of which come from previously known suppliers.

This paper is organized as follows. Section 2 describes the combination of the two perspectives (Elicitation by Decomposition and Holistic Evaluation) in the FITradeoff Method. Section 3 presents the Truck Acquisition problem. Section 4 illustrates the FITradeoff application to solve the problem. Finally, Sect. 5 remarks the conclusions.

2   FITradeoff Method: Combining Elicitation by Decomposition and Holistic Evaluation

The FITradeoff Method (Flexible and Interactive Tradeoff) emerges as an extremely relevant support tool in the decision-making process. After all, one of the most relevant challenges when using MCDM/A models is the evaluation of scale constants in the aggregation procedure [10], especially considering additive aggregation models. This method was created based on the classic Tradeoff procedure [1].

It is worth noting that the classic tradeoff procedure works based on the comparison of consequences, in which the Decision Maker needs to establish points of indifference between them, considering tradeoffs (exchanges) among the criteria. This type of information that requires the definition of indifference points demands a greater cognitive effort from the Decision-Maker (DM), which deals to inconsistencies in results [12].

In this way, FITradeoff emerges as a flexible elicitation method that works with partial information about Decision Maker (DM) preferences. In other words, this method only requires strict preference by DMs. Thus, in the FITradeoff method, the specific values of each scale constant are not obtained, instead of that, a space of scaling constants are obtained in the final of the decision process [10].

Moreover, the FITradeoff method allows the combination of two paradigms of preference modeling - the Elicitation by Decomposition [1] with the Holistic Evaluation [2] in the preference modeling process [11]. Such combination is of great relevance, since, within the context of MAVT (Multi-Attribute Value Theory), in the preference modeling process, these two paradigms are approached in an opposite/exclusive way. Therefore, in general, each method is based on only one of these two approaches [11].

Briefly, the Holistic Evaluation considers the comparison of alternatives, which is done based on graphical views (bar, bubble or radar chart) and explicit numerical data in a table provided by FITradeoff. Thus, during the holistic evaluation the DM can define dominance relations between alternatives in the middle of the elicitation process, since FITradeoff allows the user to alternate between these two perspectives of preference modeling (elicitation by decomposition and holistic evaluation) throughout the use of the Decision Support System (DSS).

On the other hand, Elicitation by Decomposition is based on the comparison of consequences, meaning that it considers the space of consequences. The answers given by the Decision Maker is based on a heuristic with compares consequences of adjacent criteria, considering an interval scale [10, 11].

Each preference expressed during the decomposition, or the holistic evaluation is included in a Linear Programming Problem (LPP). Hence, this LPP runs after each interaction with DMs seeking for solutions. After each interaction, DMS can observe partial results. The decision process stops when a solution has been found (a complete ranking for ranking problematic, for example) or when DMs wish to stop the process and consider the partial result obtained until this moment (a partial ranking, for instance). In the FITradeoff has possible to interrupt the process at any time by the Decision Maker [10].

Hence, the integration of these two paradigms provided by the flexibility of FITradeoff represents an important step in the advancement of decision support methods, since it allows a global and more in-depth view of the problems (after all, two different points of view are evaluated: one related to the space of consequences and another one to the space of alternatives) and, consequently, more assertive solutions.

This paper wishes to discuss the bases of the decision process in the FITradeoff method, specifically the combination of the paradigms of Holistic Evaluation and the Elicitation by Decomposition provided by the FITradeoff method. The axiomatic bases of this method are already widely discussed in the literature. To more details about the FITradeoff method see [10, 11].

Several applications have been developed using the FITradeoff method [13–25]. In this study, a truck acquisition problem at a midsize carrier faced with an uncertain and turbulent scenario due to the Coronavirus pandemic has been solve. Next section describes the truck acquisition problem, and Sect. 4 illustrates the decision process in the FITradeoff DSS. The FITradeoff DSS is web available at www.fitradeoff.org.

3   Purchase of the Trucks

Faced with an uncertain scenario and marked by large drops in the global financial market because of the Coronavirus pandemic that hit the whole world in early 2020, a carrier, member of the Transport sector of the Brazilian economy, realized the need to optimize all its areas. It is important to emphasize that this carrier is a medium-sized company that has approximately 300 pieces of equipment (from trucks and implements to forklifts), whose customers are, primarily, beverage multinationals — characterizing their load as heavy.

One of the points observed by the administrative sector together with the financial sector of the company was the exacerbated expense with trucks (from their purchase to their maintenance, as well as other expenses that are necessary to ensure that the routes can be completed and, consequently, the deliveries can be performed properly). Therefore, it was noticed that the selection of new trucks would be a good starting point in this scenario of change and improvement of the sectors. Thus, it was concluded that it was necessary to formulate a model capable of aiding the people responsible for these purchases, so they could define the best trucks (cost-benefit ratio) to be acquired for each operating unit. Also, one of the reasons to create such model was to ensure consistent results and to facilitate future analysis, by creating and laying a foundation that could even serve as a database for new scenarios. After all, based on the Pandemic itself, it is clear how the world is constantly changing and, for that matter, it is possible to conclude that each of the parameters used could not be valid in the next couple of years, when the necessity to acquire new trucks would appear.

However, since the company does not want the information obtained regarding the best vehicle to be purchased to be used only superficially, the objective with this model is to obtain a ranking of the trucks and not only the best alternative, so that the information can be more complete and can also be used for future analyses. After all, based on the ranking obtained, the company would have a better understanding of all the trucks and assure a clear comparison of their performances. For this reason, considering the search for determining a ranking and not just the best alternative (in this second situation, there would have been a problematic of choice) the problematic is classified as ranking [de Almeida 2015]. It is necessary to clarify that this problem would not be properly classified if determined as a portfolio problematic, since the trucks are not complementary nor excluding. Therefore, even considering the acquisition of an entire fleet, the company would not choose a specific combination of the trucks but instead opt to only acquire the one that, according to the FITradeoff Method, presented the best performance (cost-benefit ratio) to compose the whole fleet.

Regarding the agents involved in the decision-making process, since the choice of the truck to be acquired to compose the fleet has a substantial economic impact, the Financial Director is assigned to be the Decision Maker. However, the process will be cautiously supervised by one of the 3 company's partners, to ensure that the decision is according to the organization's main strategy. Also, the National Fleet Manager and the Operations Manager appear in this scenario respectively helping with the necessary background to ensure that the decision-making process is carried out based in factual information and to assist in the modelling process, since the Financial Director is highly overloaded with all the demands of the sector.

Considering the main objective of guaranteeing the greatest long-term profitability in the operationalization of the trucks, for each criterion there is an individual objective that corroborates for the achievement of the main one: the lowest possible purchase price is aimed (to reduce the price of initial investment necessary), the highest selling price (since the truck will be resold after 5 years), the highest km/L ratio, so that consumption is as efficient as possible, the lowest maintenance cost (a company always aims to minimize its costs), the least number of corrective stops, the greatest amount of km between each preventive maintenance and the smallest number of days needed for each preventive review. The last three objectives are related to the maintenance that need to be ensured on the trucks, all of which are linked to the fact that the carrier wants its trucks to stop for the shortest possible time and to minimize the necessary maintenance, to reduce costs and increase productivity (more uptime means more deliveries).

The company's Financial Director (Decision Maker) and the other agents involved used the most relevant criteria to guarantee the proper ranking of the trucks, so that the chosen model ensures lower costs and higher profits in the long run. Each of the criteria (all natural) is associated with an objective:

- **Purchase price:** vehicle's purchase price (0 km);
- **Selling price:** resale value of the vehicle after 5 years;
- **Maintenance Cost:** maintenance contract value in R$ per km driven;
- **Availability:** vehicle reliability, i.e., history of corrective stops (per year) of the vehicle;
- **Average km for each preventive maintenance review**: number of km between each preventive maintenance;
- **Average time required for each review:** number of days required for each preventive review to be completed;
- **Fuel Consumption (km/L)**: number of km driven per liter of fuel.

It is important to emphasize that the last four criteria listed above (Availability, Average km for each preventive maintenance review, Average time required for each review and Fuel Consumption), according to the Financial Director, could not be easily translated into monetary consequences because the company operates in different states of the Brazilian territory, involving divergent routes, and, consequently, a varied number of kilometers traveled per day. Also, the Financial Director among with the other agents involved, considered that the possible utilization of the average of km traveled per day would be an inadequate simplification, since the wrong choice of which truck to acquire could represent a huge financial impact for the company. Therefore, it was necessary to model this problem as MCDM problem.

In addition, the 6 current manufacturers (and the respective models of trucks that can be used in the operations) that the company knows or has already had some sort of contact with were listed so that they can be analyzed according to the 7 criteria defined for solving this problem. Hence, the alternatives are:

- **Option 1:** Volkswagen 25 420 Constellation 6 × 2 2P (Diesel)(E5);
- **Option 2:** Man Tgx 28.440 6 × 2 2P (Diesel)(E5);
- **Option 3:** Scania G 410 A 6 × 2 2P (Diesel)(E5);
- **Option 4**: Volvo Fh 420 6 × 2 2P (Diesel) (E5);
- **Option 5:** Mercedes-Benz Axor 2544 S Ls 6 × 2 2P (Diesel) (E5);
- **Option 6**: Iveco Stralis Hi Road 600S44T 6 × 2 (Dies.)(E5).

Based on this information, it is possible to illustrate the Consequences Matrix of the problem, as shown in the Table 1.

The focus of this study is to emphasize the importance of the possibility of integrating the paradigms of Holistic Evaluation and the Elicitation by Decomposition provided by

Table 1. Supplier selection decision matrix

Alt vs Crit	Purchase price (0 km – in R$)	Selling price (5 years in R$)	Maintenance cost (in R$)	Availability	Average Km	Average time (days)	Consumption (km/L)
Op1	R$381.021,00	R$170.470,00	R$1,19	10	30000	1	2,4
Op2	R$460.875,00	R$211.413,00	R$1,27	10	40000	1	2,3
Op3	R$488.150,00	R$244.075,00	R$1,48	9	40000	1	2,4
Op4	R$487.545,00	R$239.359,00	R$1,34	8	30000	1	2,45
Op5	R$408.559,00	R$237.648,00	R$1,08	15	40000	2	2,4
Op6	R$415.810,00	R$187.114,50	R$1,34	20	30000	2	2,3

the FITradeoff method. Thus, in the next section, the entire decision process performed by the DM in the FITradeoff DSS is illustrated combining the two paradigms to obtain the ranking of the trucks [9].

4   Application of the FITradeoff Method

After establishing the main information of the problem, the FITradeoff Decision Support System was used (it is available at www.fitradeoff.org) and the following order of the scale constants was obtained.

$$K_{\text{Purchase Price}} > K_{\text{Maintenance Cost}} > K_{\text{Consumption}} > K_{\text{Availability}} > K_{\text{Selling Price}} > K_{\text{Average Km}} \quad (1)$$
$$> K_{\text{Average Time}}$$

The performance of each alternative in each of the criteria is illustrated below. This graph was obtained right after the process of ordering the scale constants. After all, at this moment, no alternative stands out over the other, i.e., the ranking has only one level, as illustrated in Fig. 1.

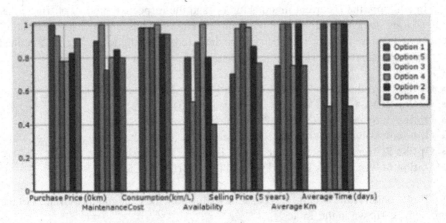

Fig. 1. Bar graph exhibiting the performance of all the alternatives

After that, the DM decides to continue the process in the elicitation by decomposition, thus several comparisons are made between the criteria, aiming to find more precise relations. Thus, questions are asked about two possible consequences (A or B), to which the DM can respond either if he prefers one of them or if he is indifferent. It is also possible for the DM to claim that he does not have an answer to a given question or even indicate that there is inconsistency.

Therefore, this process continued until the 8th question: all questions were answered through Elicitation by Decomposition. However, after answering the 8th one, the DM chose to evaluate the results obtained until that moment, since he wanted to guarantee that his answers were being consistent to what was best to the company (preferences defined). So, it was observed that there was a tie in the 3rd level of the ranking between options 2, 4 and 6. In order to understand which would be the most relevant alternatives for the Holistic Evaluation, the Hasse Diagram constructed so far was observed, as illustrated in Fig. 2. It is worth noting that the black arrows in the diagram above represent dominance relations established by the Elicitation by Decomposition. In addition, each option represents a truck that will be ordered. The name was omitted at this time to facilitate the process, as the trucks are specific and have extensive names. However, the respective trucks can be rescued by turning to the topic "Purchase of the trucks", where this relation between the options and the trucks was established.

Hasse Diagram

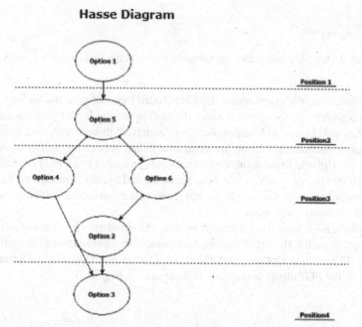

Fig. 2. Hasse diagram obtained after the 8th question during the flexible elicitation

Based on this diagram, the Decision Maker, realizing the inexistence of a clear/determined relationship between options 2 and 4, chose to make a Holistic Evaluation of these two alternatives. In ranking problematic, the Holistic Evaluation is done for pairs of alternatives that are at the same level of the ranking until then found by FITradeoff. For this, it was necessary to evaluate/compare their performance by analyzing the graphics provided by the FITradeoff DSS. Only the Bubble Chart is illustrated in Fig. 3, but it is important to note that the DM has the possibility of checking 3 different types of graphic representations: bar, radar and bubble charts - in addition to the numerical results that are always available.

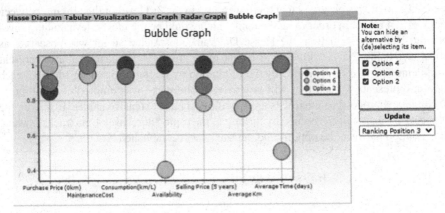

Fig. 3. Bubble graph exhibiting the performance of the alternatives 2, 4 and 6.

After analyzing the graph above, DM concluded that, between the options 2 and 4, there was a preference for option 2, since this option present higher performance in the Criteria Purchase Price and Maintenance Cost, which are those with higher scaling constant. Thus, a dominance relation has been established between these two alternatives, finalizing the Holistic Evaluation. Furthermore, it is possible to identify the Hasse Diagram illustrated in Fig. 4, which was obtained at the end of the FITradeoff application. It is also possible to notice the red arrow, that represents a dominance relation determined through the Holistic Evaluation.

Therefore, after answering 8 questions from the Elicitation by Decomposition process and one from the Holistic Evaluation, the outcome provided by FITradeoff was the following: Option 1 > Option 5 > Option 6 > Option 2 > Option 4 > Option 3. The summary of the FITradeoff application is illustrated in Fig. 5.

Hasse Diagram

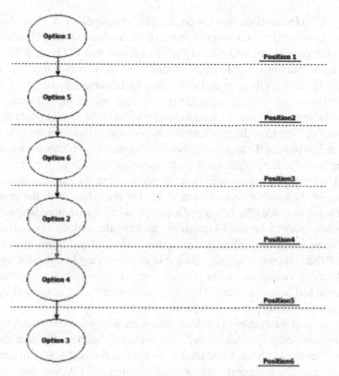

Fig. 4. Hasse Diagram obtained at the end of the FITradeoff application

Cycle	Consequence A	Consequence B: better of	Response	Number of levels
0			Ordering...	1
1	434585.500 of Purchase Price	Average Time (1)	A	1
2	434585.500 of Purchase Price	Maintenance Cost (1.075)	B	1
3	1.277 of Maintenance Cost	Consumption (2.45)	A	2
4	2.375 of Consumption	Availability (8)	A	2
5	14.000 of Availability	Selling Price (244075)	A	3
6	207272.500 of Selling Price	Average Km (40000)	A	3
7	35000.000 of Average Km	Average Time (1)	B	3
8	407803.250 of Purchase Price	Maintenance Cost (1.075)	A	4

Holistic Evaluation done?	Alternativas comparadas em (AH)	Answer (HE)	Number of levels after (HE)
No			
No			
No			
No			
No			
No			
No			
No			
Yes	Option 2, Option 4	Option 2 preferable	6

Fig. 5. Summary of the FITradeoff application

5 Conclusion

In this study the FITradeoff method has been applied to solve a truck acquisition problem in a medium-sized carrier. In that sense, through the analysis of the FITradeoff decision process, it was possible to understand the advantages that FITradeoff has due to its flexibility, since, among other features of this method, it is possible to combine the paradigms of Holistic Evaluation and Elicitation by Decomposition.

Hence, it is also important to highlight that, to demonstrate the relevance of combining the two paradigms (Holistic Evaluation and Elicitation by Decomposition) in modeling FITradeoff preferences, the problem was implemented twice: in the first application (illustrated in this paper), these paradigms were integrated, so both were used to find the final ranking linked to the problem and, in the second, only Elicitation by Decomposition was used. The results obtained in both applications were the same, demonstrating the effectiveness of the combination of paradigms. On the other hand, the process of the application using only the Elicitation by Decomposition caused more fatigue in the DM, since it was necessary to answer 14 questions, meanwhile, as described before, the combination of the paradigms resulted in a process with only 9 questions. Such time saving is crucial for the company analyzed since it is always trying to optimize its processes. This possibility of combining them is even more relevant because, over many years, this integration had been disregarded by other researchers, who, in general, defended an excluding relation between these two paradigms.

Moreover, the utilization of FITradeoff was of great importance to the carrier because with this DSS, not only time was saved – as explained before – but also the company was able to obtain, exactly as it intended, a ranking of the best trucks in terms of cost-benefit. Consequently, equipped with such information, the DM was able to reduce the exacerbated costs associated to the trucks and, in a more global analysis, he was also able to obtain the necessary basis to establish a good starting point in this scenario of change and improvement of the organization's sectors. After all, the three partners of the carrier were satisfied with the decision encountered and decided that the acquisition of a new fleet of the Volkswagen's truck would be the correct decision to be made, since it presented a good performance in the most relevant criteria for them. On the other hand, it was defined that the acquisition of the fleet would occur gradually, to reduce the expenses and ensure positive impacts on the company's financial situation and, consequently, its further development.

Therefore, in this paper a real problem has been solved with the support of the FITradeoff method. The decision process using the combination of both paradigms was presented, and as result it provides a coherent ranking according to DM preferences, and simultaneously a more efficient outcome, since the DM saves time due to the reduction on the number of questions that need to be answered. For future research, more analyses will be done to improve the FITradeoff DSS, for instance studies about inconsistency rate will be developed supported by neuroscience studies [26–31].

Acknowledgment. This work had partial support from the Brazilian Research Council (CNPq) [grant 308531/2015–9;312695/2020–9] and the Foundation of Support in Science and Technology of the State of Pernambuco (FACEPE) [APQ-0484–3.08/17].

References

1. Keeney, R.L., Raiffa, H.: Decisions with Multiple Objectives: Preferences, and Value Tradeoffs. Wiley, New York (1976)
2. Belton, V., Stewart, T.: Multiple Criteria Decision Analysis. Kluwer Academic Publishers, Dordrecht (2002)
3. Figueira J, Greco S, Ehrgott M (eds).: Multiple Criteria Decision Analysis: State of the Art Surveys. Springer, Berlin (2005). https://doi.org/10.1007/b100605
4. de Almeida, A.T., Cavalcante, C., Alencar, M., Ferreira, R., de Almeida-Filho A.T., Garcez. T.: Multicriteria and Multi-objective Models for Risk, Reliability and Maintenance Decision Analysis. International Series in Operations Research & Management Science. vol. 231. Springer, New York (2015). https://doi.org/10.1007/978-3-319-17969-8
5. Barla, S.B.: A case study of supplier selection for lean supply by using a mathematical model. Logist. Inf. Manag. **16**, 451–459 (2003)
6. Xia, W., Zhiming, W.: Supplier selection with multiple criteria in volume discount environments. Omega **35**(5), 494–504 (2007)
7. Chai, J., Liu, J., Ngai, E.: Application of decision-making techniques in supplier selection: a systematic review of literature. Expert Syst. Appl. **40**(10), 3872–3885 (2013)
8. Frej, E.A., Roselli, L.R.P., Araújo, J., de Almeida, A., de Almeida, T.: A multicriteria decision model for supplier selection in a food industry based on FITradeoff method. Math. Prob. Eng. **2017**, 1–9 (2017)
9. Ho, W., Xu, X., Dey, P.K.: Multi-criteria decision making approaches for supplier evaluation and selection: a literature review. Eur. J. Oper. Res. **202**(1), 16–24 (2010)
10. de Almeida, A.T., Almeida, J.A., Costa, A.P.C.S., Almeida-Filho, A.T.: A new method for elicitation of criteria weights in additive models: flexible and interactive tradeoff. Eur. J. Oper. Res. **250**(1), 179–191 (2016)
11. de Almeida, A.T., Frej, E.A., Roselli, L.R.P.: Combining holistic and decomposition paradigms in preference modeling with the flexibility of FITradeoff. CEJOR **29**(1), 7–47 (2021). https://doi.org/10.1007/s10100-020-00728-z
12. Weber, M., Borcherding, K.: Behavioral influences on weight judgments in multi-attribute decision making. Eur. J. Oper. Res. **67**, 1–12 (1993)
13. de Gusmao, A.P.H., Pereira Medeiros, C.: A model for selecting a strategic information system using the FITradeoff. Math. Prob. Eng. **2016**, 1–8 (2016)
14. Kang, T.H.A., Júnior, A.M.D.C.S., de Almeida, A.T.: Evaluating electric power generation technologies: a multicriteria analysis based on the FITradeoff method. Energy **165**, 10–20 (2018)
15. Carrillo, P.A.A., Roselli, L.R.P., Frej, E.A., de Almeida, A.T.: Selecting an agricultural technology package based on the flexible and interactive tradeoff method. Ann. Oper. Res. 1–16 (2018). https://doi.org/10.1007/s10479-018-3020-y
16. de Macedo, P.P., de Miranda Mota, C.M., Sola, A.V.H.: Meeting the Brazilian energy efficiency law: a flexible and interactive multicriteria proposal to replace non-efficient motors. Sustain. Cities Soc. **41**, 822–832 (2018)
17. Frej, E.A., de Almeida, A.T., Costa, A.P.C.S.: Using data visualization for ranking alternatives with partial information and interactive tradeoff elicitation. Oper. Res. Int. J. **19**(4), 909–931 (2019). https://doi.org/10.1007/s12351-018-00444-2
18. Monte, M.B.S., Morais, D.C.: A decision model for identifying and solving problems in an urban water supply system. Water Resour. Manage. **33**(14), 4835–4848 (2019)
19. Kang, T.H.A., Frej, E.A., de Almeida, A.T.: Flexible and interactive tradeoff elicitation for multicriteria sorting problems. Asia Pac. J. Oper. Res. **37**, 2050020 (2020)

20. Fossile, D.K., Frej, E.A., da Costa, S.E.G., de Lima, E.P., de Almeida, A.T.: Selecting the most viable renewable energy source for Brazilian ports using the FITradeoff method. J. Clean. Prod. **260**, 121107 (2020)

21. Santos, I.M., Roselli, L.R.P., da Silva, A.L.G., Alencar, L.H.: A supplier selection model for a wholesaler and retailer company based on FITradeoff multicriteria method. Math. Prob. Eng. **2020**, 1–14 (2020)

22. Dell'Ovo, M., Oppio, A., Capolongo, S.: Decision support system for the location of healthcare facilities SitHealth evaluation tool. PoliMI SpringerBriefs. Springer Nature, Switzerland (2020). https://doi.org/10.1007/978-3-030-50173-0

23. Camilo, D.G.G., de Souza, R.P., Frazão, T.D.C., da Costa Junior, J.F.: Multi-criteria analysis in the health area: selection of the most appropriate triage system for the emergency care units in natal. BMC Med. Inform. Decis. Mak. **20**(1), 1–16 (2020)

24. Pergher, I., Frej, E.A., Roselli, L.R.P., de Almeida, A.T.: Integrating simulation and FITradeoff method for scheduling rules selection in job-shop production systems. Int. J. Prod. Econ. **227**, 107669 (2020)

25. Frej, E.A., Ekel, P., de Almeida, A.T.: A Benefit-to-cost ratio based approach for portfolio selection under multiple criteria with incomplete preference information. Inf. Sci. **545**, 487–498 (2021)

26. Roselli, L.R.P., de Almeida, A.T.: Use of the alpha-theta diagram as a decision neuroscience tool for analyzing holistic evaluation in decision making. Ann. Oper. Res. (2022). https://doi.org/10.1007/s10479-021-04495-1

27. Roselli, L.R.P., de Almeida, A.T.: The use of the success-based decision rule to support the holistic evaluation process in FITradeoff. Int. Trans. Oper. Res. **2021**, 1–21 (2021)

28. Silva A.L.C.L, Costa, A.P.C.S., de Almeida, A.T.: Exploring cognitive aspects of FITradeoff method using neuroscience tools. Ann. Oper. Res. 1–23 (2021). https://doi.org/10.1007/s10479-020-03894-0

29. Roselli, L.R.P., de Almeida, A.T., Frej, E.A.: Decision neuroscience for improving data visualization of decision support in the FITradeoff method. Oper. Res. Int. J. **19**(4), 933–953 (2019). https://doi.org/10.1007/s12351-018-00445-1

30. Roselli, L.R.P., Pereira, L., da Silva, A., de Almeida, A.T., Morais, D.C., Costa, A.P.C.S.: Neuroscience experiment applied to investigate decision-maker behavior in the tradeoff elicitation procedure. Ann. Oper. Res. **289**(1), 67–84 (2019). https://doi.org/10.1007/s10479-019-03394-w

31. Carneiro de Lima da Silva, A.L., Cabral Seixas Costa, A.P.: FITradeoff Decision Support System: An Exploratory Study with Neuroscience Tools. In: Davis, F.D., Riedl, R., vom Brocke, J., Léger, P.-M., Randolph, A., Fischer, T. (eds.) Information Systems and Neuroscience. LNISO, vol. 32, pp. 365–372. Springer, Cham (2020). https://doi.org/10.1007/978-3-030-28144-1_40

Maturity Assessment in the Context of Industry 4.0 - an Application Using FITradeoff Method in a Textile Industry

Duan Vilela Ferreira[1]([✉]) [iD] and Ana Paula Henriques de Gusmão[1,2]([✉]) [iD]

[1] Management Engineering – PPGEP-CAA, Federal University of Pernambuco,
Campina Grande Avenue, Caruaru 55014-900, Brazil
duanvilela@gmail.com
[2] Management Engineering, Federal University of Sergipe,
Marechal Rondon Avenue, São Cristóvão 49100000, Brazil
anapaulahg@hotmail.com

Abstract. The Brazilian textile industry scenario has been unfavorable in relation to competition, mainly due to the entry of foreign products in the region. Thus, an opportunity to improve Brazil´s competitive potential in this sector can not only be perceived but also achieved by applying the technological tools of industry 4.0. Hence, this paper seeks to contribute to the organizational management of developing and applying a maturity model to evaluate companies in the textile sector in terms of technological maturity for industry 4.0, by taking a multicriteria approach based on the FITradeoff method for sorting problems. As a demonstration of the applicability of the model, three Brazilian companies were evaluated. As to results, it was possible to access the maturity levels of these three companies, and the main aspects associated with the attributes evaluated were also analyzed. Finally, it is believed that this study can serve as a support tool in the process of strategic planning for managers and others involved in companies in the textile and clothing market, who are seeking to develop strategies in relation to the aforementioned theme. In addition, this study contributes to mitigating the gap found in the literature.

Keywords: Industry 4.0 · Maturity · FITradeoff · Sorting problems

1 Introduction

In Brazil, one of the sectors of industry marked by the need to improve competitiveness is textiles and clothing. This industry, despite having significant relevance to the national economy, still has a long way to go in terms of improving competitiveness in relation mainly to Asian competitors [1]. However, in order to plan actions to improve competitiveness, it is pertinent to evaluate the current state of an organization in relation to competitive references so it can set its strategic objectives better.

The technological advance characteristic of the fourth industrial revolution has been a relevant factor in promoting the competitiveness of organizations. The change that

A. P. Cabral Seixas Costa et al. (Eds.): ICDSST 2022, LNBIP 447, pp. 151–163, 2022.
https://doi.org/10.1007/978-3-031-06530-9_12

is occurring today is based on using a set of technologies, management concepts and emerging tools that enable networks and systems to be integrated, thereby bringing flexibility, autonomy, customization and a high capacity for cooperation between processes. This facilitates the creation of new operational models [2].

These models start by applying tools such as artificial intelligence (AI) in decision-making, seeking high performance in the storage and processing of data using Big Data, transmitting information with the Internet of Things (IoT) or by operating systems and devices remotely via physical cyber systems (PCS). The use of these technologies and tools is likely to generate a consequent improvement in value generation throughout production chains and to bring benefits such as reducing costs or increasing productivity [3].

Thus, taking into account the potential organizational benefits promoted by industry 4.0 technologies, which have aroused the interest of companies, one can perceive the relevance and complexity of decisions related to planning and executing a company's business strategy with the aid of the tools appropriate to the business scenario of companies and thus to promote their competitiveness. In this scenario, maturity models (MM) emerge as frameworks that assist organizations in analyzing the current situation in terms of technological maturity towards industry 4.0, and that also propose actions to achieve higher levels [4, 5]. In other words, an MM can be used to guide the process of changing a company's business model, as well as to help understand the resources needed to implement industry 4.0 [6].

Therefore, this article seeks to contribute to the organizational management of textile companies, within the investment decision-making process to increase competitiveness. It does so by applying an MM to assess technological maturity in the context of industry 4.0. On applying the MM, an investment strategy can be defined for the companies that will increase their competitiveness within the context of industry 4.0.

In addition to the previous contribution, this research was also motivated by the fact that the MMs found in the literature do not include in their structure the particular parameters, regarding the textile industry, which are associated with a clear measurement related to the methods and variables considered [7]. Thus, the model, proposed and used in this study, is based on a multicriteria decision method (MCDM/A), combined with FITradeoff, for sorting problems.

2   Related Studies and Background

2.1   Maturity Models for Industry 4.0

Several MMs have been proposed to evaluate the performance and readiness of organizations vis-à-vis industry 4.0, and thus to identify the need for specific investments for the full application of tools and to benefit from their advantages [8]. The initiatives that result from MMs are typically carried out by academics, government agencies and marketing companies.

Based on software aimed at methods of measuring process capability (SPICE), an MM has been proposed by [9] for the evaluation of organizations. These authors argue that SPICE served as a reference due to its well-defined and commonly accepted structure for evaluation and improvements. The model, called industry 4.0-MM, aims to create a common basis for evaluating technologies, as well as to guide how to achieve higher levels of maturity to maximize economic benefits.

Besides the model proposed by [9], the Singapore Economic Development Council created an MM called the Singapore Smart Industry Readiness Index (SIRI). Information published by the development council puts forward the argument that MM is comprehensive for all sizes of companies and is supported by the following pillars of industry 4.0: technology, process and organization, thereby seeking to find a balance between technical requirements and usability of tools. Additionally, the model can be accessed in a limited version from a website (https://siri.gov.sg/) where it is possible to perform assessments interactively by answering questionnaires available in the interface [10].

In a market initiative, an MM entitled Connected Enterprise Maturity Model has been developed by [11]. The tool proposes a five-stage framework based on assessing the current state of maturity associated with evaluations of pillars focused on security, controls and data networks, the definition and structuring of data use, change management for the incorporation of data analysis, and the creation of a predictive environment of activities through the supply chain and demand.

Researchers have also conducted systematic reviews of the literature with the aim of mapping and characterizing the state of the art related to industry 4.0 MMs. In [12] a study was conducted to identify the main dimensions of industry 4.0 evaluation for organizations and 30 MMs were identified that have 158 unique dimensions in their structure. After a detailed analysis, these authors proposed a grouping of dimensions. They identified relevant groupings that are normally evaluated by MMs: technology, people, strategy, leadership, processes and innovation.

When proposing a multicriteria model for the selection of MMs, [13] stated that the number of dimensions and processes considered in an MM is a relevant attribute in the process for evaluating tools for application in organizations. In this study, the number of dimensions was established as directly proportional to the duration of the proposed maturity identification processes. In other words, the more dimensions, the longer the time required to apply the MM.

It has also been observed that it is not possible to obtain information about several MMs, such as their parametric and methodological bases, since they are the result of market activities and such information is kept confidential by companies for reasons of competitiveness. This fact makes it impossible to study some of the existing tools [13, 14]. Also, based on the distinction between the MMs available in the literature, it can be inferred that business and processes can be evaluated from a perspective of multiple criteria. So, taking these matters into account, the authors of this paper propose a model for assessing the maturity of companies in the context of Industry 4.0 using a multi-criteria approach. The proposed model has, among other advantages, the flexibility of being able to be replicated and parameterized according to the preferences of experts and decision makers (DMs), is easily understood, and presents a structured procedure for classification. In the case study, presented in Sect. 3, details of how the problem is structured are presented (definition of criteria, thresholds, classes, etc.).

2.2 FITradeoff for Sorting Problems

Multiple criteria sorting problems are common in the context of decision analysis. Problems related to recognizing health patterns, human resources management, labor allocation and others, which demand a sorting/classification analysis, are found in the literature. Thus, some multicriteria methods were developed to support this analysis [15–17].

Developed by [18], which was based on the previous concepts of [19] and [20], the FITradeoff for ordinal sorting problems addresses the idea of flexible elicitation with the use of partial information about decision-making preferences to allocate alternatives in classes by means of a structured process of flexible elicitation based on tradeoffs. The method, which has also versions for ordering and selection problems, has been applied in several areas of knowledge, such as supplier selection [21], health [22], and neuroscience [23].

The method is implemented in a decision support system (DSS) available at http://fitradeoff.org/. The overall performance of the alternatives in this method is measured according to Eq. (1):

$$v(a_j) = \sum_{i=1}^{n} k_i v_i(a_j) \tag{1}$$

This equation considers a multicriteria problem with n criteria where k_i and $v_i(a_j)$ are, respectively, the scale constant of criterion i and the marginal value function of the alternative a_j in the criterion i normalized on a scale from 0 to 1.

The flexible elicitation process is based on the traditional tradeoff procedure [24]. It maintains the robustness of the axiomatic structure, but has the advantage of not requiring exact points of indifference to be established for all pairs of criteria. In the flexible procedure, the method uses partial information from the DM to seek a solution to a linear programming problem (LP) for each new level of information obtained in order to obtain values of the scale constants of the criteria [18].

During flexible elicitation, each level of information provided by the DM related to a pair of i and $i + 1$ criteria in the form of strict preference is used to update the range of values $\left(X_i'', X_i'\right)$, $v_i\left(X_i''\right) < v_i\left(X_i'\right)$ containing the point of indifference. The thresholds of these intervals are related to the scale constants of Eq. (2):

$$\begin{aligned} v_i\left(X_i''\right)k_i &< k_{i+1} \\ v_i\left(X_i'\right)k_i &> k_{i+1} \end{aligned} \tag{2}$$

Considering a decision problem with n criteria and a ranking of scale constants such as $k_1 > \ldots > k_i > k_{i+1} > \ldots > k_n$, it is proposed to ask the DM questions in order to compare two hypothetical alternatives to infer the limits (l_1, m_1) of the range that comprises the value of indifference x_i^1. Thus, $x_1 \in (l_1, m_1)$ leading to the in equations presented in (3) in relation to the scale constants k_1 and k_2.

$$\begin{aligned} v_1(l_1)k_1 &< k_2 \\ v_1(m_1)k_1 &> k_2 \end{aligned} \tag{3}$$

Based on the DM's preference, regarding the performance of two alternatives presented, the space of scale constants is reduced based on new information obtained [18].

The method makes use makes use of boundary values (b_r) that limit the consecutive classes. Thus, considering $b_0 < b_1 < \ldots < b_k$, where $b_0 = 0$ and $b_k = 1$, Table 1 shows the definition of classes according to the b_r values.

Table 1. Definition of classes

Class	Definition
C_k	$b_{k-1} < v(a_j) \leq b_k$
C_{k-1}	$b_{k-2} < v(a_j) \leq b_{k-1}$
$\vdots$	$\vdots$
C_r	$b_{r-1} < v(a_j) \leq b_r$
$\vdots$	$\vdots$
C_1	$b_0 \leq v(a_j) \leq b_1$

In this interval, 0 and 1 represent the worst and best performance of an alternative measured by using Eq. (1) [18].

The elicitation process of FITradeoff works with viable value ranges for the scale constants of the criteria. Thus, a decision rule was adopted based on maximized and minimized performance values obtained for a given alternative [18].

To this end, the LP models detailed below (4 and 5) are solved for each alternative A_j which belongs to the discrete set of alternatives A, considering the space of scale constants φ^n obtained from the decision-making information in interactions with the DSS. This space consists of a set of possible scale constant values that each criterion could assume, according to preferential information provided by the DM so far. The space of scale constants is used in order to replace the need for exact values, as in traditional methods that work with complete information.

Thus, φ^n is represented in the form of in equations that act with restrictions in the LP model. While the DM provides more preferential information during the process, the scaling constant space is refined and the constraints updated [18].

$$s_1 = \min_{k \in \varphi^n} v(a_j) = \sum_{i=1}^n k_i v_i(a_j).$$
$$\textit{Subject to:}$$
$$v_1(X_1'')k_1 + \varepsilon \leq k_2$$
$$v_1(X_1')k_1 - \varepsilon \geq k_2$$
$$\ldots \tag{4}$$
$$v_{n-1}(X_{n-1}'')k_{n-1} + \varepsilon \leq k_n$$
$$v_{n-1}(X_{n-1}')k_{n-1} - \varepsilon \geq k_n$$
$$\sum_{i=1}^n k_i = 1$$
$$k_i \geq 0, i = 1, \ldots, n.$$

$$s_2 = \max_{k \in \varphi^n} v(a_j) = \sum_{i=1}^{n} k_i v_i(a_j)$$
$$\text{Subject to:}$$
$$v_1(X_1'')k_1 + \varepsilon \leq k_2$$
$$v_1(X_1')k_1 - \varepsilon \geq k_2$$
$$...$$
$$v_{n-1}(X_{n-1}'')k_{n-1} + \varepsilon \leq k_n$$
$$v_{n-1}(X_{n-1}')k_{n-1} - \varepsilon \geq k_n$$
$$\sum_{i=1}^{n} k_i = 1$$
$$k_i \geq 0, i = 1, ..., n.$$

(5)

Where S_1 and S_2 are the optimal solutions of LP 4 and 5 models, respectively, and ε is a small constant applied to make the strict in equations computationally treatable. After obtaining the minimum and maximum solutions for $v(a_j)$ with the resolution of the PL models, as mentioned earlier, a rule is applied to verify the possibility of allocating the alternative to any of the classes C_k, which are delimited by the range (b_{r-1}, b_r) of values. Because the method works with an ordinal sorting, the categories are established in such a way that $C_k > C_{k-1} > ... > C_1$. That is, alternatives are classified from the most preferable category (C), to the least preferable category (C_1) [18].

In this scenario, from the perspective of methods that work with compensatory rationality, there are additive methods, based on utility/value functions and unique synthesis criteria. Thus, in this research, the FITradeoff method was used for sorting problems. The method was defined based on the nature of the problem and the DM's preference structure, associated with advantageous characteristics such as the use of a flexible and interactive procedure that allows the decision model to recommend alternatives without the need for complete information [18].

The evaluation process with FITradeoff for classification problems is conducted with partial information, which does not require much cognitive effort from the DM, following interactive and flexible steps. This was taken into consideration with regard to why FITradeoff was used in this study.

3   Maturity Assessment of Textile Companies

As a result of the globalization process associated with the commercial opening of the Brazilian economy in the 1990s, there were negative impacts for the sector that began to be bombarded by imported products mainly from Asia [25]. Between 2006 and 2012, there was an average annual increase of 15% in imports, reaching US $17.5 billion annually. Brazilian participation in international trade has been small. It occupies 26th position in textile exports and 48th in the export of manufactured goods [26].

The companies evaluated in this study are inserted in the unfavorable scenario of being in a market characterized by strong competition. They are Brazilian small- and medium-sized companies and showed interest in participating in the process to acquire an understanding of their level of maturity in relation to the concepts of industry 4.0. Although they make use of some technological tools, they still did not have specific strategies for increasing their level of maturity.

3.1 Problem Structuring

Considering the organizations' main motivation for carrying out the maturity assessment, reported earlier, the problem was structured and the parameters defined according to the validation of two experts – academics and professionals working in the context of Industry 4.0 for the textile industry.

Initially, based on a literature review, comprising the main MMs and textile tools associated with industry 4.0, the set of criteria needed to evaluate the company was established. Thus, the following criteria were defined: strategy and innovation (E&I), technology and processes (T&C), Sustainability (Sus), People (Pess) and Leadership (Lid). As a way of obtaining the performance of the decision alternatives (three companies) in the criteria included in the problem, a Likert scale of 5 points was used, with 1 being the least preferable in relation to the objective of the problem, and 5 the most preferable.

Then, also based on the literature review and experts' opinions, the different levels of business maturity were defined. Thus, 6 classes were proposed to evaluate the maturity of companies operating in the textile sector, in order to improve maturity, respectively: non-existent, basic, intermediate, experienced, specialist and convergent.

It is important to highlight that, considering the compensatory methodological procedure adopted in this application, companies can be allocated to a certain class, without necessarily strictly meeting all the aspects expected for a class. Thus, the denomination of levels serves as a general reference of maturity of the organizations.

3.2 Maturity Assessment Using FITradeoff

Regarding the infrastructure currently available in the organizations, in general, part of the machinery uses sensors to generate real time information and, in addition to that, some machines have automation characteristics and autonomy for adjustments. Some information systems are used but they are not directly integrated with each other for the purposes of information sharing.

In relation to sustainability, the companies do not have actions to reduce emissions or their consumption of scarce resources, nor do they even use sustainable materials in the structure of the components of their products. Moreover, the companies' employees do not yet have many skills and competencies related to industry 4.0, but there are plans to train them in these. Leaders recognize the importance of acquiring new skills and competencies and understand that new challenges are opportunities for their companies to develop. Therefore, initially they are defining their digital transformation strategy for some areas.

Based on the information collected, MM was applied by using FITradeoff's DSS for sorting problems. Thus, to start the process, some steps related to specifying the parameters of the model in the software are required. In the context of the problem situation under evaluation, the criteria were established as discrete maximization, given the nature of the problem and the Likert scale used in the questionnaire.

The profiles were specified, based on the experts' opinions, and are presented in Table 2. In this table, the thresholds (b_k) of the profiles are presented. These profiles

Table 2. Thresholds and categories

Threshold (b_k)	#Class	Maturity
0.2	C1	Nonexistent
0.4	C2	Basic
0.6	C3	Intermediate
0.8	C4	Experienced
0.9	C5	Expert
1	C6	Convergent

reflect the 6 maturity levels (categories) placed on a scale from 0 to 1, in which, to obtain k categories, k-1 profiles are required.

The experts established the values of b_k considering the desired performance in each class is. Also, following the guidelines in [18], they set percentages in the range between 0 and 1 and the values of b_k were defined in such a way that each alternative could be assigned to one class.

After specifying the parameters, the companies were evaluated against the criteria provided by the companies' managers and the data were entered into the DSS. Thus, the first interaction of the tool was initiated with the DM – a specialist responsible for implementing the standards of industry 4.0 for the first time in South America in a textile plant in in the clothing sector. He is also a professional active in the market, with extensive experience. In the first interaction, the DSS presents a hypothetical alternative with the worst performance in each criterion and asks the DM to choose one of the criteria to improve the performance to the maximum. Criteria can be selected about which the DM is indifferent. This step is repeated until the DSS can establish an ordering of the criteria. Thus, the following order of relative importance of the criteria was established: Lid > E&I > Pess > F&P > Sust, which can be seen in Fig. 1.

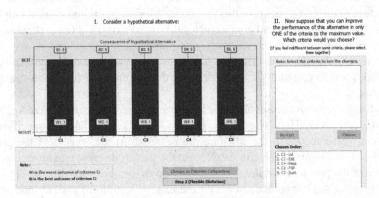

Fig. 1. Holistic assessment

In this context, still in relation to Fig. 1, it can be understood that the scale constant (weight) of the leadership criterion is greater than that related to strategy and innovation, and this is greater than that of the criterion related to people, which, following this logic, is greater than the factory attribute and processes and sustainability, respectively.

Then, the DM initiated the flexible elicitation procedure with the objective of exploiting the space of consequences of the problem. At this point, the DM answers questions regarding two hypothetical alternatives that have distinct performances between two of the evaluated criteria. In the interaction, the DM must choose an answer from among the alternatives made available to him/her, by considering the performances in the criteria presented in the situation.

Throughout the process, the DM can choose to visualize the partial results (sorting and weight space) after each question presented. The process ends at the moment when the DSS establishes a sorting of the alternatives according to the space of weights measured from the linear programming models or, if the DM is satisfied with the information generated at that point, the process may be stopped.

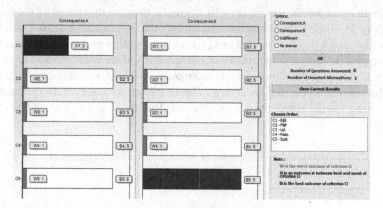

Fig. 2. Flexible elicitation in FITradeoff

In this stage, presented in Fig. 2, the DM opted for alternative A. During the flexible elicitation, the DM answered 4 questions, to the point where the DSS established the final sorting of the company according to the space of weights obtained from the information provided. The details of what questions were put and what the DM chose are set out in Table 3.

Table 3. Questions answered

Iteration	Consequence A	Consequence B	DM's choice
1	Lid 3	Sus 5	A
2	Lid 3	E&I 5	B
3	E&I 3	Pess 5	B
4	Pess 3	F&P 5	Indifferent

Table 4 shows the company's minimized (S_1) and maximized (S_2) global values and the conditions of the DSS decision rule applied to sort the company's maturity.

Table 4. Global values and conditions for sorting

Alternative	S_1	S_2	Cond. 1	Cond. 2	Class
Company A	0.271	0.333	$S_1 > 0.2$	$S_2 < = 0.4$	2
Company B	0.438	0.600	$S_1 > 0.4$	$S_2 < = 0.6$	3
Company C	0	0	$S1 >$	$S2 < = 0$	1

The final sorting of the companies is carried out with reference to the minimum and maximum global values of the alternative applied to the DSS decision rule, which has two constraints related to the extreme values of each profile. For instance, company B had values of S1 and S2 which were limited according to the profiles of the intermediate category. In other words, the value of S1 is greater than the maximum of the beginner category (0.4), while S2 is below the minimum of the experienced category (0.6).

It is also worth mentioning that in FITradeoff for sorting problems the exact values of the weights (k) are not determined and, consequently, there is also no way to calculate the overall values of the alternatives in the model. However, possible combinations of values between the upper and lower thresholds of the weight space established at the end of the process should reflect the results obtained. This space of weights can be observed in Fig. 3.

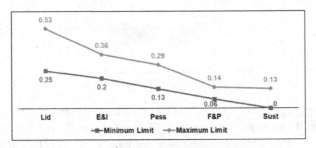

Fig. 3. Weights space

As can be seen in Fig. 3, the weights of the Lid and E&I criteria have longer ranges of values that could be assumed. This fact is aligned with the initial holistic evaluation of the criteria made by the DM, who judged these two criteria as being the most relevant in the problem. In addition, the ranges of scale constant values (weights) for each of the criteria are presented. The extent of these intervals represents the extent to which the scale constants can vary without changes in the sorting of alternatives.

For instance, considering the class of the company B at the intermediate level (3), the results obtained were congruent with the situation of the company in its operational reality, according to the opinions of the DM and managers of the organization evaluated.

In general, according to the specialist, the points observed in the maturity assessment show the possibility of a better development of strategic plans that include actions focused on aspects such as integration between information systems, in addition to the incorporation of equipment that has characteristics that contribute to sustainability, such as reducing tailings or applying sustainable materials. Additionally, points related to the need to develop employees' skills and abilities with regard to industry 4.0 were observed.

Thus, the companies' leaders stated that they recognize the importance of and understand the challenges related to industry 4.0, and, based on the results obtained in the maturity assessment, the have taken initiatives to seek a better structuring of the strategic planning processes with possible support from consultancies.

4 Final Remarks

This study has presented a multi-criteria approach for assessing the maturity of companies, in the context of industry 4.0. A case study was conducted in which three companies were evaluated and this provided information about their processes and structure for incorporation into the MM. As a result, the maturity levels of these companies were obtained and discussed, and improvement points were presented in the attributes considered in the MM.

When carrying out a general analysis of the evaluation process and interactions with the DSS, the DM highlighted the agility of the process itself, as an advantage from a practical point of view. This feature makes it quick to apply in market organizations, where managers have resources constraints (time, people) for decisions that need to be structured.

In addition, the assessed organizations provided their impressions regarding the results of the maturity assessment, demonstrating an understanding of the points identified by applying the MM. Specifically, the companies indicated the incorporation of aspects such as people development and sustainability in its strategic planning for investments in technological tools, for example. Additionally, the evaluation process also contributed to their knowledge of new perspectives and concepts related to industry 4.0 and its technologies applied to the textile and clothing sector that hitherto the company had not been aware of.

From a practical point of view, it is worth highlighting the flexibility of the MM, which allows it to be replicated in other textile business contexts, and the MM also enables new parameterizations associated with the scenarios and DM involved to be undertaken. Regarding the theoretical aspect, the contribution of this work comprises the development of knowledge in the textile area focused on MMs, based on a review of the vast literature, the contextualization of the problem and the generation of results that demonstrate the applicability of the MM.

For future studies, it is intended to improve the model by incorporating new evaluation parameters, and by applying it in other companies in the textile market, either with a strategic bias or for other specific processes.

References

1. SEBRAE, Estudo econômico do Arranjo Produtivo Local de confecções do Agreste Pernambucano, 2012, p. 151 (2013)
2. Schwab, K.: The Fourth Industrial Revolution, 1st edn, vol. 1. World Economic Forum, Switzerland (2016)
3. Lom, M., Pribyl, O., Svitek, M.: Industry 4.0 as a part of smart cities. In: 2016 Smart Cities Symposium. Prague, SCSP 2016, pp. 1–6 (2016)
4. de Andrade, C.T.A., de Gusmão, A.P.H., Silva, W.: World class manufacturing performance measurement using a maturity model and the FlowSort method. Int. J. Prod. Res. 59(24), 7374–7389 (2021)
5. Wagire, A.A., Joshi, R., Rathore, A.P.S., Jain, R.: Development of maturity model for assessing the implementation of Industry 4.0: learning from theory and practice. Prod. Plan. Control 32(8), 603–622 (2020)
6. Lin, T.C., Wang, K.J., Sheng, M.L.: To assess smart manufacturing readiness by maturity model: a case study on Taiwan enterprises. Int. J. Comput. Integr. Manuf. 33(1), 102–115 (2020)
7. Ferreira, D.V.: Modelo de maturidade daindústria 4.0 para avaliação de processos têxteis, Universidade Federal de Pernambuco (2021)
8. Simetinger, F., Zhang, Z.: Deriving secondary traits of industry 4.0: a comparative analysis of significant maturity models. Syst. Res. Behav. Sci. 37(4), 663–678 (2020)
9. Gökalp, E., Şener, U., Eren, P.E.: Development of an assessment model for industry 4.0: industry 4.0-MM. In: Mas, A., Mesquida, A., O'Connor, R.V., Rout, T., Dorling, A. (eds.) SPICE 2017. CCIS, vol. 770, pp. 128–142. Springer, Cham (2017). https://doi.org/10.1007/978-3-319-67383-7_10
10. Singapore Economic Development Board, The Singapore Smart Industry Readiness Index: Catalyzing the transoformation of manufacturing, pp. 1–46 (2018)
11. Rockwell Automation, The Connected Enterprise Maturity Model (2014)
12. Hizam-Hanafiah, M., Soomro, M.A., Abdullah, N.L.: Industry 4.0 readiness models: a systematic literature review of model dimensions. Information11(7), 1–13 (2020)
13. Van Looy, A., De Backer, M., Poels, G., Snoeck, M.: Choosing the right business process maturity model. Inf. Manag. 50(7), 466–488 (2013)
14. Ferreira, D.V., De Gusmão, A.P.H., Sousa, E.E.M.: Industry 4.0 maturity models assessment - a multicriteria approach. In: The 7th International Conference on Decision Support System Technology – ICDSST 2021, p. 36 (2021)
15. Doumpos, M., Zopounidis, C.: Multicriteria Decision Aid Classification Methods. Kluwer Academic Publishers, New York, Boston (2004)
16. Rigopoulos, G., Askounis, D.T., Metaxiotis, K.: NeXCLass: a decision support system for non-ordered multicriteria classification. Int. J. Info. Tech. Dec. Mak. 9(1), 53–79 (2011). https://doi.org/10.1142/S0219622010003622
17. Costa, A.S., Figueira, J.R., Borbinha, J.: A multiple criteria nominal classification method based on the concepts of similarity and dissimilarity. Eur. J. Oper. Res. 271(1), 193–209 (2018)
18. Kang, T.H.A., Frej, E.A., de Almeida, A.T.: Flexible and interactive tradeoff elicitation for multicriteria sorting problems. Asia-Pacific J. Oper. Res. 37(5), 1–22 (2020)
19. De Almeida, A.T., De Almeida, J.A., Costa, A.P.C.S., De Almeida-Filho, A.T.: A new method for elicitation of criteria weights in additive models: flexible and interactive tradeoff. Eur. J. Oper. Res. 250(1), 179–191 (2016)
20. Frej, E.A., de Almeida, A.T., Costa, A.P.C.S.: Using data visualization for ranking alternatives with partial information and interactive tradeoff elicitation. Oper. Res. Int. J. 19(4), 909–931 (2019). https://doi.org/10.1007/s12351-018-00444-2

21. Roselli, L.R.P., de Almeida, A.T.: Using FITradeoff method for supply selection with decomposition and holistic evaluations for preference modelling. In: Jayawickrama, U., Delias, P., Escobar, M.T., Papathanasiou, J. (eds.) ICDSST 2021. LNBIP, vol. 414, pp. 18–29. Springer, Cham (2021). https://doi.org/10.1007/978-3-030-73976-8_2

22. Dell'Ovo, M., Frej, E.A., Oppio, A., Capolongo, S., Morais, D.C., de Almeida, A.T.: Multicriteria decision making for healthcare facilities location with visualization based on FITradeoff method. In: Linden, I., Liu, S., Colot, C. (eds.) ICDSST 2017. LNBIP, vol. 282, pp. 32–44. Springer, Cham (2017). https://doi.org/10.1007/978-3-319-57487-5_3

23. Reis Peixoto Roselli, L., de Almeida, A.T.: Analysis of graphical visualizations for multicriteria decision making in FITradeoff method using a decision neuroscience experiment. In: Moreno-Jiménez, J.M., Linden, I., Dargam, F., Jayawickrama, U. (eds.) ICDSST 2020. LNBIP, vol. 384, pp. 30–42. Springer, Cham (2020). https://doi.org/10.1007/978-3-030-46224-6_3

24. Keeney, R.L., Raiffa, H.: Decisions with Multiple Objectives: Preferences and Value Trade-Offs, no. 7. Wiley, New York (1976)

25. Kon, A., Gomide, R.P., Coan, D.C.: Transformações da indústria têxtil brasileira: a transição para a modernização. Rev. Econ. Mackenzie **3**(3), 11–34 (2005)

26. Mayumi, R., Fujita, L., Jorente, M.J.: A Indústria Têxtil no Brasil: uma perspectiva histórica e cultural. Rev. ModaPalavra e-Periódico **8**(15), 91–105 (2015)

Sustainable Mobility Engagement and Co-planning; a Multicriteria Analysis Based Transferability Guide

Glykeria Myrovali[✉] ⓘ and Maria Morfoulaki ⓘ

Hellenic Institute of Transport/Centre for Research and Technology Hellas (HIT/CERTH),
6th km Charilaou-Thermi Road, 57001 Thessaloniki, Greece
{myrovali,marmor}@certh.gr

Abstract. Engagement in sustainable mobility planning seems to act as a starting point to unlock a new era of responsible and sustainable behaviors. After almost a two-years experience of a global crisis (COVID-19) revealing that the only way out is through jointly walking on the way into sustainability and resilience, engaging people in shifting to sustainable mobility options has become an imperative need. The current paper exploits Multi-Criteria Decision Analysis (MCDA) in building a methodological 5-step framework for evaluating the transferability potentials of good practices (GPs) in citizens' sensibilization and engagement in sustainable mobility. 10 good practices were selected in order to cover the whole cycle of sustainable mobility planning (SUMP cycle) while representatives from different EU Regions were involved in the assessment procedure resulting in this way in a general transferability guide. The guide, tailored to each case, can be a very useful tool in the hands of single authorities while making their mobility engagement plan.

Keywords: Sustainable mobility · Engagement · Co-planning · Multicriteria decision analysis · PROMETHEE method · Transferability · COVID-19

1 Introduction

Engagement in sustainable mobility planning seems to be a key to unlock real change. Years ago, the term 'sustainable mobility' was a faraway goal set by visionaries in transport sector, however today, after almost a two-years experience of a global crisis (COVID-19) revealing that the only way out is through jointly walking on the way into sustainability and resilience, it has become an urgent call for action [1, 2].

Multi-causal and complex issues like engagement in sustainable mobility planning asks for collaborative strategies [3]. Sustainable mobility planning is all about planning for all the people while incorporating the various and potentially contradicting needs – 'planning for all with all'. While the traditional transport planning approach was considering travelling as a derived demand and tried to find an optimal compensation among travel time and travel costs [4], sustainable mobility planning is based on a different approach; it recognizes travelling as both a derived demand as well as an activity, it

© Springer Nature Switzerland AG 2022
A. P. Cabral Seixas Costa et al. (Eds.): ICDSST 2022, LNBIP 447, pp. 164–176, 2022.
https://doi.org/10.1007/978-3-031-06530-9_13

is structured around notions as accessibility and connectivity, inclusiveness and accept-ability, it gives car alternatives place to flourish and it aims to safeguard sustainability pivotal dimensions (social, economic, environmental).

Acceptability – this word is not a trend, is an imperative call if we need to really support shift to sustainable mobility. Effective mobility plans are plans developed for the people (better 'co-developed' by people and decision makers), serving their needs, well-communicated to people, co-agreed and therefore accepted [5, 6]. Engagement in sustainable mobility planning starts from political level common understanding, goes to cross-sectorial high level clear commitment for working into sustainability path, is dif-fused to regional and local administrations and from there continues its trip to competent authorities' staff, to stakeholders and to the whole community. Acceptance comes as a result of this intense engagement procedure in the planning process that enables multiple parties to work together, to give birth to an ecosystem for discussing and solving mobility related environmental, social, and economic issues [7, 8]. Knowing and understanding travelers' needs (citizens, tourists and newly arisen categories as telework tourists, dig-ital nomads) on the above topics, is at the center of a successful planning, therefore for fulfilling the goals clearly set in the recent European Commission 'Sustainable and Smart Mobility Strategy' for green and digital transformation and a resilient future (incorpo-rating lessons learned from recent COVID-19 pandemic) [9], decision makers should reform the way they decide – from forced measures to co-creation of solutions.

Identifying the most effective motivational feature for attracting travelers' in sus-tainable mobility options and in engaging them in sustainable mobility planning is an effortful challenge; permanent interaction with decision makers, real time personalized notifications and digital assistants supporting shift to sustainable modes, social influ-ence, token and reputation building [10], solutions real-testing can bring us closer to a citizens-led planning. In a similar with the psychological continuum model (PCM) used in sport and event consumer behavior understanding, that defines four stages—awareness, attraction, attachment and allegiance to describe users' level of involvement [11], also in passengers transportation we can find out the following steps for reach-ing; training the traveler on sustainable mobility benefits (awareness), receiving positive experience from testing solutions (attraction), progressing into attachment – being part of traveler's everyday life (attachment) and changing behavior to sustainable mobil-ity options, car-free lifestyle adoption, responsible choices, valuable contribution while reaching co-planning goal (allegiance).

Being the public participation the cornerstone of effective policies and plans, it is vital to keep the participation process active even in times of unforeseen crisis. Although unprecedented situations (i.e. COVID-19 social distancing measures) have posed obsta-cles to the traditional co-planning approach, new approaches have emerged support-ing a new format of interaction. Thanks to technology, efforts to involve citizens in decision-making kept alive even remotely - interaction and effective engagement proved to be survivors; exploitation of, the most appropriate per target group, online tools, combination of traditional channels (phone surveys, traditional paper mailing, printed material/brochures/banners) with more interactive elements (voting platforms and appli-cations, interactive boards), smart use of social media i.e. Instagram polls, constant commenting on twitter and instant questions and answers, collection of comments and ratings, live videos for direct information seem able to spark the attention of different target groups [12].

2   Methodology and Materials

2.1   The Methodology

The current paper exploits Multi-Criteria Decision Analysis (MCDA) in building a methodological framework for evaluating the transferability potentials of good practices (GPs) in citizens' sensibilization and engagement in sustainable mobility. The 5 step framework applied in the paper is presented in Fig. 1.

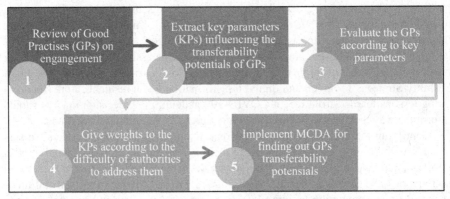

Fig. 1. The 5-step methodological framework of estimating good practices transferability potentials

As a first step, a review of relevant good practices took place in order to understand their objectives, the tools and means that have been used, the target group(s) and the final achievements. For the scope of the current work, 10 good practices (GPs), able to cover different steps of sustainable mobility planning procedure (awareness, co-analysis, co-creation, co-monitoring) were selected.

During the second step, key parameters (KPs) related to transferability potentials of the selected GPs were extracted. This procedure required the understanding of capacity and skills that the relevant to SUMP staff/ stakeholders have, the problems and the barriers that they usually face as well as authorities efficiency to overcome these problems. For this reason, a dialogue with the authorities and stakeholders took place in order to develop a list of the most important issues that should be addressed for implementing an engagement strategy. In total seven KPs were extracted.

During the third step of the framework, the list with the selected GPs were evaluated from the responsible for their implementation as well as from marketing and communication experts. The scope was to find out how difficult is to implement each GP as regards the specific parameters that were set in the previous step (budget needed, specific skills needed, time and the effort required etc.). For each GP a grade between 1–5 was given in each KP (1: very easy to 5: very difficult to be fulfilled).

As for the fourth step, the list with the seven KPs was given to the different key actors of the authorities, therefore, the community who will implement relevant actions, in order to evaluate the difficulty of their authority to address each parameter. The current evaluation resulted in the weights given to each KP and as a matter of fact, the weights of each criterion that the MCDA will use for the GPs transferability ranking.

The final step of the framework was the implementation of the MCDA methodology, using the parameters, criteria and weights that were described above, and the ranking of the GPs according to the needs and capacity of each authority.

2.2   Step 1; GPs on Engagement Identification

In this section, we briefly present ten characteristic good practices (GPs) in citizens' engagement (covering the different steps of sustainable mobility planning, starting from awareness actions and going up to co-planning boosting activities) identified in the framework of e-smartec Interreg EUROPE 2014–2020 project [13].

GP1 Voltaro event; It is an annual event taking place in the seafront of Thessaloniki, GR, aiming to promote cycling, walking and alternative sustainable modes and ways of transport with the help of volunteers (both companies directly and indirectly linked to mobility services and young people – lovers of active mobility) that act as sustainability ambassadors.

GP2 REFORM; The practice established a permanent regional cooperation for increasing capacity of the Municipalities in Region of Central Macedonia (RCM), GR and facilitating the deployment of their Sustainable Urban Mobility Plans (SUMPs). RCM developed a dedicated to SUMP support web platform for Greek Municipalities (https://www.keyp-svak-rcm.imet.gr/). Guidance, training, capacity building and dialogue area creation are among the principal goals of this SUMP competence center.

GP3 PEDIBUS; PEDIBUS supports primary school managers to encourage pupils and families to walk to school safely in organized groups following fixed safe routes. The main purpose of the initiative is to foster the interaction and trust among parents in order to stimulate a mutual support, in accompanying children to school as a group.

GP4 Trensportal card game; A good example of the interaction and optimal involvement of stakeholders and citizens during the co-development step of the vision of North Limburg (Netherlands Region) is the Trendsportal card game. The initiative uses gamification and gaming techniques through digital (web portal) and non digital (focus groups) channels.

GP5 Cargobike Trendsportal – Competition; It is a competition with an electric cargo bike aiming to create attention and involvement in policy making. People were invited to take a cycling related photo and share it on social media with the remark of how they envision mobility in the region in 2040 aiming to increase co-planning levels. The municipality awarded the bike among the participants of the photo contest.

GP6 MOTIVATE app; MOTIVATE app is an integrated crowdsourcing – game initiative towards transforming travelers into active agents of change of the new low carbon era. The MOTIVATE app is a cloud based tool that collects data and provides first level overview of daily trips and travelers' opinions [14]. As an online tool, given the appropriate promotion, it can complement/replace (to the desired degree) physical consultation procedures and events. It can also act as a permanent communication channel for citizens - administrators on mobility issues.

GP7 Coventry Recycling Club; It is a scheme to reward residents for recycling. If residents recycle more than the previous year, or reduce the amount of general rubbish, they are rewarded with points. In return, the points can be given to a Good Cause.

GP8 Sacravelo; It is a combination of two different aspects in one product to attract a broader group of people with an aim to promote active transport for sacral tourism. In this practice the added value is created by adding sacral tourism to the concept of active transport in the cross-border region. People can visit pilgrimage sites during their trips, enjoy rich cultural heritage of the Hungarian-Slovak border region and combine this experience with the beauties of the natural environment and an active leisure time activity.

GP9 Active Mobility Toolbox; A selection of standardized materials for awareness raising and advertising on active mobility gives local authorities the possibility of promoting active mobility in different formats with a high publicity effect at low costs and effort. In order to be able to present active mobility more effectively within the framework of municipal events, municipalities can order an exhibition counter, roll-up displays, tables and photo walls.

GP10 Energy transition game; The Energy transition game is a game played on a map – searching for potential locations for windmills and solar fields - that guides an informal discussion about the energy transition in a municipal level. By playing the game the participants (local council, energy cooperation's, energy suppliers, farmers, industry, citizens and other environmental organisations) share opinions that are enlightening for the policy makers.

2.3   Step 2; Defining KP of Transferability Potentials

Through consulting with responsible bodies or local linked actors with good knowledge of the above GPs while further diving into the available published information for the GPs, authors extracted KPs related to transferability potentials. This information that regards specific parameters that should be taken into account when an authority would like to implement a specific GP, is presented below:

A.   **Advanced knowledge/capacity requirement for GP adoption and transferring**; This criterion is based on the estimation of the responsible public authority's knowledge/capacity requirement compared to traditional and simpler communication activities i.e. development of a leaflet (in most cases, collaboration with external experts is necessary both for the planning and implementation phase).

B.   **Advanced ICT exploitation related knowledge/capacity for GP adoption and transferring**; This criterion is based on the estimation of the responsible public authority's knowledge/capacity requirement for the development and management of ICT tools i.e. need to develop a crowd-sourcing app (in most cases, collaboration with external experts is necessary for the development of the ICT tool and the public authority contributes with feedback during the development and takes over the management and maintenance).

C. **Necessary budget for replication of the GP**; This criterion is based on the estimation of total cost required for both the design and implementation of the GP.

D. **Necessary estimated effort for a full replication of the GP**; This criterion is based on the estimation of total man-months required for designing/developing/implementing and monitoring the GP by an average public employee with no specific expertise on a certain sector but with previous experience in similar projects (i.e. ICT, communication, participatory practices).

E. **Level of synergies required for the replication of the GP**; This criterion is based on the estimation of the required level of synergies with public or private stakeholders for the effective replication of the GP with increased outreach to the specific project's target groups.

F. **Level of effectiveness of the GP for engaging wide audience/diverse targets**; This criterion is based on the estimation of the anticipated level of effectiveness of the GP, focusing specifically on the increased diversity of the engaged audience.

G. **Requirement for strong access to more advanced communication channels**; This criterion is based on the estimation of the responsible public authority's experience/capacity requirement for the design and coordination of communication campaigns with increased reach out and strong communication strategy that usually require broad stakeholder engagement for securing collaboration. i.e. media coverage.

2.4   Step 3; Evaluating the Response of the GPs to the KPs

During step 3, marketing/engagement experts evaluated the response of each GP per KP. More specifically, they gave grades from 1 to 5 according to how demanding is the GP on the specific parameters (5 is equal to the need for high ICT skills, long time of development, high level of synergies etc.). Information collected is depicted in Table 1.

Table 1. Response of GPs to KPs

		KP1	KP2	KP3	KP4	KP5	KP6	KP7
GP1	Voltaro event	2	1	3	3	4	4	4
GP2	REFORM	4	2	3	3	3	4	2
GP3	PEDIBUS	4	1	2	4	4	4	3
GP4	Trensportal card game	4	1	2	2	4	5	1
GP5	Cargobike	4	2	2	3	4	5	5
GP6	MOTIVATE app	4	4	4	4	3	4	4
GP7	Coventry recycling club	4	3	4	4	3	4	4
GP8	Sacravelo	4	1	3	4	4	3	4
GP9	Active mobility toolbox	3	1	3	3	4	4	3
GP10	Energy transition game	3	1	3	2	3	4	2

2.5   Step 4; Evaluating the Difficulty of the Authorities to Address the KPs

The criteria used in the evaluation of the GPs at the previous step were transformed into engagement challenges. Representatives of European Regions and cities (Region of Central Macedonia, West Midlands, Bratislava, Lazio Region, State of Hessen and North Limburg) were asked to give weights to assess the level of difficulty of their Municipality/Region to respond to specific requirements for implementing and following a strong mobility engagement strategy (comparative assessment between the criteria, the higher the difficulty, the higher the weight).

In total 31 questionnaires were collected (profile; transportation planners, local and regional authorities' staff, decision makers, Business Delivery Managers, Sustainability Advisors, Road Traffic and Civil Engineering Office staff, urban planners, Communication - marketing specialists).

The current evaluation resulted in the weights of the parameters that will be used as criteria of the MCDA for the GPs transferability ranking. Table 2 presents the average weight per KP.

Table 2. Average weights of transferability KPs

		Average weight (%)
KP1	Advanced knowledge/capacity	17.83
KP2	Advanced ICT knowledge/capacity	16.42
KP3	Necessary budget for replication	11.33
KP4	Necessary estimated effort	13.85
KP5	Level of synergies	18.03
KP6	Level of effectiveness	13.13
KP7	Requirement for strong access communication channels	9.41

The evaluation per criterion assigned to each GP (from 1-low to 5-high) and the "difficulty of applicability" parameters that was based on the stakeholders' questionnaires were imported in the databases that were developed in the PROMETHEE MCDA (Multicriteria Decision Analysis) software.

2.6   Step 5; MCDA for Prioritization of GPs According to Perceived Level of Easiness and Applicability

In the current approach, PROMETHEE has been chosen as the most appropriate method in order to formulate and implement the methodological framework for ranking engagement actions according to real challenges. PROMETHEE method has been used to evaluate real life problems, among which also transportation related issues, with ultimate goal to select the optimal actions from an existing portfolio [15–17].

The preference ranking organization method for enrichment of evaluations (PROMETHEE) method, which is used for the current work, belongs to the outranking family of MCDA (Multicriteria Decision Analysis) methods and is developed by

[18] and [19]. The method has been later on complemented by geometrical analysis for interactive aid (GAIA), an attempt to represent the decision problem graphically in a two-dimensional plane. This interactive visual module can assist in complicated decision problems. PROMETHEE results in a ranking of actions (as the alternatives are known in the method's terminology) based on preference degrees. Briefly, steps include the pairwise comparison of actions on each criterion, then the computation of uni-criterion flows, and finally, the aggregation of the latter into global flows. It has been applied successfully in various application areas; Application domains include nuclear waste management, the productivity of agricultural regions, risk assessment, web site evaluation, renewable energy, environmental assessment, selection of contract type and project designer.

According to [20], PROMETHEE is designed to tackle multicriteria problems, such as the following;

$$max\{g1(a), g2(a), \ldots, gn(a) | a \in A\} \tag{1}$$

where:
A is a finite set of possible alternatives {a1, a2, $\cdots$, am}
and {g1($\cdot$), g2($\cdot$), $\cdots$, gn($\cdot$)} a set of evaluation criteria either to be maximized or minimized.

The decision-maker needs to construct the evaluation table as in the following table. The second row of this table is about the weights associated with each of the criteria, and Eq. (1) holds true (Table 3):

$$\sum_{j=1}^{n} wj = 1, j = 1, 2, \ldots, n \tag{2}$$

Table 3. Evaluation table

a g1($\cdot$) g2($\cdot$) $\cdots$ gn($\cdot$)
w1 w2 $\cdots$ wn
a1 g1(a1) g2(a1) $\cdots$ gn(a1)
a2 g1(a2) g2(a2) $\cdots$ gn(a2)
...
am g1(am) g2(am) $\cdots$ gn(am)

It must be pointed out that MCDA techniques in general place the decision-makers in the center of the process, and different decision-makers can model the problem in different ways, according to their preferences (it also must be mentioned here that the methods assist the decision-maker, they do not make the final decision; thus, the word "aid" in the MCDA acronym. The responsibility for the final decision rests with the decision-maker alone). In PROMETHEE, a preference degree is an expression of how one action is preferred against another action. For small deviations among the evaluations of a pair of criteria, the decision-maker can allocate a small preference; if the deviation can be considered negligible, then this can be modelled in PROMETHEE too. The exact opposite stands for large deviations where the decision-maker must allocate a large preference of one action over the other; if the deviation exceeds a certain value set by the decision-maker, then there is an absolute preference of one action over the other. This preference degree is a real number always between 0 and 1 [21]. Value 1 represents a strong preference of alternative a over b while 0 shows indifferent preference value. Six types of preference functions have been proposed by the developers of the PROMETHEE methodology: Usual criterion, Quasi criterion (U-shape), Criterion with linear preference (V-shape), Level criterion, Linear criterion, and Gaussian criterion. Due to the evaluation methodology that was used for the GPs, the Usual criterion of PROMETHEE was used. This is the simplest of all preference functions. It has no thresholds and returns a binary result:

- Two actions with equal values (difference = 0) are indifferent (preference degree = 0).
- Two actions with different values (difference > 0) generate a full preference
- (preference degree = 1) even if the difference is very small.

3 Results

The multicriteria positive (Phi+), negative (Phi-) and net (Phi) flows are displayed in the next table together with the diagram of the complete ranking. As it is depicted in Fig. 2, the most easily transferable practice for the participated Regions is the Energy Transition followed by the VOLTARO and the Active Mobility Toolbox practices.

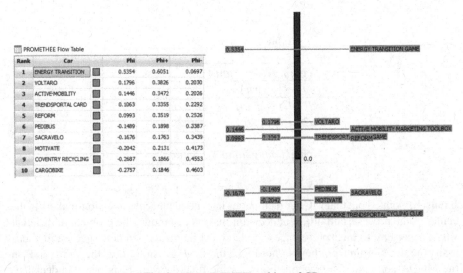

Fig. 2. PROMETHEE ranking of GPs

The specific ranking is also confirmed in the diamond diagram of PROMETHEE (Fig. 3a). From the diamond ranking we can see that there are (correlation) lines are close enough but there is also an overlapping between the cones of the low choices, which means that there is a clear preference ranking between the high preference good practices with no incomparable cases. The ENERGY TRANSITION GAME is clearly the most preferred, while MOTIVATE app is not so easily comparable with the other practices probably due to high ICT requirements.

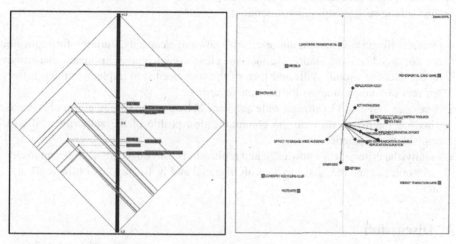

Fig. 3. a) PROMETHEE diamond ranking b) PROMETHEE-GAIA visual analysis graph.

Additionally, the PROMETHEE-GAIA Visual Analysis resulted is diagram of Fig. 3b that shows the U-V plane of:

1. Actions that are represented by points.
2. Criteria that are represented by axes.
3. The weights of the criteria and the PROMETHEE II ranking that are represented by the decision axis.

In this diagram we can identify four different types of good practices (that are very close to each other).

- VOLTARO and Active Mobility TOOLBOX (very close so similar to each other) together with ENERGY TRANSITION GAME (not so closed but in the same quadrant)
- Coventry recycling club and MOTIVATE (very close so similar to each other) in the same quadrant
- PEDIBUS, Sacravelo and Cargobike not so closed but in the same quadrant
- Reform and Energy Transition Game closed enough and in the same quadrant.

To better understand the differences between these four groups of practices, we can have a look at the criteria. Each criterion is represented by an axis drawn from the center of the GAIA plane. The orientation of the axes is important as it indicates how closely the criteria are related to each other:

- Criteria expressing similar preferences have axes that are close to each other.
- Conflicting criteria have axes that are pointing in opposite directions.

It is thus possible to identify groups of criteria expressing similar preferences and to better understand the conflicts that have to be solved in order to make a decision. In this analysis, three such groups can be identified:

- Overall effort, implement/monitor effort, knowledge/capacity, duration for replicate and advanced communication channels are close to each other. This means that based on the data the overall skills and time of the staff needed to implement the practice are very crucial parameters for the transferability.
- Synergies and effect to engage wide audience belong to the second group of criteria. This has mainly to do with the communication profile of the authority who will implement the practice.
- Finally, the criteria ICT knowledge and replication cost/budget are not relevant to any other criteria, and they have to do with financial and ICT capability of the replicator area.

4 Discussion

The 5-step framework presented in the current paper for finding out transferability potentials of an engagement related good practice is a stable methodology to be tailored per case. In the current analysis, 10 indicative good practices were selected in order to cover the whole cycle of sustainable mobility planning (SUMP cycle) while representatives from different EU Regions were involved in the assessment procedure resulting in this way in a general transferability guide. The input for a tailored transferability analysis should include GPs precisely selected for covering specific needs (i.e. awareness raising, crowdsourcing data for AS IS situation analysis, prioritizing interventions via participatory approaches) while rankings of KPs should be collected from a wide range of stakeholders and staff involved of the specific Municipality. Furthermore, the transferability potentials presented here refer to the transferring of all the aspects of a presented GP – this means that when getting inspiration from specific aspects/dimensions of a GP (partial transferring or 'free' transferring of a GP), the situation can be totally different. Finally, we could say that the final decision of choosing a GP or a specific dimension of a GP to be transferred depends on top priorities - political will – that can be in total contrast with the current situation/capacity of a Municipality i.e. a medium advanced ICT city, given a large investment plan and funding on digitalization transformation, could select to implement engagement and co-planning measures that require high ICT exploitation levels even if the current relevant capacity of its staff is not rich enough.

References

1. Banister, D.: The sustainable mobility paradigm. Transp. Policy **15**(2), 73–80 (2008)
2. Myrovali, G., Morfoulaki, M., Vassilantonakis, B.M., Mpoutovinas, A., Kotoula, K.M.: Travelers-led innovation in sustainable urban mobility plans. Period. Polytech. Transp. Eng. **48**(2), 126–132 (2020)
3. Lönngren, J., Van Poeck, K.: Wicked problems: a mapping review of the literature. Int. J. Sustain. Dev. World **28**(6), 481–502 (2021)
4. Van Audenhove, F. J., Korniichuk, O., Dauby, L., Pourbaix, J.: The future of urban mobility 2.0: imperatives to shape extended mobility ecosystems of tomorrow (2014)
5. Jutra, A., Zupančič, T.: Influencing urban mobility through public engagement process: traditional and digital methods for public participation in urban design. Open Urban Stud. Demography J. **1**(1), 52–61 (2015)
6. Tsay, S.P., Herrmann, V.: Rethinking urban mobility: sustainable policies for the century of the city, pp. 68-p, Carnegie Endowment for International Peace, Washington (2013)
7. COM/2020/789 final, Communication from the commission to the European parliament, the council, the European economic and social committee and the committee of the regions Sustainable and Smart Mobility Strategy – putting European transport on track for the future
8. Gabrielli, S., et al.: Design challenges in motivating change for sustainable urban mobility. Comput. Hum. Behav. **41**, 416–423 (2014)
9. Funk, D.C., James, J.: The psychological continuum model: a conceptual framework for understanding an individual's psychological connection to sport. Sport Manag. Rev. **4**(2), 119–150 (2001)
10. e-smartec project Interreg Europe 2014–2020. Del. Handbook for success tips on marketing techniques (2020). https://www.interregeurope.eu/e-smartec/library/
11. e-smartec project Interreg Europe 2014–2020. Del. State-of-the art on marketing techniques for citizens' engagement in e-smartec Regions (2020). https://www.interregeurope.eu/e-smartec/library/
12. Myrovali, G., Tsaples, G., Morfoulaki, M., Aifadopoulou, G., Papathanasiou, J.: An interactive learning environment based on system dynamics methodology for sustainable mobility challenges communication & citizens' engagement. In: Dargam, F., Delias, P., Linden, I., Mareschal, B. (eds.) Decision Support Systems VIII: Sustainable Data-Driven and Evidence-Based Decision Support. ICDSST 2018. Lecture Notes in Business Information Processing, pp. 88–99, vol. 313, Springer, Cham (2018). https://doi.org/10.1007/978-3-319-90315-6_8
13. Brans, J.P., Mareschal, B., Vincke, P.: PROMETHEE: a new family of outranking methods in MCDM. Oper. Res. Int. J. **3**, 477–490 (1984)
14. Brans, J.P., Vincke, P.: Note—a preference ranking organisation method: (The PROMETHEE method for multiple criteria decision-making). Manage. Sci. **31**(6), 647–656 (1985)
15. Brans, J.-P., Mareschal, B.: Promethee methods. In: Multiple Criteria Decision Analysis: State of the Art Surveys, pp. 163–186. Springer, New York (2005). https://doi.org/10.1007/0-387-23081-5_5
16. Morfoulaki, M., Papathanasiou, J.: Use of PROMETHEE MCDA method for ranking alternative measures of sustainable urban mobility planning. Mathematics **9**, 602 (2021). https://doi.org/10.3390/math9060602
17. Brans, J.-P., De Smet, Y.: PROMETHEE methods. In: Greco, S., Ehrgott, M., Figueira, J.R. (eds.) Multiple Criteria Decision Analysis. ISORMS, vol. 233, pp. 187–219. Springer, New York (2016). https://doi.org/10.1007/978-1-4939-3094-4_6
18. Zhaoxu, S., Min, H.: Multi-criteria decision making based on PROMETHEE method. In: 2010 International Conference on Computing, Control and Industrial Engineering, vol. 1, pp. 416–418. IEEE (2010)

19. Oubahman, L., Duleba, S.: Review of PROMETHEE method in transportation. Prod. Eng. Arch. **27**(1), 69–74 (2021). https://doi.org/10.30657/pea.2021.27.9
20. Nikolaeva, A., Adey, P., Cresswell, T., Lee, J.Y., Nóvoa, A., Temenos, C.: Commoning mobility: towards a new politics of mobility transitions. Trans. Inst. Br. Geogr. **44**(2), 346–360 (2019)
21. Van Brussel, S., Huyse, H.: Citizen science on speed? Realising the triple objective of scientific rigour, policy influence and deep citizen engagement in a large-scale citizen science project on ambient air quality in Antwerp. J. Environ. Plan. Manage. **62**(3), 534–551 (2019)

A DSS for the Multi-criteria Vehicle Routing Problem with Pickup and Delivery and 3d Constraints

Themistoklis Stamadianos⬭, Magdalene Marinaki⬭, Nikolaos Matsatsinis⬭, and Yannis Marinakis(✉)⬭

School of Production Engineering and Management, Technical University of Crete, Chania, Greece
marinakis@ergasya.tuc.gr

Abstract. The Vehicle Routing Problem (VRP) with three-dimension (3D) constraints (3L-CVRP) is a variant of the VRP with many possible applications in real-world scenarios. The purpose of this paper is to propose a Decision Support System for the VRP with pickup and delivery and 3D constraints (3L-CVRP-PD), considering multiple criteria. A Graphical User Interface (GUI) is developed, aiming to provide a better interaction experience with the software. The GUI includes a 3D representation of the loading bay for each vehicle, a feature that makes solutions easier to comprehend. The routing segment of the 3L-CVRP-PD is solved using a heuristic method, while item packing takes place in an exhaustive manner and multiple solutions are generated for each problem. The solutions are ranked by a Multi-Criteria Decision Method (MCDM). Two MCDMs are tested in this paper, the Preference Ranking Organization Method for Enrichment of Evaluations (PROMETHEE) and the UTility Additives* (UTASTAR), on modified instances from the literature.

Keywords: Vehicle routing problem · Multi-criteria VRP · Three dimensional loading · Graphical user interface

1 Introduction

Vehicle Routing Problems have been a popular subject since their conception [4]. Throughout the years they have become more complex, to better represent the real world and to account for many variables such as traffic, weather, and others.

One of these variants, 3L-CVRP, is concerned with the physical dimensions of the items, as well as their weight. Besides the need to determine vehicle routes, the placement of the items must also be determined. 3L-CVRP has yet to receive the attention other variants have experienced, partly because it is a very niche problem and partly due to its difficulty to be solved.

© Springer Nature Switzerland AG 2022
A. P. Cabral Seixas Costa et al. (Eds.): ICDSST 2022, LNBIP 447, pp. 177–189, 2022.
https://doi.org/10.1007/978-3-031-06530-9_14

Since making deliveries of large items is considered, there are cases where delivery demands will exceed capacity. This may occur during periods of high interest in transportation such as holidays, high tourism seasons, or even humanitarian crises. An application of 3L-CVRP could be useful in city logistics scenarios, where the use of small vans with limited space is the only method of transportation.

The purpose of the present paper is to solve the problem of large item deliveries and present it in a DSS environment that enhances the user experience and makes the use of the software and the interpretation of the results easier. An extension of 3L-CVRP that includes pickup and delivery (3L-CVRP-PD) is considered. An algorithm is used to solve 3L-CVRP-PD many times, with the intention to generate many different solutions. These solutions are ranked according to the preferences of the Decision Maker (DM), and the most suitable solution is presented. For the process of ranking, a MCDM has to be used. For this application, two methods, PROMETHEE and UTASTAR, were tested and compared.

The rest of the paper is structured in the following manner. In Sect. 2, a brief literature review concerning VRPs, DSSs, and MCDM is presented. In Sect. 3, a brief description of the VRP variant solved is discussed. Further insights in the MCDM methods employed are given in Sect. 4. In Sect. 5, the DSS and its components are presented. The numerical experiments are presented in Sect. 6 and the conclusions follow on the last section.

2   Literature Review

The most relevant research topic to this paper is DSSs with VRP integration. [6] combined waste collection VRP with an Analytical Hierarchy Process (AHP) and a GUI. [20] solved Dynamic Unmanned Aerial System Routing Problems (DUASRPs), using AHP, PROMETHE, along with mathematical programming. [27] tackled a multi-criteria, heterogeneous fleet VRP and developed a DSS. Solution quality was determined by the number of served customers. [32] and [10] presented two-stage solutions. They, both, created groups of customers first and then the delivery plans. It is not rare to deal with different types of vehicles depending on the items carried or the destination. [7,8], and [23], solved VRP variants employing heterogeneous fleets in a DSS setting.

Another highly relevant research topic is that of 3L-CVRP. [33] improved upon previously published heuristics for item loading. [1] proposed a hybrid algorithm, employing a Tabu Search for the VRP and a tree search to load the items. [13] presented a hybrid algorithm, including the Greedy Randomized Adaptive Search Procedure (GRASP) and Evolutionary Local Search (ELS). A hybrid Honey Bees Mating Optimization algorithm was proposed by [22], declaring new best solutions for many instances from the literature. [28] suggested a new heuristic based on space management, aiming to maximize the amount of used space.

[14] is the only research in regards to 3L-CVRP-PD. Multiple models were developed and tested on new instances for the three Dimensional Pickup and

Delivery Problem. Some relevant Pickup and Delivery VRPs are those of [5], and [26]. The first considered a PD-VRP with partial collaboration, while the latter added time-dependent deliveries and suggested hiring vehicles when needed. They both highlighted the potential for city logistics application of their proposals.

Case studies in realm of city logistics have also taken place in the last decade ([17,19,30], etc.). Some have also proposed alternative vehicles, such as bikes and EVs ([16,18]).

Lastly, there are some worth-mentioning surveys on the subject of MCDM. A survey was carried by [12] on the subject of multi-criteria VRP. It contains a detailed review of papers presented between 2008 and 2014. Another study is presented by [31]. Their bibliographic study includes an in-depth analysis of both multi-criteria formulations, as well as multi-objective and goal programming studies.

The research of the present paper aims to enrich the DSS space of VRPs by providing 3D tools to aid with solution interpretation. While DSSs with VRP integrations have been presented, none of them were concerned with any 3L-CVRP. Moreover, papers concerned with 3L-CVRP and its variants, did not include a DSS with a GUI environment. Furthermore, to the best of the authors knowledge, this is the first application of PROMETHEE and UTASTAR in the field of 3L-CVRP.

3   The Vehicle Routing Problem

3.1   Problem Description

The 3L-CVRP-PD can be described as follows: vehicles, starting at the depot, travel toward pickup points, pickup items and deliver them. This version differs significantly from the traditional courier practice of having all the items at the depot and planning deliveries from there.

A notable aspect of the 3L-CVRP-PD is the requirement to have unobstructed access from the loading gate to the next customers' items, meaning, no item must be moved in order to complete the delivery, following the Last-In-first-Out (LIFO) principle. This attribute greatly affects the results.

Previous studies on 3L-CVRP have suggested algorithms that create solutions assuming same size boxes for each customer, creating either layers or stacks and having the advantage of decreased execution times. In this paper, the method of maximal spaces that uses the actual dimensions is employed.

3.2   Generating Solutions

The solution algorithm of the 3L-CVRP-PD is intended to run multiple times and generate many alternative solutions; therefore, it should be simple enough to be fast, but powerful enough to provide good solutions. To help achieve that, the initial solution generation mechanism of GRASP was used. When using this mechanism, for each customer, a small list of potential customers to be visited next is generated before the solution algorithm starts. The lists are updated during the solution phase, as customers are served. The criterion upon which the groups are created is distance. A pseudo-code of the algorithm used to solve 3L-CVRP-PD is presented in Algorithm 1.

Algorithm 1: VRP solver

Data: Customer Information, Vehicle Information, Depot coordinates.
Result: Feasible VRP Solution
$customer = pick\_customer();$
while *true* **do**
  $truck \leftarrow truck + 1$
  if $served(customer) == true$ **then**
    $customer = pick\_customer();$
  end
  while $terminate == false$ **do**
    if $vehicle\_weight + customer\_weight <= capacity$ **then**
      if $fit\_in\_loading\_space(customer\_items) == true$ **then**
        $served(customer) \leftarrow truck;$
      end
    end
    $customer \leftarrow pick\_customer();$
    if $iter > iter\_max$ **then**
      $terminate \leftarrow true;$
    end
  end
  if $all\_served() == true$ **then**
    break;
  end
end
Add the delivery points to the route.

---

4   The Multi-Criteria Decision Methods

This research relies on being able to consistently select solutions close to the preferences of the person in charge, the DM. Each VRP is solved multiple times before the best solution is presented to the DM. The process through which solutions are selected is highly important. Two different MCDMs are employed. The first is PROMETHEE and the second is UTASTAR. Each of them operates in different ways. One of their main differences is the process through which data regarding the DM's preferences are collected.

In both PROMETHEE and UTASTAR, the solutions will be judged upon four criteria. The first criterion is the total load of the carried items, and the second criterion is their total volume. They help to efficiently utilize the cargo space of the vehicles. The third criterion considers the total distance that the vehicles travel to deliver the items they carry, while the last criterion is the number of served customers. The distance criterion is usually a good indicator of operational costs and the last criterion, the number of served customers helps the DM provide service to more customers. The importance of each criterion for the DM is set differently by each method and is described in the following subsections.

4.1 Preference Ranking Organization Method for Enrichment of Evaluations - PROMETHEE

PROMETHEE is a valued member of the MCDM field, first proposed during the nineteen-eighties in [2]. It is an outranking method, useful when there are conflicting criteria. Many versions have been developed to deal with different types of problems, but, in this case, PROMETHEE II is chosen over the others since it provides a complete ranking. PROMETHEE I can also be used in case of extreme differences between the criteria values of each solution. PROMETHEE can be used to assess both qualitative and quantitative criteria, but, since the method is based on comparisons between all the alternatives, if the alternatives are altered new comparison have to be made, and the solution process must be repeated.

Table 1. Promethee parameters

Criterion	Load	Volume	Distance	Served customers
Weight	50%	10%	30%	10%
Max/Min	Max	Max	Min	Max
Criteria type	1	1	5	5
Indifference threshold	N/A	N/A	2	2
Preference threshold	N/A	N/A	1	1
Intermediate value	N/A	N/A	N/A	N/A

The DM is given the choice to use as few as two criteria if deemed beneficial, but a minimum of two criteria must be used, otherwise, the problem cannot be characterized as multi-criteria. For each criterion used, the DM can select the preference function out of the six predefined ones, to determine the level of preference. The values displayed in Table 1 were used for all the PROMETHEE tests. All of the parameters contained in the Table are described in detail in [3].

4.2 UTASTAR

UTility Additives (UTA), originally developed by [11], is a method of Multi-Attribute Utility Theory (MAUT). Various methods can be employed in order to attain information about the DM's value system, including previous decisions of the DM or the creation of a set of representative alternatives for the DM to rank. The provided alternatives are a list of imaginary routing plans. This information is used to create a function or functions, able to provide rankings according to the DMs values. These functions are referred to as additive utility functions and when combined they form a model which can be used to evaluate future routing plans.

Table 2. UTASTAR alternatives

Alternative	Distance	Serviced	Load	Volume	Ranking (DM)
1	100	12	225	525	8
2	100	19	340	660	7
3	250	19	260	830	6
4	250	19	390	720	5
5	250	26	660	750	4
6	400	37	700	1080	2
7	400	19	870	920	1
8	400	26	660	940	3

In this research paper, an extension of the UTA method was used, UTASTAR (or UTA*), introduced in [25]. It includes both an underestimation and an overestimation error index, as opposed to a single error index of the original UTA, allowing for the creation of a better ordinal regression model. This seemingly small difference was proven to consistently outperform the classic UTA method. Some cases of UTASTAR being employed in a Decision Support System can be found in [24,34] and [15].

The most important part of UTASTAR is the data related to the DM's preferences, regardless of the method employed to acquire them. In this case, the DM is presented with a total of 8 different plans to rank, as shown in Table 2. The DM has to be consistent to avoid errors. The ranking was determined in accordance to the criteria values of PROMETHEE to ensure a fair comparison.

5   The Decision Support System

The attribute of 3L-CVRP-PD that sets it apart from the vast majority of VRPs is the 3D aspect of the problem. Presenting solutions in text format would not be as big of a problem in other cases, but in 3D problems, attempting to convey the relative position of the items inside the loading bay of the vehicle would not be practical.

To help alleviate this problem, a visual representation of a vehicle is necessary. It helps the DM to check that the loading plan is indeed viable and desireable, and it would help the workers that load the vehicles understand the loading pattern, avoiding the need to decipher text instructions.

Visual tools and other useful tools concerning the VRP data were encased in DSS environment presented in the following subsections.

5.1   Graphical User Interface

The proposed GUI can be split in three phases, data input, data processing, and presentation of the results. The processing part includes the solution phase and the ranking phase. Data input is the most rigorous part since vast amounts of data are needed from the algorithm; however, there is the option of data input via spreadsheets. The necessary data are the following:

- the number of customers,
- the number, the size and the total weight of their items,
- pickup and delivery coordinates,
- the dimensions, as well as the maximum capacity of the vehicles,
- the depot coordinates, and
- the PROMETHEE parameters.

5.2   Components

To begin with, Fig. 1 exhibits the interface through which the customer data may be inserted manually. There exist some fail-safe mechanisms to ensure the DSS will operate properly. For example, when the number of customers needs to be edited, no changes can be made to customer data until the number of customers is set. Vehicle data is inserted in the same fashion.

The GUI incorporates a menu and shortcuts. Figure 2 presents the menu structure and the shortcut bar of the interface. From left to right, the shortcuts include quick save, import and run button, the tools used to manipulate the 3D graph, the C, V, D, and P button that represent the (C)ustomers, (V)ehicles, (D)epot, and MCDM (P)arameters. To quickly check the function of any short-cut, hovering the mouse cursor over it, prompts a pop-up window with more information. The parameters window allows the DM to select the preferred MCDM method and insert the desired parameters for it.

5.3   The Solutions within the DSS Environment

User-friendliness is a significant factor to consider. The goal is to have a simplified experience for the DM to decipher the results. The requirements from the DM are clear and simple. After entering the necessary customer and vehicle information, along with the parameters for PROMETHEE or UTASTAR, the DM is just a click away from a solution.

A cumulative graph including the routes of all the vehicles is the default visual representation of the chosen solution, as seen in Fig. 3 for a solution of instance 2. The ranked list of alternative solutions is on the left-hand side, and a list of all the routes is displayed beside it. The best solution is the default selection, and the first route is displayed. An information box below contains the load of the selected vehicle, the distance, and the number of served customers. The graph is

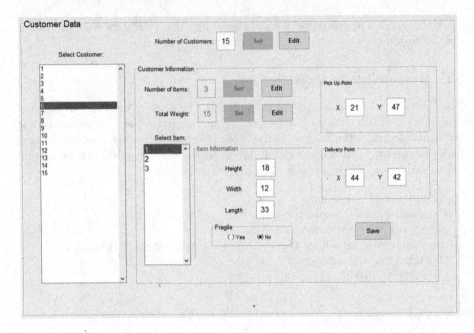

Fig. 1. Example of manual data logging (customer data)

Fig. 2. Menu and shortcuts of the interface

the centerpiece of the interface and serves as a display for two different purposes. The route of the selected vehicle is displayed there by default, and the user may switch to a 3D representation of the loading space with the ability to rotate, and view any angle imaginable, as portrayed in Fig. 4. The license plate and the driver of the vehicle are above the graph.

When a specific vehicle is selected, then, only the route of that vehicle is displayed. The entered information and parameters can be saved and used again in the future. The results can be saved as well, in a separate file, to be reviewed later.

6   Numerical Experiments

Like the GUI, the solution algorithm is implemented in MATLAB and tested on an Intel i3 8130u Laptop Computer with 6.0 GB of 2400 MHz DDR4 RAM.

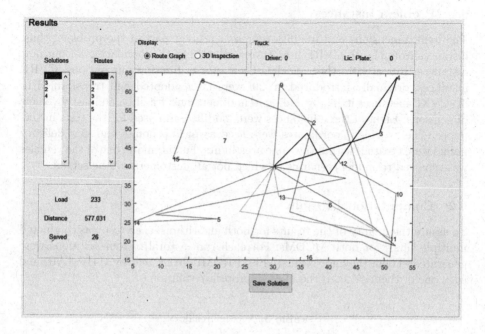

Fig. 3. Routes for a solution of instance 2

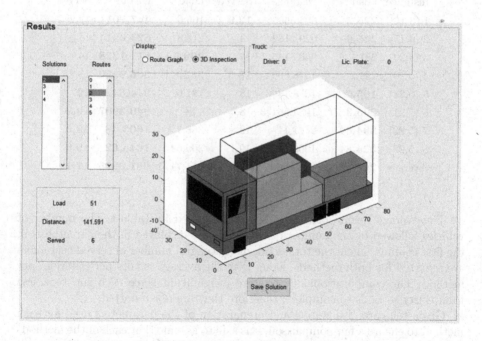

Fig. 4. 3D view of a vehicle for a solution of instance 2

6.1   Problem Instances

The item dimensions and fragility represent a great part of the problem; thus, instances from the 3L-CVRP literature were used as the foundation for our new instances. Research in this field has been sparse, limiting our options. CVRP instances, originally introduced in [29] were later adopted and transformed to 3L-CVRP instances in [9], by adding item dimensions, fragility, and lastly vehicle dimensions. Eight of these instances were modified and used for the tests in this paper. The provided coordinates were used as pickup points and new delivery points were created, within the same area limits. Furthermore, one of the vehicles was removed to model scenarios in which not all customers can be served.

6.2   Computational Results

To assure the quality of the results for both algorithms, each test was conducted multiple times for both MCDMs. For each run, a total of four solutions were generated. Then, they got evaluated by PROMETHEE and by UTASTAR, and each one of them selected the most appropriate solution.

Table 3. Average results

Instance	PROMETHEE			UTASTAR		
	Load	Distance	Served	Load	Distance	Served
1 (3,15)	**225,2**	608,5686	**12,9**	166,6	**447,701**	12,2
2 (4,15)	**225,6**	629,2182	13	218,8	**524,6914**	13
3 (4,20)	281,1	960,8146	**17**	**299,6**	**811,1228**	16
4 (5,20)	299,2	1078,8064	**18,5**	**332,8**	**966,9320**	18,2
5 (5,21)	**195,6**	1058,1366	18	181,6	**914,6421**	19
6 (5,21)	**205,3**	1084,56143	18,8	178	**940,3907**	19,2
7 (5,22)	**394,57**	2021,11	18,8	358,7	**1603,48**	19,6
8 (5,22)	**324,84**	1908,14	19,1	309,64	**1645,62**	19,6
Average	**268,9263**	1168,6695	17,0125	255,7175	**981,8225**	17,1

The average results of those tests are provided in Table 3. The number of vehicles followed by the number of customers are displayed in the parenthesis in the first column. Then, the total load, distance, and number of served customers are reported for both methods, along with the average results per criterion, per method. The computational times were insignificant since each run took less than thirty seconds to complete; therefore they are not reported.

Given the careful planning and preparation of the parameters used for each method to ensure a fair comparison, it is safe to assume that each of the methods would be suitable for different applications, while UTASTAR would be appropriate for cases where travel distance is more important. The difference between the results of the two methods may be attributed to their different mechanics and techniques used to acquire the results. The two methods use different techniques to evaluate the alternatives and suggest the one closes to the DM's preferences. Comparing the two methods, or any MCDMs, is not advised [21]. In multi-criteria applications there is no correct answer, but an answer that will satisfy the DM the most.

7   Conclusions

The aim of this paper was twofold, solving the 3L-CVRP-PD, and providing a DSS tool equipped with an intuitive graphical interface. The combination of the two could be of great assistance in urban applications, where vehicles of smaller size are employed and size becomes important.

The 3L-CVRP-PD was solved using an exact method for loading the items of the customers and a GRASP-derived algorithm to route the vehicles. To be able to provide results that would satisfy the DM's preferences, two different MCDMs were tested, each bearing their own benefits. For both methods, four criteria were used to help find solutions according to the DM's preferences.

The developed DSS tool includes a very intuitive GUI. The GUI provides a 3D visual representation of the loaded vehicles, representing each customer of the vehicle with a different color, with the ability to conform to any vehicle size, and with the ability to move around the vehicle and check the loading bay from any desired perspective. This visualization tool helps expedite the vehicle loading phase, since it is easier to comprehend compared to instructions in text format. Additionally, the GUI provides all the tools necessary to import data from spreadsheets and easily manipulate it. A shortcuts bar provides easy access to the most commonly used tools. It is worth noting that this tool could be easily used to solve other VRPs and is not limited to this application only.

Future research on the 3L-CVRP-PD could be on employing heuristic methods that could expedite the loading phase of the problem and could probably help serve more customers per vehicle route. Another option would be the use of alternative fuel vehicles accompanied with MCDM parameters that would favor them. As of the DSS, emphasis should be given on support for more types of input file-types, more tools in regards to the 3D representation of the vehicles, and most importantly the possibility of allowing the DM to manually move the items around the loading bay if needed.

References

1. Bortfeldt, A.: A hybrid algorithm for the capacitated vehicle routing problem with three-dimensional loading constraints. Comput. Oper. Res. **39**(9), 2248–2257 (2012)
2. Brans, J.P.: L'ingénierie de la décision: l'élaboration d'instruments d'aide a la décision. Université Laval, Faculté des sciences de l'administration (1982)

3. Brans, J.P., Vincke, P.: Note-a preference ranking organisation method: (The PROMETHEE method for multiple criteria decision-making). Manag. Sci. **31**(6), 647–656 (1985)
4. Dantzig, G.B., Ramser, J.H.: The truck dispatching problem. Manage. Sci. **6**(1), 80–91 (1959)
5. Farvaresh, H., Shahmansouri, S.: A coalition structure algorithm for large-scale collaborative pickup and delivery problem. Comput. Ind. Eng. **149**, 106737 (2020)
6. Ferreira, J.A., Costa, M., Tereso, A., Oliveira, J.A.: A multi-criteria decision support system for a routing problem in waste collection. In: Gaspar-Cunha, A., Henggeler Antunes, C., Coello, C.C. (eds.) EMO 2015. LNCS, vol. 9019, pp. 388–402. Springer, Cham (2015). https://doi.org/10.1007/978-3-319-15892-1_26
7. Gayialis, S.P., Tatsiopoulos, I.P.: Design of an IT-driven decision support system for vehicle routing and scheduling. Eur. J. Oper. Res. **152**(2), 382–398 (2004)
8. Gencer, C., Kızılkaya Aydoğan, E., Çetin, S.: Simultaneous pick-up and delivery decision support systems. Decis. Support Syst. Adv. Croatia, INTECH 203–214 (2010). https://doi.org/10.5772/39398
9. Gendreau, M., Iori, M., Laporte, G., Martello, S.: A tabu search algorithm for a routing and container loading problem. Transp. Sci. **40**(3), 342–350 (2006)
10. Gonzalez-Feliu, J., Salanova-Grau, J.M.: VRP algorithms for decision support systems to evaluate collaborative urban freight transport systems. Enterp. Interoperability: IESA **14**, 196–201 (2015)
11. Jacquet-Lagreze, E., Siskos, J.: Assessing a set of additive utility functions for multicriteria decision-making, the UTA method. Eur. J. Oper. Res. **10**(2), 151–164 (1982)
12. Labadie, N., Prodhon, C.: A survey on multi-criteria analysis in logistics: focus on vehicle routing problems. In: Benyoucef, L., Hennet, J.C., Tiwari, M. (eds.) Applications of Multi-Criteria and Game Theory Approaches, vol. pp. 3–29, pp. 3–29. Springer, London (2014). https://doi.org/10.1007/978-1-4471-5295-8_1
13. Lacomme, P., Toussaint, H., Duhamel, C.: A GRASP× ELS for the vehicle routing problem with basic three-dimensional loading constraints. Eng. Appl. Artif. Intell. **26**(8), 1795–1810 (2013)
14. Männel, D., Bortfeldt, A.: A hybrid algorithm for the vehicle routing problem with pickup and delivery and three-dimensional loading constraints. Eur. J. Oper. Res. **254**(3), 840–858 (2016)
15. Matsatsinis, N.F., Siskos, Y.: MARKEX: an intelligent decision support system for product development decisions. Eur. J. Oper. Res. **113**(2), 336–354 (1999)
16. Montwiłł, A., Pietrzak, O., Pietrzak, K.: The role of integrated logistics centers (ILCs) in modelling the flows of goods in urban areas based on the example of Italy. Sustain. Cities Soc. **69**, 102851 (2021)
17. Nathanail, E., Karakikes, I., Mitropoulos, L., Adamos, G.: A sustainability cross-case assessment of city logistics solutions. Case Stud. Transp. Policy **9**(1), 219–240 (2021)
18. Nürnberg, M.: Analysis of using cargo bikes in urban logistics on the example of stargard. Transp. Res. Procedia **39**, 360–369 (2019)
19. Pulawska, S., Starowicz, W.: Ecological urban logistics in the historical centers of cities. Procedia Soc. Behav. Sci. **151**, 282–294 (2014)
20. Ries, J., Ishizaka, A.: A multi-criteria support system for dynamic aerial vehicle routing problems. In: CCCA12, pp. 1–4. IEEE (2012)
21. Roy, B., Słowiński, R.: Questions guiding the choice of a multicriteria decision aiding method. EURO J. Decis. Process. **1**(1–2), 69–97 (2013)

22. Ruan, Q., Zhang, Z., Miao, L., Shen, H.: A hybrid approach for the vehicle routing problem with three-dimensional loading constraints. Comput. Oper. Res. **40**(6), 1579–1589 (2013)
23. Sakhala, N.K., Jha, J.: Developing decision support system for heterogeneous fleet vehicle routing problem using hybrid heuristic. Int. J. Logist. Syst. Manage. **26**(2), 253–276 (2017)
24. Siskos, Y., Spyridakos, A., Yannacopoulos, D.: MINORA: a multicriteria decision aiding system for discrete alternatives. J. Inf. Sci. Tech. **2**(2), 136–149 (1993)
25. Siskos, Y., Yannacopoulos, D.: UTASTAR: an ordinal regression method for building additive value functions. Investigaçao Operacional **5**(1), 39–53 (1985)
26. Sun, P., Veelenturf, L.P., Hewitt, M., Van Woensel, T.: Adaptive large neighborhood search for the time-dependent profitable pickup and delivery problem with time windows. Transp. Res. Part E: Logist. Transp. Rev. **138**, 101942 (2020)
27. Szczepański, E., Jachimowski, R., Żak, J.: Decision support system in freight transport based on vehicle routing problem with quality criterion. Arch. Transp. Syst. Telematics **11**, 49–56 (2018)
28. Tao, Y., Wang, F.: An effective tabu search approach with improved loading algorithms for the 3L-CVRP. Comput. Oper. Res. **55**, 127–140 (2015)
29. Toth, P., Vigo, D.: The vehicle routing problem. SIAM (2002)
30. Viana, M.S., Delgado, J.P.M.: City Logistics in historic centers: multi-criteria evaluation in GIS for city of Salvador (Bahia-Brazil). Case Stud. Transp. Policy **7**(4), 772–780 (2019)
31. Zare Mehrjerdi, Y.: Multiple criteria decision making combined with VRP: a categorized bibliographic study. Int. J. Supply Oper. Manag. **2**(2), 798–820 (2015)
32. Zhao, Q., Zhou, C., Pedrielli, G., et al.: A decision support system for data-driven driver-experience augmented vehicle routing problem. Asia-Pac. J. Oper. Res. (APJOR) **37**(05), 1–23 (2020)
33. Zhu, W., Qin, H., Lim, A., Wang, L.: A two-stage tabu search algorithm with enhanced packing heuristics for the 3L-CVRP and M3L-CVRP. Comput. Oper. Res. **39**(9), 2178–2195 (2012)
34. Zopounidis, C., Matsatsinis, N., Doumpos, M.: Developing a multicriteria knowledge-based decision support system for the assessment of corporate performance and viability: The FINEVA system. Fuzzy Econ. Rev. **1**(2), 2 (1996)

A Multicriteria Tool to Support Decision-Making in the Early Stages of Energy Efficiency Investments

Aikaterini Papapostolou⬝, Filippos Dimitrios Mexis⁽⊠⁾⬝, Charikleia Karakosta⬝,
and John Psarras⬝

Decision Support Systems Laboratory, School of Electrical and Computer Engineering,
Energy Policy Unit National Technical University of Athens, Athens, Greece
`pmexis@epu.ntua.gr`

Abstract. The energy demand of modern communities contributes significantly to climate change, increasing the release of greenhouse gases into the atmosphere. Energy efficiency is recognised as the key pathway to reducing energy usage while sustaining an equivalent, contemporary economic activity. In other words, to avoid climate change, mainstreaming energy efficiency finance is considered a top priority. This study focuses on introducing a rating system based on a Multi-Criteria Decision Analysis method that aims to promote the implementation and financing of energy efficiency investments. To this end, a benchmarking Tool is being deployed in order to materialise the proposed methodology and introduce a standardised procedure for benchmarking energy efficiency potential projects during the preliminary stages of investment conceptualisation. The proposed Tool exploits the Multi-Criteria Decision Analysis method ELECTRE Tri, taking into account major key performance indicators that are broadly used by investors and financing institutions to identify bankable energy efficiency investments and promote green transition. The methodology has been applied to benchmark 114 energy efficiency investments from eight different European countries. It should be mentioned that for the successful and effective development of the proposed Tool, input and feedback has been received by a variety of stakeholders from the energy sector and financing community, who also tested the Tool and confirmed that the approach proved to be extremely helpful to those seeking for sustainable investments in energy efficiency. The analysis resulted in the conclusion that the Tool covers the necessity for a standardised benchmark, providing added value to the energy efficiency market.

Keywords: Green transition · Energy efficiency · Sustainable investments · Benchmarking · Decision support

1 Introduction

Climate change and rising energy consumption are two interrelated phenomena. To a considerable extent, energy production and consumption are responsible for greenhouse

© Springer Nature Switzerland AG 2022
A. P. Cabral Seixas Costa et al. (Eds.): ICDSST 2022, LNBIP 447, pp. 190–202, 2022.
https://doi.org/10.1007/978-3-031-06530-9_15

gas (GHG) emissions and pollution in the environment. In order to minimise the growing energy demand in the European Union (EU), numerous targets and initiatives for Energy Efficiency (EE) have been set, while tentative national targets are to reduce energy consumption at a pan-European level [1]. When talking about EE investments, their needs have been quantified as around EUR 62.6 bn, while the European Commission (EC) estimates that at least EUR 185 bn per annum should be motivated, resulting in a much higher investment gap over the next decade [2].

Despite the fact that many worthwhile EE investments exist at the development stage, only a tiny percentage of them are ultimately funded. This issue has been named the "efficiency paradox," often known as the "EE gap" [3]. Hence, an effort is needed to stir investments in EE projects to reduce the EE gap as rapidly as possible. The lack of evidence on the performance of EE projects and the lack of available data on successfully implemented EE investments constitute a significant drawback to mainstreaming EE investments, making it difficult for project developers to benchmark their projects [4].

In this direction, the present manuscript introduces an applied methodology that aims to support the decision making of EE investments in order to facilitate investors to undertake such projects. The proposed methodology has been incarnated by an online tool, which takes into account principal Financial, Risk and Sustainable Development Goals (SDG) criteria. It uses the Multi-Criteria Decision Analysis (MCDA) method, ELECTRE Tri, to benchmark the project ideas in different classes according to their performance [5]. The ELECTRE-Tri was chosen to be used in the benchmarking procedure as it handles both qualitative and quantitative data, meaning that it can deal with the imperfect nature of knowledge [6].

The developed Tool has been applied to benchmark projects from different sectors of activities in eight European case study countries, namely: Bulgaria, the Czech Republic, Germany, Greece, Italy, Lithuania, Netherlands, and Spain, under the activities of the EU H2020 funded "Enhancing at an Early Stage the Investment Value Chain of Energy Efficiency Projects - Triple-A" project. The Triple-A scheme tries to identify which investments can be considered Triple-A investments, fostering sustainable growth while also having an extreme capacity to meet their commitments from the first stages of investments generation and pre-selection/pre-evaluation [7]. The results reveal that the vast majority of the identified and benchmarked projects pertain to the Building Sector, while almost half of the submitted projects have a great capacity to meet their financial commitments.

Following the introductory Section, the 2 Section of the manuscript presents the methodology that has been developed, Sect. 3 analyses the application of the proposed methodology through the selected MCDA method, while Sect. 4 presents and analyses the results of the application of the method through the online benchmarking Tool in the eight European case study countries. Finally, Sect. 5 summarises the main aspects of the paper.

2   Methodology

The proposed methodology aims to assess and benchmark EE projects based on their bankability, risk, and sustainability. The methodology is being applied to a web-based

Tool; the benchmarking is conducted by a Python 3.0 script running in the background. The Tool's benchmarking of the project ideas is organised in four main steps, as depicted in Fig. 1.

Fig. 1. Tool methodological steps

2.1 Project Data and User Preferences

The data collection is being performed by a user interface in which the Tool requires the user to provide the necessary data to calculate the Key Performance Indicators (KPIs) and perform the MCDA that follows. The user has to provide details on the project's basic information, such as name, country and region, sector of the project, and some contact details of the user to receive the results. In addition, the user should provide information related to the risks by answering 10 related questions. Facts and figures are also needed concerning the project's financial, energy, and CO_2 data, the preferred KPIs for the evaluation and the weights these criteria should have. The order of the data input is summarised in Fig. 2.

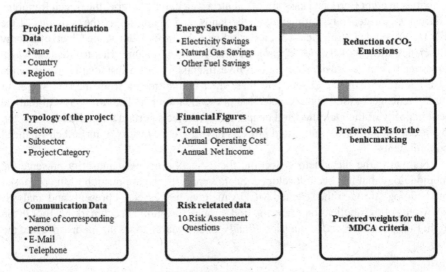

Fig. 2. Tool's input data

The typology of the sectors and project categories covered by the Tool is presented in Table 1 [8].

Table 1. Project sectors and categories

Sectors	Project categories
Buildings	Building envelope retrofits
	Heating, Ventilation, Air conditioning (HVAC&R) retrofits
	Lighting appliances' retrofits
	Automatic control retrofits
	Renewable energy sources (RES) installations
	Construction of new buildings
Manufacturing	Manufacturing-specific retrofits
Transportation	Purchase of new vehicles
District energy networks	District energy networks retrofits/Expansion
Outdoor lighting	Outdoor lighting retrofits

2.2 Calculation of Evaluation Criteria and KPIs

At this step, the KPIs used as benchmarking criteria are calculated based on the user's input and project data [9] Table 2.

Table 2. Key performance indicators

Key performance indicators	
Financial criteria	
Net present value (NPV)	NPV reflects the risk and cash flows discount by quantising it through the discount rate the profitability of the investment by involving the yearly income calculations
Discounted payback period	The discounted payback period is the number of years necessary to recover the project cost of an investment while accounting for the time value of money
Internal rate of return (IRR)	IRR is a rate of return used in capital budgeting to measure and compare the profitability of investments
Cost-effectiveness	Cost-effectiveness measures whether an investment's benefits exceed its costs, calculated based on the project cost per kWh saved
Risk criteria	
Behavioural risk	The criterion consists of the rebound effect, expressed as a ratio of the lost benefit compared to the expected environmental benefit when holding consumption constant
Energy market & Regulatory risk	It reflects the uncertainty about energy prices and affects the decision to undertake an EE investment

(continued)

Table 2. (*continued*)

Key performance indicators	
Financial criteria	
Economic risk	The economic risk will be monitored by the interest rates volatility factor. Fluctuation in interest rates may lead to an unexpected cost of capital deriving from changes in the cost of debt for the borrower, preventing the accurate estimation of savings
Technology, Planning & Operational risk	It considers the maturity of the technology, the construction, operation and maintenance risk, and the capacity to predict the energy savings accurately
SDG criteria	
Arrears on utility bills	It reflects the share of (sub) population (%) having arrears on utility bills,
Total population living in a dwelling with a leaking roof, damp walls, floors or foundation, or rot in window frames or floor	It indicates the share (%) of the population experiencing at least one of the following basic deficits in their housing condition: a leaking roof, damp walls, floors or foundation, or rot in window, frames, floor
Population unable to keep home adequately warm by poverty status	It indicates the share (%) of the population who cannot keep home adequately warm. Data for this indicator are being collected as part of the EU Statistics on Income and Living Conditions (EU-SILC)/
Primary energy consumption	It quantifies the Gross Inland Consumption in tonnes of oil equivalent (toe), excluding all non-energy use of energy carriers
Energy import dependency	The share (%) of total energy needs of a country met by imports from other countries
Final energy consumption in the industry sector	It includes all the energy supplied to the industry sector in toe, excluding deliveries to the energy transformation sector
Final energy consumption in the transportation sector	It measures the energy consumption of the transportation sector in toe, excluding deliveries to the energy transformation sector
Final energy consumption in other sectors or commercial and public services	It indicates the energy supplied to non-categorised sectors, commercial and public services in toe
Final energy consumption in households per capita	The indicator measures how much electricity and heat every citizen consumes at home in Kilogram of oil equivalent (kgoe/capita), excluding energy used for transportation
GHG emissions from energy consumption	The data are based on the European Environmental Energy Agency measures and represent the GHG emissions in thousand tones of CO_2 equivalent
GHG emissions from the industrial sector	This KPI reflects the GHG emissions (in thousand tones of CO_2 equivalent) caused by the industrial sector

Sources: [10–12]

The financial criteria are based on scientific and economic equations corresponding to each indicator. In detail:

NPV is calculated based on the following equation:

$$\text{Net Present Value} = -C + \sum_{y=1}^{Y} \frac{CF_y}{(1+i)^n} \tag{1}$$

Where:

C = Initial Investment Cost
CF = Cash Flow for the year y

The cash flow for each year is being calculated based on the energy savings of the candidate project:

$$\sum_{y=1}^{Y} CF_y(€) = (S_{el} \cdot p_{el})_y + (S_{gas} \cdot p_{gas})_y + (S_{oil} \cdot p_{oil})_y + \Delta Cost_y \tag{2}$$

Where,

S_{el} = energy savings: electricity (kWh)
S_{gas} = energy savings: gas (kWh)
S_{oil} = energy savings: other fuel (kWh)
$p_{el}, p_{gas}, p_{other}$ = fuel prices,

and

$$\Delta Cost_y = \text{Annual Maintenance Cost before EE measures} -$$
$$\textbf{Annual Maintance Cost after EE measures} \tag{3}$$

The **Discounted Payback Period** is calculated as follows:

$$\textbf{Payback Period} = A + \frac{B}{C}. \tag{4}$$

Where,

A = the last period number with a negative cumulative discounted cash flow;
B = absolute value of cumulative discounted net cash flow at the end of period A;
C = the total discounted cash inflow during the period following period A;

The Discounted Cash Inflow of each period is being calculated according to:

$$\text{Discounted Cash Inflow} = \frac{\text{Actual Cash Inflow}}{(1+i)^n} \tag{5}$$

Where,

i is the discount rate, and

n is the period to which the cash inflow relates.

The **Internal Rate of Return** is calculated as follows:

$$0 = \mathbf{NPV} = \sum_{t=1}^{T} \frac{C_t}{(1 + IRR)^t} - C_0 \tag{6}$$

Where:

C_t = Net cash inflow during period t
C_0 = Total initial investment costs
IRR = the Internal Rate of Return
t = number of time periods

Cost-Effectiveness is calculated based on the project cost per kWh saved, according to the following equation:

$$\mathbf{Cost\ Effectiveness} = \frac{\text{Life Cycle Cost (€)}}{\text{Savings (kWh)}} \tag{7}$$

All the parameters needed to calculate the above financial indicators are based on the EU Directives and Regulations on Cost-Benefit Analysis of Investment, also reflected in EU official statistics by deploying a unique methodology for each case study country [13]. The risk criterion is calculated based on answers to 10 questions related to the project design, conceptualisation and legal requirements [14]. The questions require information regarding, among others, the calculations of the energy baseline, the energy savings assessment, the related project permits, the experience of the technical development team, the quality of the equipment, as well as the creditworthiness of the borrower.

The **Total Risk** is calculated as the aggregation of the risks identified in Table 2, in values that range from 0 to 1.

$$K_3 = \frac{B_1 + \ldots + B_n}{n} \tag{8}$$

Where:

$B_{i\ldots n}$ = The identified Risks

Finally, the **SDG** criterion is the average of the respective criteria, as presented in Table 2.

$$K_4 = \frac{C_1 + \ldots + C_n}{n} \tag{9}$$

Where:

C_i = each SDG criterion
n = the number of SDG criteria

The SDG criterion is a quantitative analysis that examines factors derived mainly from Eurostat indicators. These metrics indicate the current state of EE, energy poverty, and pollution of the country of the EE project idea. The methodology produces a parameterised SDG progress estimation (per project country and sector). The chosen indicators, primarily related to the energy industry and environmental protection, are linked to the United Nations Sustainable Development Goals Agenda [15].

3   MCDA Application

To run the MCDA, the user selects four criteria. The ELECTRE Tri algorithm is executed based on the user's input and settings. A set of two financial KPIs (one default and one selected by the user), the total risk and the SDG criterion are applied to the ELECTRE Tri MCDA to build a consistent family of criteria [16]. The default financial KPI is cost-effectiveness, while the other can be chosen between the NPV, the Discounted Payback Period and the Internal Rate of Return.

ELECTRE Tri is an MCDA method proposed by Yu [17] and Mousseau et al. [18] and used for classification problems and, more specifically, in discrete classification problems, where the alternatives of the problem should be classified into predefined categories. The classification is made using pair-wise comparisons between the alternatives and the reference profiles based on concordance and discordance checks. The ELECTRE Tri was chosen to be used in the benchmarking procedure as it handles both qualitative and quantitative data, meaning that it can deal with the imperfect nature of knowledge [35]. In ELECTRE Tri, each outranking relation is constructed after comparing each alternative to a predefined category limit. As a result, if a new alternative should be later added to the classification process, the new alternative compares with the existing profile limits.

According to the nature of each KPI, the criteria values are directly input as determined in equivalent units, and the project is classified into one of three predefined categories. The first category is named "Triple-A", which contains projects that merit attention from the funding organisations. The Triple-A projects are extremely capable of meeting their energy-saving targets, already from their conceptual phase (where they are still considered project fiches).

The second category consists of "Reserved" projects. These projects have a good but not outstanding performance in the MCDA criteria. They are projects capable of repaying the initial capital invested and contributing significantly to the site's energy savings.

The last category contains projects marked as "Rejected". The rejected projects are the ones that have an unsatisfactory total performance in the examined criteria. They may have a risk higher than the maximum threshold, or they do not seem capable of recovering the total investment.

The classification thresholds have been defined using the input gathered through several stakeholder consultation activities (e.g., email exchanges, bilateral meetings, phone calls, questionnaires, structured interviews, webinars, workshops, etc.) within the framework of the Triple-A project. The Tool user is enabled to adjust the weights of the ELECTRE Tri criteria according to the importance of each factor based on the user's preferences. The importance of each factor is expressed through the linguistic variables "Very high", "High" ", Medium", "Low", and "Very Low". An arithmetic value is assigned to each linguistic variable, as depicted in Table 3:

Table 3. Assignment of weights

Linguistic values	Arithmetic values
Very high	5
High	4
Medium	3
Low	2
Very low	1

Based on the user selection of weights, the values are normalised to the total sum of the weights equal to one, as shown in the following equation:

$$W_{Sum} = \sum_1^4 W_i \tag{10}$$

$$W'_i = \frac{W_i}{W_{Sum}} \tag{11}$$

Where:

$W_i =$ *the arithmetic weight selected by the user for each criterion*
$W_i =$ *the normalized weight*

Additionally, the weights are given some default values if the user does not wish to set some specific values. The default values are equal for all the criteria.

4 Result Analysis

The developed Tool has been used and tested by several EE professionals, investors, policymakers, and EE stakeholders. An extended stakeholder consultation approach has been realised, in which demonstrations and testing of the Tool have been conducted in bilateral meetings and training workshops to gather feedback in real-time when each step of the Tool was live presented. In these meetings and workshops, related key actors have participated, such as energy efficiency companies and project developers, financiers and investors interested in sustainable financing. As a matter of fact, 133 users have signed up and utilised the online Tool.

Though the stakeholder consultation, the Tool has received 114 EE investment ideas. The projects have been collected from the relevant stakeholders in the case study countries: (i) by directly using the Tool and inserting their projects and (ii) filling a predefined template. Thus, quality control of the input data provided by the users has been done and extensive debugging and optimisation of the Tool, using real projects data. The consultation followed a bottom-up procedure to build the respective Tools in a way that is practical to the energy efficiency business actors. The selection of the criteria and the deployment of the methodology have been realised in close cooperation with stakeholders. In this process, a real demonstration of the Tool has been performed to receive feedback and reinforce the methodology. In addition, hands-on webinars and bilateral meetings have been conducted, in which stakeholders provided real project ideas that have been entered into the Tool, and the stakeholders have commented on the benchmarking results. The comments, inputs and feedback received have been the major developing force for the Tools, while the potential issues and imprecisions have been rectified.

The chart in Fig. 3 reveals that most EU projects in need of private funding pertain to the building sector. These project ideas include, primarily, retrofits in the building envelope, HVAC&R and lighting upgrades. This result is reasonable, as the building sector is responsible for almost one-third of total global final energy consumption and nearly 15% of direct CO_2 emissions and efforts have been intensified towards decarbonising this sector [19]. On the other hand, the Manufacturing sector received just one (1) project into the Tool, demonstrating the urgent need to boost energy efficiency measures. The lack of projects in that sector can be explained by various reasons. First, the industry seems to prioritise other types of investments, such as expanding the production capacity rather than energy efficiency. Another reason is that the energy efficiency in industry is achieved along with other modifications of the production line, so energy efficiency measures are not treated as standalone investments. Finally, industries that do prioritise energy efficiency usually allocate equity for these measures, so there is no need to use such kind of Tool to seek financing.

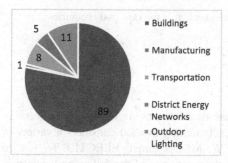

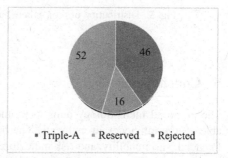

Fig. 3. Number of projects per sector

Fig. 4. Classification of projects by the developed tool

In Fig. 4, statistics of the classified projects by the Tool are presented. As it can be seen, more than half of the projects (62 out of 114) have been classified as either Triple-A or Reserved. This demonstrates that many project developers are taking the future financial performance of their EE projects seriously. In addition, this indicates that they are not seeking any public tender to finance their EE projects, but they are stirring towards private funding, which could be challenging for projects with abysmal financial indicators. Nevertheless, a significant number (52) of Rejected projects also appears, which means there is a huge potential for development and capacity building for stakeholders to design profitable and bankable EE project ideas [20].

As depicted in Fig. 5, most projects entered into the Tools come from Lithuania, while most Triple-A projects are recorded in Bulgaria. Lithuania, even if it has a significant amount of EE project ideas, the majority of them have been classified as Rejected. Through the proposed Tools, these projects could identify their weaknesses and be redesigned to deliver a more attractive financial profile. As derived by the Tools' results, a significant role in the cashflows of EE projects play the estimated energy savings, along with the respective energy price. Suppose the impact of the Covid-19 pandemic on the energy sector [21] and the latest increase of 2022 in energy prices are considered, EE become even more crucial. Higher energy prices indicate that some Rejected projects could be easily redesigned to increase their overall rating and achieve a positive financial balance.

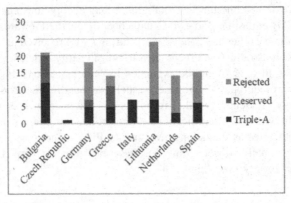

Fig. 5. Distribution of project benchmarking across the case study countries

5   Conclusions

The proposed methodology aims to promote decision-making in identifying sustainable energy efficiency investments. The benchmarking method considers a variety of financial, sustainability, and risk indicators. An MCDA namely ELECTRE Tri, is used to benchmark the project ideas, classifying them into one of the following categories: "Triple-A", "Reserved", or "Rejected". The methodology has been materialised through an online Tool that aims to support users in assessing and benchmarking their project ideas when they are in their early stages when seeking financing.

The Tool has been tested and validated by different stakeholders from the financing and energy sector, who gave feedback and input in all the implementation phases of the methodological steps. According to their feedback, the proposed Tool proves to be essential since it allows for quick identification of bankable project ideas through a user-friendly environment, establishes a common framework, and provides background material for project developers and investors to negotiate.

The benchmarking results reveal that almost half of the project ideas inserted and benchmarked in the Tool are classified as Triple-A, which means they are worth financing due to their outstanding performance in the KPIs. The results also indicate the Tool's potential to identify bankable EE investments, supporting investors in the EE investments decision making procedure. On the other hand, projects classified as "Rejected" would be able to identify their weaknesses in specific factors to try to improve their performance and then be more likely to find funding. In addition, project developers can easily benchmark their projects to get a preliminary insight on the estimated risk, profitability, and overall design of their EE project ideas. In conclusion, the proposed Tool proves to be able to address the challenges that emerge when seeking financing to implement an EE project, while it could assist the related key actors in identifying which investments can foster sustainable growth while also having a strong capacity to meet their commitments.

Further results could be extracted when more stakeholders use the Tools, and the project's database will be enriched with projects from various sectors, benchmarking and countries. By deploying further statistical data of the projects' benchmarking, more profound evidence and clues regarding the energy efficiency gap. Correlation between countries, sectors and poor project design could be achieved. In addition, the poor performance in certain financial indicators that cause the energy efficiency projects to fall short in private financing could be examined. In addition, further research with additional projects could be realised to perform a sensitivity analysis of the Tool and fine-tune the benchmarking results.

Acknowledgement. The present paper is based on research done as part of the EU Horizon 2020 project "Triple-A: Enhancing at an Early Stage the Investment Value Chain of Energy Efficiency Projects" (grant agreement no. 846569, https://aaa-h2020.eu), which aims to support financial institutions and project developers increase their capital deployment in energy efficiency by making investments more precise, reliable, and enticing. The paper's authors are solely responsible for its content, which does not necessarily reflect the views of the European Commission.

References

1. United nations: Paris agreement to the united nations framework convention on climate change (2015). https://ec.europa.eu/clima/policies/international/negotiations/paris_en
2. Fi-compass factsheet: the potential for investment in energy efficiency through financial instruments in the European Union (2020)
3. Decanio, S.J.: The efficiency paradox: bureaucratic and organizational barriers to profitable energy-saving investments. Energy Policy **26**, 441–454 (1998). https://doi.org/10.1016/S0301-4215(97)00152-3
4. Energy Efficiency Financial Institutions Groups (EFFIG): Energy Efficiency – the first fuel for the EU Economy. How to drive new finance for energy efficiency investments. https://ec.europa.eu/energy/en/news/new-report-boosting-finance-energy-efficiency-investments-buildings-industry-and-smes. Accessed 04 Apr 2020
5. Doukas, H.: On the appraisal of "Triple-A" energy efficiency investments. Energy Sources Part B: Econ. Plann. Policy **13**(7), 320–327 (2018). https://doi.org/10.1080/15567249.2018.1494763

6. Roy, B., Figueira, J.R., Almeida-Dias, J.: Discriminating thresholds as a tool to cope with imperfect knowledge in multiple criteria decision aiding: theoretical results and practical issues. Omega **43**, 9–20 (2014). https://doi.org/10.1016/j.omega.2013.05.003

7. Mexis, F.D., Touloumis, K., Papapostolou, A., Karakosta, C.: Final Triple-A Standardised Tools, Deliverable 4.2 of the triple-a project funded under the European Union's Hozizon 2020 research and innovation programme GA No. 846569 (2021). https://aaa-h2020.eu/res ults

8. Mexis, F.D., Papapostolou, A., Karakosta, C., Psarras, J.: Financing sustainable energy efficiency projects: the triple-a case. Environ. Sci. Proc. **11**, 22 (2021). https://doi.org/10.3390/environsciproc2021011022

9. Koutsandreas, D., Kleanthis, N., Flamos, A., Karakosta, C., Doukas, H.: Risks and mitigation strategies in energy efficiency financing: a systematic literature review. Energy Rep. **8**, 1789–1802 (2022). https://doi.org/10.1016/j.egyr.2022.01.006

10. Allan, G., Gilmartin, M., McGregor, P., Swales, J.K., Turner, K.: Economics of energy efficiency. Int. Handb. Econ. Energy. **2**, 144–163 (2009). https://doi.org/10.1016/b0-12-176480-x/00228-x

11. Short, W., Packey, D., Holt, T.: A manual for the economic evaluation of energy efficiency and renewable energy technologies. (1995). No. NREL/TP-462-5173

12. Jakob, M.: Marginal costs and co-benefits of energy efficiency investments. Energy Policy **34**, 172–187 (2006)

13. European Commission (EC): Guide to Cost-Beneft Analysis of Investment Projects (2014)

14. Kleanthis, N., Koutsandreas, D., Exintaveloni, D.S., Karakosta, C., Ristau, P., Flamos, A.: Final Report on Risks of Energy Efficiency Financing and Mitigation Strategies Typology" Deliverable 3.2 of the Triple-A project funded under the European Union's Hozizon 2020 research and innovation programme GA No. 846569" 2020. (2019)

15. Eurostat: Sustainable Development Goals Indicators. https://ec.europa.eu/eurostat/web/sdi/indicators. Accessed 11 May 2020

16. Mexis, F.D., Papapostolou, A., Karakosta, C., Sarmas, E., Koutsandreas, D., Doukas, H.: Leveraging energy efficiency investments: an innovative web-based benchmarking tool. Adv. Sci. Technol. Eng. Syst. J. **6**(5), 237–248 (2021). https://doi.org/10.25046/aj060526

17. Yu, W.: Aide multicritère à la décision dans le cadre de la problématique du tri: concepts, méthodes et applications (1992)

18. Mousseau, V., Slowinski, R., Zielniewicz, P.: ELECTRE TRI 2.0 a Methodological Guide and User's Manual (1999)

19. International Energy Agency (IEA): Buildings: A source of enormous untapped efficiency potential. https://www.iea.org/topics/buildings. Accessed 22 Feb 2022

20. Loureiro, T., Gil, M., Desmaris, R., Andaloro, A., Karakosta, C., Plesser, S.: De-risking energy efficiency investments through innovation. Proceedings **65**, 3 (2020). https://doi.org/10.3390/proceedings2020065003

21. Karakosta, C., Mylona, Z., Karásek, J., Papapostolou, A., Geiseler, E.: Tackling covid-19 crisis through energy efficiency investments: decision support tools for economic recovery. Energy Strateg. Rev. **38**, 100764 (2021). https://doi.org/10.1016/j.esr.2021.100764

Author Index

Printed in the United States
by Baker & Taylor Publisher Services

Printed in the United States
by Baker & Taylor Publisher Services